MW00721041

Certificate for Music Educators Guidebook

Certificate for Music Educators Guidebook is focused on the learning outcomes of the Certificate for Music Educators in the UK, accredited by the Office of Qualifications and Examinations Regulation (Ofqual), and validated by Trinity College London (TCL) and the Associated Board of the Royal Schools of Music (ABRSM).

Through reflective questions, readers become acquainted with research findings relevant to teaching children and explore ways for enacting best teaching practice in day-to-day teaching. It offers strong foundations in teaching music in contemporary diverse settings, in both instrumental and vocal teaching; early years, primary and secondary schools and community-based contexts.

This book is directly aligned with the CME Level 4 course modules, units and areas of study and its desired learning outcomes. It is a key companion for students enrolled in a validated centre, as well as the teachers and mentors involved in the design and delivery of the CME.

Lilian Simones is Director and founder of Enact Music (Belfast, UK), and Researcher Development Consultant at Queen's University, Belfast, UK.

"The first part of the book provides a strong research-base for interested readers, and the final part offers a compendium on the practicalities of teaching in contemporary diverse settings including studio, school and community, all in a single volume. This is a strong book with little competition that fills a gap in the market."

Oscar Odena, *School of Education, University of Glasgow, UK*

Certificate for Music Educators Guidebook

Teaching Children and Young People

Lilian Simones

Routledge
Taylor & Francis Group

NEW YORK AND LONDON

First published 2022
by Routledge
605 Third Avenue, New York, NY 10158

and by Routledge
2 Park Square, Milton Park, Abingdon, Oxon OX14 4RN

Routledge is an imprint of the Taylor & Francis Group, an informa business

© 2022 Lilian Simones

Library of Congress Cataloging-in-Publication Data
Names: Simones, Lilian, author.
Title: Certificate for Music Educators guidebook : teaching children
    and young people / Lilian Simones.
Description: New York : Routledge, 2021. | Includes bibliographical
    references and index.
Identifiers: LCCN 2020055585 (print) | LCCN 2020055586 (ebook) |
    ISBN 9780367336127 (hardback) | ISBN 9780367336110
    (paperback) | ISBN 9780429320811 (ebook)
Subjects: LCSH: Music—Instruction and study. | Music—Instruction
    and study—Great Britain.
Classification: LCC MT1.S529 C47 2021 (print) | LCC MT1.S529
    (ebook) | DDC 780.71—dc23
LC record available at https://lccn.loc.gov/2020055585
LC ebook record available at https://lccn.loc.gov/2020055586

ISBN: 978-0-367-33612-7 (hbk)
ISBN: 978-0-367-33611-0 (pbk)
ISBN: 978-0-429-32081-1 (ebk)

Typeset in Times New Roman
by Apex CoVantage, LLC

To all those who contributed in one way or another to my musical learning and personal growth. This includes my parents, siblings, partner, children, teachers, colleagues, friends and my students throughout the years.

Contents

List of Tables   xiii
List of Figures   xiv
List of Abbreviations   xv
Acknowledgements   xvi
Preface   xvii

Introduction   1
Becoming a Qualified Music Teacher 5
What Is the Certificate for Music Educators (CME),
*   Level 4? 7*
*   Are You Eligible for the Course? 10*
*   Choosing the Right Course Provider 11*
*   Ensuring Success in Your Application 12*
*   Ensuring Success in Your CME Interview 13*
*   Getting the Most Out of Your Mentor 15*
References 16

SECTION I
The Importance of Music in Children and Young People's Lives   17

1   How Children and Young People Learn and Develop
**   Their Musicality**   19
Introduction 19
Musical Beginnings 19
*   Musical Worlds and Musical Learning 22*
*   Musical Development 25*
*   Nature Versus Nurture 25*
*   Cognitive Constructivism: A Brief Overview 26*
*   A Humanist Approach: Learning Power Theory 28*
*   Reflective Questions 34*

Further Reading 36
References 36

2   Self-Expression Through Music Shaping Musical Identities   40
Introduction 40
Musical Identities: What *and* How? *40*
Listening 43
Singing 45
   Young Children's Singing 45
      Spontaneous Singing 46
      Production of Standard Songs 47
   Children and Young People's Singing 48
      Learning Songs Taught by Others 48
      Self-Directed Learning of Songs Alone 49
      Self-Directed Learning of Songs With Peers 49
      Inventing Songs 50
Interacting and Playing Musical Instruments 51
   Young Children 52
   Children and Young People: Motivations for Instrumental
      Music Learning 52
      Development of Metacognitive and Practice Skills 54
      The Importance of Developing Self-Regulated
         Learners 55
Composing and Inventing Musical Notation 56
   Inventing Musical Notation 58
      Technology Mediating Creative Musical Self-Expression
         Through Composition 60
Improvising: Alone and With Others 62
Movement Play, Moving to Music and Dancing 64
Reflective Questions 66
Further Reading 68
References 69

3   Multidimensional Benefits of Music   74
Introduction 74
   Communicational, Social and Personal Development 74
   Perceptual, Cognitive and Intellectual 75
      Music Develops Enhanced Perceptual and Language
         Skills 75
      Music Aids the Development of Literacy Skills 76
      Music Aids Intellectual Development 77

Music Aids General Attainment 78
Creativity 79
Emotional and Physical Well-Being 79
Reflective Questions 81
Further Reading 82
References 82

SECTION II
Planning, Leading and Assessing Musical Learning   85

**4 Preparing for the Development of Inclusive Learning
   Environments**   87
Introduction 87
Inclusion, Equality and Diversity 88
  Identifying Barriers to Music Learning 90
    School System and Society 90
    Intrapersonal Barriers 91
    Informational Barriers 91
    Physical Learning Environment Barriers 91
    Informational and Physical Barriers 92
  Learning Styles 92
  Difficulties With Learning 96
    General Learning Difficulties 96
    Specific Learning Difficulties 98
  Very Gifted Children 99
  Cultural Diversity 102
  Motivation for Learning 106
    Intelligence and Beliefs About Personal Ability 106
    Value Placed on Music 107
    *Developing a Musical Identity: A Decisive Factor
      in Developing Motivation 108*
    Music Fulfilling Psychological Human Needs 109
  Promoting and Developing Motivation 109
  Promoting Positive Behaviour 110
    Procedures for Promoting Positive Behaviour 113
    Dealing With Inappropriate Behaviour 114
    Expectations/Rules and Boundaries 116
    Rewards and Sanctions 116
    When to Refer Inappropriate Behaviour to Others 117
  Reflective Questions 118

Further Reading 120
References 120

5   Planning for Inclusive Teaching and Learning   124
Introduction 124
Universal Design Learning 125
  Creating Inclusive Lesson Plans 126
    Step 1: Know Your Learner/s and the Educational
      Context 128
    Step 2: Outline Learning Outcomes and Learning
      Objectives 128
    Step 3: Develop the Lesson Introduction 133
    Step 4: Plan Specific Learning Activities and Teaching
      Methodologies 133
    Step 5: Plan to Check for Understanding 136
    Step 6: Develop a Lesson Conclusion 136
    Step 7: Create a Timeline 137
    Step 8: Consider the Resources Available to You and
      Your Learners 137
    Step 9: Consider Potential Risks and Hazards 137
    Step 10: Plan for Reflection on Your Lesson Plan
      and Lesson Delivery 139
  Reflective Questions 142
Further Reading 144
References 144

6   Leading Music Learning   146
Introduction 146
  Early Years 147
  Primary School 150
  Secondary School 158
  Vocal and Instrumental Music 163
    Approaches to Instrumental and Vocal
      Teaching 165
    Scaffolding and Teachers' Teaching Behaviours 168
  Community Music 176
    Principles and Approaches 178
    Inclusion, Hospitality and Ethics of Care 180
    Facilitation and Workshops 181
  Reflective Questions 186
Further Reading 188
References 189

7 **Assessing Music Learning** 193
  Introduction 193
  The Purposes of Assessment 193
    What Should be Assessed? 195
    Formative Assessment and Feedback 196
    Summative Assessment 198
    Methods and Tools 200
      Teacher Observation 200
      Teacher-Designed Tasks and Tests 201
      Work Samples and Portfolios 201
      Projects 201
      Records of Learners' Achievements 202
      Self- and Peer Assessment 202
    Reflective Questions 204
  Further Reading 205
  References 205

SECTION III
The Music Educator and Their Wider Professional Role 207

8 **Safeguarding and Child Protection in Music Education** 209
  Introduction 209
    The UK Context: Legislation, Guidelines, Policies
      and Procedures 210
    The Roles of Different Individuals and Agencies 211
    Understanding and Recognising Different Forms
      of Abuse 213
    What to Do If You are Concerned About a Child or
      Young Person's Well-Being 217
    What to Do If a Child Confides Abuse to You 218
    Promoting Safe Practice in the Use of ICT, the Internet
      and Social Media 219
    Avoiding Risks and Possible Consequences to Self When
      Working With Children and Young People 225
    Reflective Questions 229
  Further Reading 231
  References 231

9 **Promoting Collaboration and Partnerships to Support**
  Musical Learning 233
  Introduction 233
  Why are Partnerships Important? 233

Types of Partnerships 234
Initiating Partnership Work 237
   Developing Effective Partnerships With Parents 240
   Developing Effective Partnerships With Schools and the
     Wider Community 245
  Evaluating the Effectiveness and Impact of Partnership
   Work 247
  Reflective Questions 250
Further Reading 251
References 251

10   Becoming a *Reflective* and *Reflexive* Practitioner   253
Introduction 253
Reflective *Versus* Reflexive *Practice 253*
  A Selection of Theories and Models 256
  Continuing Your Professional Development 261
  Reflective Questions 264
Further Reading 267
References 267

Index   268

Tables

1.1	Types of musical learning contexts	22
1.2	Learning dispositions in Learning Power Theory	31
1.3	Some types of professional relationships teachers can establish with their learners	32
2.1	A model of vocal pitch-matching development for learning standard songs	47
4.1	Learning styles categories, definitions and implications for music learning and teaching	95
4.2	Developing psychological health and fulfilling basic human psychological needs through music teaching	111
5.1	Example of a proposed learning outcome and aligned learning objectives for a Music Theory lesson	129
5.2	Summary of lesson planning steps and some aspects to consider	140
6.1	Categorisations used in the Teacher Behaviour and Gesture Framework (TBG)	169
6.2	Pillars of effective instrumental music teaching and constituent elements	172
8.1	Categorisation of risks to online safety	220
10.1	Possible questions to guide reflection when using Gibbs Reflective Cycle (1988)	260
10.2	A proposed Continuous Professional Development (CPD) model for music teachers	262

Figures

5.1 Domains of learning (cognitive, affective and psycho-motor)
     based on the work of Bloom et al. (1956) and some of his
     followers   130
6.1 Annotation template example A   170

Abbreviations

ABRSM:	Associated Board of the Royal Schools of Music
A levels:	Advanced level qualifications
AOS:	Area of study
CW:	refers to this book's Companion Website
CME:	Certificate for Music Educators
CPD:	continuous professional development
DNS:	Domain name system
e.g.:	for example
EU:	European Union
GCSE:	General Certificate of Secondary Education
HTTPS:	Hypertext Transfer Protocol Secure
ibid.:	as mentioned in the previous reference
ICT:	Information and Communication Technology
i.e.:	that is, or, in other words
IT:	Information Technology
LCM:	London College of Music
LPT:	Learning Power Theory
Ofqual:	Office of Qualifications and Examinations Regulation
PC:	Personal computer
PDP:	Professional Development Plan
PIN:	Personal identification number
RPL:	Recognition of Prior Learning
STEM:	Science, Technology, Engineering and Mathematics
TCL:	Trinity College London
U:	Unit
UDL:	Universal Design Learning
UK:	United Kingdom
US:	United States of America
VPN:	Virtual Private Network

Acknowledgements

There are several people whose help and support contributed in various ways to the completion of this book. I would like to express my gratitude to the editor of the book, Constance Ditzel, and the Routledge Editing Team which has overseen this book from proposal to publication. I am particularly indebted to its anonymous reviewers and Dr Oscar Odena for their expert guidance and relevant review insights, which contributed to substantial improvements being made. Last, but not least, I am grateful to the following people: all music and CME learners I have taught and mentored over the years for what they have managed to teach me; Dr Salah Sharief (Wordsmiths Director); and the Wordsmiths team for advice and suggestions on writing style; and to my partner, son and daughter for their continued love, support and patience.

Lilian Simones
December 2020

Preface

My experiences as a mentor and course director for the Certificate for Music Educators (CME) Level 4 course have enabled me to gain unique insights into the learning needs of CME learners and the support they require to succeed in the course. Having been validated by both the Associated Board of the Royal Schools of Music and Trinity College London (both in the UK), I soon realised that the long list of learning outcomes imposed by different validating bodies required a 'fit-for-purpose' guidebook which encompassed both. Specifically, a book that CME learners, mentors and others involved in course design, delivery and assessment could use to quickly grasp the latest research and practice insights on music teaching and learning. CME learners, and those involved in CME course management, are often people who multi-task between multiple professional and family related responsibilities. It is my belief that they will benefit from a tailored resource, such as this book, which will enable them to quickly become acquainted with the content required to successfully complete (or guide completing) the various course assignment tasks.

Keeping the previous ideas in mind, my aims in writing this book were as follows.

- To provide, in a single volume, strong foundations in the practicalities of teaching music in contemporary diverse settings. These include instrumental and vocal teaching; early years; primary and secondary schools; and community-based contexts;

- To align the latest insights of up-to-date literature on the course contents clearly and directly with the course learning outcomes. This will aid students, mentors and others involved in course design, delivery and assessment to more easily navigate the learning outcomes (at times quite intricate) prescribed by the CME validating bodies;

- To support CME learners, mentors and others involved in course conceptualisation, delivery and assessment in optimising their co-shared learning, teaching and mentoring. This will enhance both their learning and professional engagement experiences;

- To promote both a *reflective* and *reflexive* music teacher and educators' landscape in all music teaching contexts and settings.

Although directly aligned with the learning outcomes of the CME course, this book is inclusive of a wider readership. This includes those *engaged* and those *not engaged* in a CME course. This is because it was specifically written for all those who wish to reflect more deeply on their teaching and take it to the next level. It will certainly prove handy for those wishing to establish a port-folio teaching career, particularly in a world demanding that musicians acquire multi-faceted knowledge, skills and qualifications. More specifically, this book is for you if you fall into any of the following categories.

- A teacher in studio settings (instrumental or vocal), an early year's music educator, a primary or secondary school music teacher or assistant or a community music practitioner;

- An amateur, traditional and pop/rock/jazz musician with an interest in teaching or who is already teaching with or without a formal music or teaching qualification;

- A novice or experienced music educator, working in formal and informal settings in your home country or across the world;

- A current music student or a recent music graduate considering a career in teaching;

- A CME student based in the UK or elsewhere;

- A mentor, teacher or assessor at a CME course provider;

- A music teacher or educator in a college, conservatoire or university. This can be nationally and/or internationally, working across various programs but with an element of music teaching and learning.

The book is organised thematically and is divided into three sections. The first section (Chapters 1–3) provides a strong research-base for interested readers, centred on understanding children and young people's musical learning and the impor-tant contribution music makes in their lives. The second section (Chapters 4, 5, 6 and 7) focuses on planning for inclusive teaching and learning, leading and assessing music learning. The third section (Chapters 8, 9 and 10) considers the roles of music teachers and educators in safeguarding and child protection. It also examines the importance of promoting collaboration and partnerships to support musical learning and guidance on becoming a *reflective* and *reflexive* practitioner.

To CME Learners and ALL Those Intending to Develop Their Music Teaching Further

To support and enhance your learning experience, this book includes the following.

- A section at the start of each chapter entitled 'To Guide Your Reading' where the main content of each chapter is directly linked with specific CME learning outcomes as per the requirements of both the ABRSM and TCL;

- Reflective questions at the end of each chapter directly align with the CME learning outcomes and assessment criteria, alongside examples of possible ideas on how to address the questions. Additionally, these reflective questions are linked to the numbered criteria as given by the specifications of the validating bodies;

- For those who enjoy reading further, in addition to references to relevant literature provided throughout the text and compiled at the end of each chapter, a list of selected references for suggested sources for further reading is also provided at the end of each chapter;

- The book is also supplemented by an Online Companion Website, where you can access supplementary materials and resources. Access and login instructions are provided in the Introduction.

To the CME Mentor, and Others Engaged in Design, Delivery and Assessment

This book assists you in the following ways.

- It provides you with up-to-date content and references to both research-based work and practice-led literature which you may enjoy discovering (if new to you), or which you may find useful to signpost to your learners. Additionally, the content at the heart of this book may help you in developing or updating learning resources for your learners;

- The alignment provided of reflective questions to the numbered criteria given by the specifications of the validating bodies makes the book easy to navigate for all centres following either the ABRSM or the TLC validated route;

- The examples of ways for addressing the Reflective questions at the end of each chapter is comprised of aspects I have discussed with CME learners I have mentored. It may be useful for those new to CME mentoring, or for the purposes of training new mentors. Furthermore, the examples provided may in some instances provide more experienced mentors (or even assessors) with new insights through a realisation of how others approach what is being required by the CME validating bodies.

The diversity of music, and the music teaching and learning landscape, offers many opportunities not always followed up by those involved. This can be for music teachers to work together, learn together and help shape a large community of practitioners guided by a common vision of elevating standards in music teaching. This book aims to provide a contribution at this level by helping to build a music education landscape that fulfils its mission in society. This will be realised through the highest possible standard of teaching in all contexts where we work and for each of our students. I firmly believe that in today's world, such standards can only be reached through an inclusive and transformational agenda. This must be embedded in solid respect and appreciation for different styles of music, inclusive music learning and development of collaborative and inclusive teaching approaches across genres, contexts and cultures.

Lilian Simones
7 December 2020

Introduction

If you have picked up this book, it is likely that you are interested in taking your music teaching capabilities to a higher level. Of course, this could be, for example, for one or several reasons:

- You want to get up to date with current music teaching best practices to ensure that you deliver high-quality learning experiences to your students;

- You are facing specific challenges in teaching and are proactively seeking solutions to overcome them;

- You have realised the importance of having a credible, recognised music teaching qualification not only in terms of personal and professional development but also for enhancing your employability;

- You desire to establish your music teaching business on a credible knowledge-based foundation while positively differentiating yourself from local competitors and thereby attract new learners;

- You are seeking career progression within your current music teaching context(s);

- You intend – or are likely to hold – positions of increased responsibility, associated with increased professional recognition and (hopefully) increased earnings;

- You are considering a career change having realised that music teaching could provide you with the work-life balance you have always aspired to – for example, having a more flexible schedule suited to your interests and needs.

This book is designed to help you become aware of recent research findings in music learning and teaching practices in order to facilitate your further development as both a *reflective* and *reflexive* teacher. It will give you an excellent head start in improving your skills regardless of the pedagogical environments where you teach, the particular musical genres you work with or whatever stage you may be at in your career.

If you desire to connect more effectively with learners and provide them with meaningful learning experiences, then reflective learning on your own teaching and learning experiences requires specific understandings of *what*, *why* and *how* we do things so that they can be modified in order to best serve the interests of your students. Naturally, self-reflexive critique such as this will undoubtedly be enriched whenever teachers are up-to-date on latest insights guiding music teaching as a field of both theory *and* practice. Moreover, teachers who are able to professionally justify their teaching approaches are more likely to be successful both pedagogically and financially.

Although directly aligned with the learning outcomes of the Certificate for Music Educators (CME) Level 4, as validated by the UK's Associated Board of the Royal Schools of Music (ABRSM) and Trinity College London (TCL), this book is aimed at:

- All music teachers and educators in any part of the world who want to learn more about music teaching and learning regardless of whether they are enrolled in a CME course or not;

- Music graduates considering a career in studio teaching;

- Those enrolled in the CME course Level 4 at a validated centre;

- Teachers, mentors and individuals involved in the design and delivery of the CME course.

The book is divided into three sections. Section I (Chapters 1, 2 and 3) focuses on understanding children and young people's musical learning, while also considering the important contribution of music in their lives. It examines how they express themselves through music in a variety of different and combined ways, as well as the benefits of musical engagement more generally.

Section II (Chapters 4, 5, 6 and 7) centres on planning, leading and assessing music learning. The focus of these chapters represents the core idea of this book: our main mission as music teachers and educators is to enhance every learner's growth as a musician and to enable each learner to achieve their unique potential. At this level, I argue that the combined use of Learning Power Theory and Universal Design Learning can build a solid foundation for developing and enacting inclusive music learning environments in learner-centred ways.

Section III (Chapters 8, 9 and 10) focuses upon the music educator and wider professional roles, emphasising the importance of promoting collaboration and partnerships to support musical learning. It also considers the roles of music teachers and educators in safeguarding and child protection.

The final chapter, on becoming a *reflective* and *reflexive* practitioner, is intended both as 'an ending' of your reading of this book but also a 'new beginning'. The insights you will have gained from the previous sections of the book will inform your teaching practices and promote deeper, more informed reflections. Coupled with the learnings you acquire from your students, colleagues, mentors and other professionals in your community of practice, this book will assist you in continuously developing yourself both as a person and a teacher.

Each chapter begins with a short section entitled 'To Guide Your Reading' where the main ideas and theoretical concepts of the chapter are linked to questions related to specific CME learning outcomes as per the requirements of both ABRSM and TCL. This will keep your reading focused and thus keep you on track in relation to the course overall. At the end of each chapter, reflective questions, linked to some of the CME course learning outcomes, provide a framework for your thinking and give you opportunities to advance with some of the required coursework tasks. Tips on suitable content to include, as well as angles from which to tackle the mentioned questions, are also provided.

In order to get the most from this book, I suggest keeping a diary of your learning journey. In this, you can take notes relevant to your reading and write down answers to the reflective questions posed. This diary can assist you framing your Personal Development Plan (PDP). References to relevant literature are given throughout the text and compiled at the end of each chapter. Hence, you can choose the *exact* material that you wish to explore in more detail on issues pertinent to you and your working environment. You will also find specific instances where you will be redirected to the Book Online Companion Website, where you can access supplementary materials and resources. To access the Companion Website (CW) go to http://enactmusic.com/certificate-for-music-educators-guidebook-companion-website-resources and use the following password: access176789

The categorisation of stages and ages used in this book are described here and can differ from what you may find in other sources. They are:

- Infant: 0–12 months;

- Pre-school: 3–5 years;

- Early years/young children: 0–5 years;

- Child: 5–12 years;

- Adolescent/young people: 12–18 years.

Please note that the terms adolescent, young person or the plural young people are used across this book interchangeably. Moreover, to ensure clarity, the following terms in bold are also used.

- **Music educator, music teacher** and **practitioner** are used interchangeably to refer to those working in a professional capacity as music teachers and/or educators in a variety of different settings, whether they work privately, in music hubs, orchestras, schools, community music organisations or other settings.

- **Applicants to the CME Course** refers to those who have formally submitted an application to enrol in the CME course and are awaiting the outcome of their application.

- **CME candidate and CME learner** refers to those enrolled in studying for the CME course at an accredited centre.

- **Learner and learners** can refer to either those enrolled in the CME course, or to those children and young people learning independently or being taught by music teachers and educators in a variety of contexts. The meaning needs to be considered in relation to the wider context of the writing.

- **CME UNITS** (also called modules by some CME course providers), refers to the CME learning units or modules.

- **CME Assessor,** an individual involved in assessing the work of CME candidates.

- **Learning outcomes** describe or list measurable and essential knowledge, skills and competencies that learners need to demonstrate to have achieved by the end of a lesson or course.

- **Professional practice** denotes the knowledge and skills expected of music teachers and educators in their professional conduct in accordance with defined standards, policies and ethical principles.

- **Community of practice is** used to refer to a group of music teachers, educators, practitioners who share professional interests and concerns and who collectively contribute to professional advancements with regard to professional practice.

- **Instrumental music teaching and instrumental music** when the term appears alone, it denotes both vocal and instrumental music teaching or music.

- **Parents,** where the term appears in isolation it refers to both parents and guardians.

This book was written with the belief that by reading it, you will further develop yourself as a practitioner who more clearly understands the purposes of music education, is keen to enhance the musical learning of children and young people and can demonstrate the real value of music and music teaching professions to society and the wider world. Only by elevating standards in music teaching professions will it become possible to build a music education landscape that fulfils its mission in society while also advocating for a transformational agenda of music for all. It is my sincere hope that this book provides a contribution at this level and will promote dialogue which considers the varied polyphony of discourses of learners, researchers and teachers across different music teaching contexts.

Becoming a Qualified Music Teacher

Music teaching is an extremely common activity for most musicians. It is often combined with other roles such as performing; composing; music production; collaborations with practitioners working in the arts and non-arts sectors; and a variety of different musical and non-musical occupations (Bennett et al., 2012; Smilde, 2012). Several interconnected teaching routes in music include:

- Early years sector;
- Primary schools;
- Secondary schools;
- Instrumental and vocal music teaching;
- Community music facilitation.

The previous routes are not mutually exclusive. Indeed, they often interlink, and this confers added depth and nuance to the music teaching process. When these connections are recognised and conscious efforts are made to optimise them, learning and music making can become fluid, dynamic and exciting yet also rigorous. For instance, instrumental and/or vocal music teaching can take place in any of the aforementioned contexts. Community music facilitation often includes elements of both instrumental and vocal learning and it can take place in schools and in many community-based environments. New teaching routes into musical education can occur in any of these contexts. An example of this is found in the debate as to whether Disc Jockeys (DJs) manipulation of and improvisations on pre-recorded music in order to generate new sound effects can be considered as a legitimately "new" branch within instrumental music, or merely a synthesis of those already existing (Broughton & Brewster, 2003). Regardless of where new music teaching routes may or may not fit within the previous mainstream teaching routes, the reality is that each of these contexts is wide-ranging and requires specific contextual and musical knowledge and a particular set of practical skills. In turn, these need to be developed primarily through:

- Acquiring appropriate teaching qualifications;
- Engaging in lifelong continuous personal and professional development;
- Being an active member of a community of musicians and teachers sharing experiences, best practices and helping to create new knowledge in order to advance teaching and learning in their own contexts and beyond.

The requirements for becoming a qualified music teacher vary from country to country, and you must familiarise yourself with these. In the UK for instance, Qualified Teacher Status (QTS) is a compulsory teaching preparation for teachers of children in *all* subjects when working in maintained schools[1] and special education schools[2] throughout England and Wales. Several routes can lead to QTS status via registration with either the Teaching Regulation Agency in England, or the General Teaching Council for Wales. Examples include having completed an undergraduate degree and a teacher training programme, or having other education-based qualifications such as a Postgraduate Certificate of Education (PGCE). Teachers in Scotland and Northern Ireland achieve what can be considered equivalent to QTS when they register with their respective General Teaching Council (GTC) and which only registers candidates who have successfully obtained teaching qualifications such as a Bachelor Degree in Education (B.Ed.), Postgraduate Certificate of Education (PGCE) or a Professional Graduate Diploma in Education (PGDE).

Several new courses provide qualified teacher status to vocal and instrumental music teachers in Australia and Europe, albeit with substantial differences in systems of professional music training across countries in these continents (Smilde, 2012). Other courses intending to provide teaching insights for vocal and instrumental music teachers include the ABRSM, TCL and LCM teaching Associate and Licentiate music teaching Diplomas.

Although music in early childhood, has enjoyed consistent growth over the past 20 years, it is noteworthy that although there is wide variety of **short** courses for educators working in early years music, there are only a few options when it comes to becoming fully qualified as a teacher. In the UK, this consists of a new postgraduate course focusing on early years music education at Birmingham City University in partnership with the Centre for Research in Early Childhood (CREC) and a CME course specifically on early childhood music, currently on offer at CREC.

The UK has been a prolific environment for training for community musicians, particularly from 1994 onwards. Training has been delivered through various providers, such as:

*   Local providers such as Youth Music, Sound it Out, Music Leader, Community Music Wales and various others;

*   Conservatoires such as the Royal College of Music, Birmingham Conservatory and Leeds College of Music, which have also widened up their offerings to include programmes in community music at the postgraduate level;

*   Universities such as the University of Edinburgh and the University of York which have also followed suit.

Beyond the UK, there are various training opportunities for community musicians including: the Irish World Academy of Music and Dance; the Universities of Washington, New York and Boston; the University of Witwatersrand in Johannesburg; and in Japan via the Creating Music Culture Foundations organisation which delivers a variety of lifelong learning programmes deeply connected to the facilitation of community music (Higgins, 2012).

In a world where musicians and music teachers increasingly work within emergent and evolving portfolio careers, in multiple teaching environments (Bennett et al., 2012), the Certificate for Music Educators (CME) course offers a personalised and tailored music qualification approach by:

- Providing you with numerous opportunities to focus solely on the specificities of music teaching in the contexts where *you* work;

- Taking account of and then begins with your identified needs of development no matter what stage you are at in your career;

- Providing you with a mentor who will guide you through all steps of your CME learning journey, particularly on how to achieve the development goals you set yourself and how to effectively demonstrate achievement of the required learning outcomes via coursework tasks.

- Offering you the flexibility to combine a busy lifestyle, other life responsibilities and duties with your CME learning and coursework.

What Is the Certificate for Music Educators (CME), Level 4?

The CME Level 4 is a qualification for music teachers and educators. It has been created as a result of the Henley Review (2011) and the UK government's 2011 National Plan for Music Education. It provides a teaching qualification and means of recognition for music teachers and educators working with children and young people, whether in the classroom environment or outside of school, across a range of music teaching and learning contexts. The first stage of development of the CME was chaired by the Arts Council England and Creative & Cultural Skills. It involved representatives from across the music education sector in order to determine precisely what this qualification should assess and at what level. This intensive process concluded with a decision that the CME qualification should be comprised of six mandatory units. These are:

- Understanding children and young people's musical learning;

- Planning, facilitating and evaluating children and young people's musical learning;

- Reflective practice and professional development;

- Promoting positive behaviour;

- Equality, diversity and inclusion;

- Safeguarding.

Furthermore, it was also decided that the qualification should be aligned with the Qualifications and Credit Framework (QCF) Level 4. This corresponds to a Certificate of Higher Education, typically attained following one year of undergraduate-level study (or its equivalent). The ABRSM and TCL are accredited by Ofqual (regulatory body for qualifications in England) for awarding the CME, and both operate this qualification as a devolved qualification. This means that the CME is offered by providers who are validated by these awarding bodies (i.e., the ABRSM and TCL). Providers approved by the awarding bodies include hubs; schools; colleges; conservatoires; universities; and other organisations that work with music educators. Delivering the CME course under the specifications of the awarding bodies (ABRSM, 2014; TCL, 2013, 2019) the participating providers register, work with and assess CME candidates on the course.

Generally speaking, those achieving a Level 4 qualification need to be able to demonstrate an ability to critically engage with principles, theories, concepts, fundamental debates and relevant statutory and policy frameworks in their area of work and study. Furthermore, they must demonstrate that they can identify professional development needs and with guided support, act effectively upon these needs. A certain degree of autonomy has been given by the awarding bodies to providers in regard to tailoring their training and assessment to meet the specific needs of the music educators enrolled on the CME. This has resulted in some variations across providers with regard to the particular number and names of course units. Additionally, while the Trinity College 2013 CME course specification refers to the course learning content as "units", this term was replaced with "areas of study" in the 2019 documentation. Although the mentioned areas of study cover the same learning outcomes as the 2013 course specification, they offer an alternative model of delivery to centres to that outlined in the original specification and centres are welcome to use either model. Despite differences in the wording of the unit names, learning outcomes and the nature of the assessment tasks across CME course providers validated by the ABRSM and Trinity College, it is fair to say that there is a high degree of similarity across these courses. Specifically:

- Learning outcomes and core content;

- Accommodating music teachers from a variety of different teaching contexts and traditions, regardless of their career stage and/or musical genres;

- CME candidates are not required to have previous formal music or teaching qualifications. However, course providers undertake an initial assessment (usually via an interview) of individuals who apply for the course to ensure that they are eligible for the course (more on this later);

- There is a procedure for recognition of prior learning (RPL), in consideration of CME candidates who are less experienced at teaching versus those with more experience so as to tailor learning to their specific needs and circumstances;

- CME candidates are assigned a mentor by the course provider to ensure expert guidance particularly with regard to engaging in reflective practice and advice on how to demonstrate effectively their achievement of required learning outcomes;

- CME candidates are required to develop a professional development plan (PDP), outlining their strengths and weaknesses in development and how such self-awareness informs their development plans. The PDP is reviewed at various points during the course and is considered a tool to be consistently used by reflective practitioners long after course completion;

- Assessment is performed via a portfolio comprised of all the work the CME candidate has developed during the course. Also, the course **must be completed within 24 months from the registration date**. In my experience at Enact Music, the majority of candidates complete the course within nine to 12 months;

- To be awarded the CME Level 4, the Portfolio must adequately demonstrate that the CME candidate has successfully met the assessment criteria for each of the course units;

- **To enrol in the course, CME candidates need to be teaching at least two learners at the start, and for the entire duration of, the course**. The real gain acquired via this qualification is the practical application of knowledge and skills to the day-to-day teaching of music practitioners. Therefore, it also enhances the necessary preparation for, delivery of and reflection upon skills embedded in this process and which constitute an integral element of the course assessment tasks;

- As per the requirements of the awarding bodies, course providers are required to have in place a set of policies on a variety of topics, including complaints against assessment outcomes, dealing with staff's malpractice and equal opportunities.

Given differences in the name and number of units across different providers, and the type and nature of requested assessment tasks, it is advisable that you take sufficient time to **thoroughly** familiarise yourself with these elements as given by your intended course provider at the earliest possible stage. Although highly similar in many aspects, they are not identical. This will help you avoid later confusion, or even failure owing to a missed component required by your respective awarding body.

Are You Eligible for the Course?

Although the CME has no specific qualification requirements, there are nevertheless important entry requisites to consider. Applicants need to:

- Demonstrate sufficient and regular teaching (e.g., weekly) at the time of application and for the *entire* duration of the course. **If you are not currently working as a music teacher in any context, you will not be able to register for the course**.

- Have or be able to obtain an up-to-date enhanced Disclosure and Barring services (DBS) check, Access NI (specific for Northern Ireland) or Criminal Record check from the country where you reside (issued within last 12 months). International applicants from countries where it is difficult to obtain a Criminal Record Check should discuss their situation with the course provider directly. As the course entails working with children and young people, it is vital that all CME candidates are appropriately checked.

- Have a level of competence (both theoretical and practical) appropriate to the learning setting(s) where they work. You must consider evidence to provide at this level. In cases where you don't have written evidence (e.g., exam certificates, degree level certificates, a reference letter from an employer or line manager etc.) you will likely be asked to undertake an audition or provide a video recording of yourself working in your particular setting. During this demonstration, your level of competence in music practice and knowledge appropriate to the specific context needs to be evident. Course providers consider each case on its own merits, and if you feel you don't have enough evidence, **still go ahead and submit an application.** Providers will then be able to advise you on the best course of action for obtaining what may be required for successful entry.

- Have appropriate interpersonal, communication and musical skills that enable them to inspire confidence in, and evoke musical responses from, their learners. Most of this is assessed via the interview, as well as other supporting evidence and by references from your referees.

- Be able to cope with the learning and assessment demands of the qualification. These include:

  1. Time commitment: on average, the course will take 185 hours in total. For a CME candidate intending to complete the course in one year (considered as 52 weeks), this equates to an average of four hours of engagement in coursework per week. More experienced candidates may take less time. Furthermore, through 'recognition of prior learning' (which takes into account your existing strengths and experience) the overall time can also be reduced.

2. Dedication to the course: this involves engagement in the learning activities and course delivery mode proposed by the provider, attendance of meetings (both online and/or in-person) and commitment to completing the assessment tasks required, which will form a crucial part of your final portfolio.
3. The ability to be proactive with regard to your own development: this is an **essential** aspect of the course, and by considering enrolling in a course such as the CME, you demonstrate that you are a proactive person seeking to continuously learn and take your teaching to the next level.
4. Excellent organisational skills to adequately fit the course with other life commitments and priorities. You may be asked in the interview how you plan to organise your time in order to be able to study effectively.
5. In most cases, in order to access the course you will need a computer with reliable internet access, and you should be confident using basic IT (word processing, web browsing, etc.).

Choosing the Right Course Provider

Approved course providers are listed on the appropriate ABRSM and TCL CME webpages. Once you have the list of providers, please take time to obtain **as much information as possible** on their application process and on how each centre has organised their CME provision. You need to carefully consider how your needs will match with a specific course provider in order to make an informed decision. Pertinent questions to ask yourself include:

- What are the course delivery methods used by providers and which would be more appropriate for you given your current work and commitments? Online course delivery, or a course which has the content of units delivered in scheduled group sessions, or a mixture of both?

- What are the provider's main requirements for course enrolment?

- How many hours the provider has reserved for guided learning, and how much of these are included in the course fees?

- Is there a requirement for guided learning to be done in person? Will you need to travel to the provider, or can the course be completed remotely and entirely online?

- What happens if work you submit is not of the standard required? What type of support will you receive as a CME candidate in cases where you are required to submit several drafts for the same assignment?

- What learning resources will be available for you? Are they sufficient for your needs throughout the entire course?

- What type of assessment tasks are CME candidates required to undertake and how comfortable are you with preparing such work?

- Who are the mentors? How do their skills and life as music educators relate to your own learning aims and priorities for development?

- What are the course fees and possible payment options? Does the course provision and learning support on offer equate to value for money?

- What are the terms and conditions that you will be signing up for as a CME candidate?

Ensuring Success in Your Application

At the application stage, you will fill out and submit an application form. The information you provide will be decisive in determining whether or not you are invited for a CME interview. Ensure you fill the form appropriately, and that in sections asking about your previous teaching experience you provide **as much detail as possible**. If there is an option for submitting supporting information, please consider doing so. Supporting information can take many forms, for example: a link to online information about you and your work; awards you may have received; media coverage; or a video of yourself performing music. If you plan to submit supporting information ensure that the information you provide showcases you as competent to work in your context. If including children and young people's evidence such as pictures, videos or classwork, you must:

- Seek parental permission for the inclusion of this material in your application, and you must state in the application that you were permitted to submit said content;

- Appropriately anonymise any information that could lead to the identification of those involved.

Due to the nature of the course (where you will be required to teach children and young people), providers are legally obliged to seek further assurances about you via criminal record checks and by approaching your designated referees (normally there are two). Remember to ask permission from referees to provide their contact details on your CME application form and ensure they know you in a professional capacity (line manager, school principal, work colleague, teacher, parents of learners, adult learner, etc.). Referees should be able to make judgements about your suitability to work with children and young people, your level of musical competence and its appropriateness to the context where you work, as well as your ability to cope with the requirements of the CME programme overall. Therefore, providing some background information to your referees about the CME course and what it entails will help them in preparing and submitting a truly useful reference for your application.

Ensuring Success in Your CME Interview

Efficient CME interview preparation entails three main aspects. I call these 'knowings':

- Knowing 1: doing research aimed at knowing more about the CME course provider and the specific CME course you have applied for.

- Knowing 2: knowing what knowledge, skills and abilities you should demonstrate at the interview.

- Knowing 3: knowing who the interviewers are. This will help you frame your answers in a meaningful way for your specific interviewers.

With regard to Knowing 1, it is important to showcase yourself as a well-informed applicant who has really taken the time to understand what the course units are and what the course will entail as garnered from a specific provider's available information. This will help interviewers to assess your level of commitment to your development; acknowledge your inquisitive mindset; and see your independent learning skills at work. All of these are essential for the course and therefore the more prepared you are along these lines the better.

For Knowing 2, you must do the following. First, demonstrate that you have a level of competence and knowledge which is appropriate to the context where you work. For example, if you are a self-taught guitar teacher with no certificates of graded guitar exams, you might be asked to perform a piece of your choice. If this is the case, ensure that the repertoire you choose for the audition is of an appropriate standard and that your performance showcases your musical and technical knowledge of guitar playing and performance. Second, and equally important, you need to demonstrate appropriate musical, communication and interpersonal skills. Be prepared to concisely:

- Talk about yourself as a musician and as a music teacher/educator while describing your current work environment. Here, ensure you give some **details about yourself as a musician, music learner and music teacher** (e.g., For how long have you been learning or studying music? Has this learning taken place in formal or informal learning settings? What music genres you tend to work with more frequently? What musical instrument(s) do you play? In what musical contexts do you operate? What music really represents you? Why have you decided to become a music educator?). You must also provide some **background information regarding your teaching context** (e.g., In what music education setting or settings have you worked before? Where do you work now? Who are your learners? Specifically, what is their age range, musical preferences, proficiency levels? Describe your teaching setting: large class teaching, small class teaching, one-to-one, other or a combination of settings? How many learners and classes do you teach?) And, **briefly state what is your teaching philosophy** (i.e., What do you value as a teacher? What do you, generally speaking, want your learners to take away from your lessons? How do you ensure that this is the case? What is your vision for your learners?).

- Identify the challenges you face in your current work environment and explain how you have (or are proactively seeking a solution to) these challenges. Even if the interviewer does not explicitly ask for such an explanation, providing it nonetheless shows that you are a resilient individual who proactively seeks solutions in order to overcome problems.

- Identify at least three strengths and three weaknesses in yourself as a music educator. Being able to identify your own strengths and weaknesses is an **integral** aspect of being a reflective practitioner, and you **must** show a good level of self-awareness about where you are in terms of your development but also what needs to be improved. When stating your strengths, emphasise how these benefit learners and explain how you enact such strengths in your teaching, and specifically how these strengths positively influence the quality of the educational provision you deliver in general. If asked to refer to your weaknesses, don't simply state your weaknesses. Rather, explain what you have been doing to overcome the identified weaknesses and how effective or ineffective your strategies have been. A specific interviewer may very well have had similar difficulties themselves at some point and hence see you as an ideal student! The point is not to showcase yourself as a 'super person' who does everything right. Instead, it is to demonstrate how you have identified weaknesses and how you are (and have been) proactively engaged in overcoming obstacles in your teaching career.

- Explain how you think that achieving the CME qualification would enhance your professional credentials. It might be helpful to consider where you see yourself in three or five years and how you think that attending the CME course can help you achieve your professional and developmental goals. Consider the following questions. Why have **you** applied for this course? What do you think you will get out of it? How can you answer these questions while demonstrating that you are aware of the course contents and what it entails? Be ready to expand upon your answers with examples of your teaching where appropriate.

For Knowing 3 (knowing the interviewers, their specialisms, interests, etc.), if at the interview invitation stage it is *not* disclosed to you who the interviewer or interviewers are, you may contact the provider to ask them if it is possible that they provide you with this information. However, if for some reason the provider is unwilling to do so, do not insist. If the provider reveals the interviewers' names, take time in advance to obtain information on what they do and how their work may or may not relate to yours. Consider the following questions. Where do they work? What do they value? What is interesting to them? Knowing these elements will greatly assist you in preparing and delivering interview answers that resonate more clearly with their interests and which are therefore more likely to create a good first impression. One crucial aspect to keep in mind is to never approach interviewers directly before or after your interview **unless** they happen to be the main point of contact between you and the course provider.

Getting the Most Out of Your Mentor

Your designated mentor will likely be an experienced music teacher and educator, whose primary role is to support you in your development as a music educator. They will help you identify needs in your development and to fulfil your potential. To do so, he or she will prompt you to realise a vision for yourself while supporting you to recognise and gradually enact your leadership qualities as a music teacher and educator, both in the short and long term. They will also help you to consider:

- What can you do to have an active role in shaping the landscape of music education in the context(s) where you currently work and beyond?

- What partnerships can you establish with others in order to achieve common goals?

- What strategies can you implement to improve your teaching? What resources do you need to do so? If resources are required and not available, how can **you** help to materialise the necessary resources? When and how would you do this?

- What are the priorities concerning your identified development needs and why?

- How to develop a PDP which is meaningful and realistic in light of your current life and professional circumstances, resources and other aspects?

- How to tackle the learning required for the CME course, assessment tasks and additional evidence in a timely fashion?

- How can you ensure that you effectively demonstrate achievement of the CME learning outcomes and that your work is of the standard required for submission?

- What learning resources are most appropriate for you (i.e., books, articles, webpages, videos, etc.)?

To make the most out of your mentor, it is vital that you take ownership of your development by placing yourself in the 'driving seat' of the mentor/ mentee relationship. You must also be continuously proactive in reflecting on your learning and maintaining an open mind with regard to trying out new things. Take the initiative for agreeing the number, frequency and duration of meetings from day one and devise a plan for each meeting to ensure you obtain the answers and support you are looking for and whenever you need it the most. When requesting feedback on your work, ensure you send the material to be reviewed at a reasonably early date and within a mutually workable timeframe. I suggest agreeing in advance dates for provision of feedback and submission.

As the mentoring relationship progresses, assess regularly if your mentor/ mentee relationship is providing you with the right amount of support and guidance. Consider discussing at specific intervals your expectations versus benefits of the relationship for both of you. The mentor's role is **not** to provide you with all the answers. Instead, it is to empower you to find your own way through, to help you find and believe in your potential and to draw your attention to different resources and strategies which may be of more use to you.

Notes

1. Maintained Schools in the UK are schools maintained by the Local Authority, and in which the national curriculum must be followed, in addition to national teacher employment conditions and guidelines.
2. Special education schools in the UK are schools where special education provision is made for children and young people with special education needs (SEN). These schools can be maintained by the local authority. However, there are a number of non-maintained special schools and independent special schools.

References

Associated Board of the Royal Schools of Music (ABRSM) (2014). *Level 4 certificate for music educators: Assessment framework*. ABRSM.

Bennett, D., Beeching, A., Perkins, R., Carruthers, G., & Weller, J. (2012). Music, musicians and careers. In D. Bennett (Ed.), *Life in the real world: How to make music graduates employable* (pp. 3–9). Common Ground.

Broughton, F., & Brewster, B. (2003). *How to DJ right: The art and science of playing records*. Grove Press.

UK Government National Plan for Music Education, Department for Education and Department for Media, Culture and Sport (DfE and DMCS) (2011). *The importance of music: A national plan for music education*. Department for Culture, Media and Sports. http://publications.education.gov.uk/

Henley, D. (2011). *Music education in England*. Department for Education and the Department for Culture, Media and Sport.

Higgins, L. (2012). *Community music in theory and in practice*. Oxford University Press.

Smilde, R. (2012). Change and the challenges of lifelong learning. In D. Bennett (Ed.), *Life in the real world: How to make music graduates employable* (pp. 99–123). Common Ground.

Trinity College London (TCL) (2013). *TCL level 4 certificate for music educators: Specifications*. TCL.

Trinity College London (TCL) (2019). *TCL level 4 certificate for music educators areas of study*. TCL.

Section I

The Importance of Music in Children and Young People's Lives

1   How Children and Young People Learn and Develop Their Musicality

---

To Guide Your Reading

• Why do many children and young people value music and why are music and music learning important?

• How can children and young people engage in musical activity and learning without the need of a formal music education?

• How are formal, informal and non-formal learning contexts important to young people's musical development?

• Musical development: nature or nurture?

• What is 'scaffolding'?

• How Learning Power Theory can provide a reliable 'ethos' for music teaching?

Introduction

This chapter provides a review of key literature on musical development, highlighting that musical learning and development results from the interactions that children and young people have with others and their surrounding environments as they grow and develop. Learning is considered as a multifaceted process which takes place in many different ways, and not solely through formal teaching. A brief, historically sequenced overview of major theories and key ideas on musical development is provided in order to contextualise the topic, leading into a deeper review on Learning Power Theory (LPT). The chapter concludes with a discussion of how LPT can offer a reliable and up-to-date conceptual basis that music teachers and educators can use in order to conceptualise their teaching philosophy and approach.

Musical Beginnings

All children are born with a capacity to be musical. As humans, we have the potential to express ourselves through music at all stages of our lives, including into adulthood. This has been demonstrated by a number of researchers dedicated to studying the foundations of musical behaviour (MacDonald, 2008). The major implication of such findings is that children and people in general are all musical, regardless of their own perceived levels of musicianship; willingness to engage in music making; and whether or not they consider themselves as 'musicians'. The innate musicality of children is a natural, inborn biological predisposition towards music. However, it is nonetheless shaped by people, groups, social institutions and situations that they encounter as they grow and develop in a particular culture (Hargreaves et al., 2012; Hargreaves & Lamont, 2017) Hence, musicality is both a biological and social phenomenon which begins developing at the early stages of life.

Many of the early experiences of language learning and social interaction have musical characteristics and can be recognised as intrinsically musical. Babies initiate their language learning by focusing on the rhythm and loudness of syllables in speech as well as the changes between low and high pitch sounds (i.e., speech intonation). In turn, parents and caregivers tend to emphasise these aural changes as they communicate with infants. These early communicative interactions between parent and infant are crucial for early communication and language learning. They are referred to as 'motherese' or 'communicative musicality' in the pertinent literature (Malloch & Trevarthen, 2018).

Communicative musicality is a shared interactive act between parent/caregiver and infant, and leads to meanings being constructed. As innately social beings actively engaged in creating and responding to musical elements, infants engage in rhythmic play (i.e., tickling, stroking and rocking), the reinforcement of 'no' and 'yes' with non-verbal equivalents such as shaking and nodding the head (all embedded in the 'motherese') as well as lullabies and play songs. Through musical exchanges of infant-directed speech, the infant progressively constructs relationships with known caregivers while simultaneously developing a sense of trust and enjoyment. These communicative interactions have overlapping educative and communicative functions which reiteratively combine to activate the innate musicality of children. The type and amount of stimulation that infants are exposed to directly relates to socio-cultural caregiving practices and environmental circumstances (North & Hargreaves, 2008).

An environment which offers opportunities for musical interactions can have a substantial impact upon promoting active engagement in music making activities and hence the development of musical skills (Marsh & Young, 2016). This was well documented in one of the earliest reports of young children's creative music making, "The Pillsbury Study" (Moorhead & Pond, 1978). Although conducted more than 40 years ago, it remains a highly valuable and relevant account of how young children engage in spontaneous music making when provided with a rich and supportive musical environment.

This study brought together a developmental psychologist and a composer in order to examine the spontaneous music making of children aged from 2–8 years old. It was conducted via observations and recordings undertaken in unstructured play settings at the Pillsbury Foundation School in Santa Barbara, California. The researchers believed that young children have an innate musicality and, if granted the freedom to play in a productive environment, their spontaneous music making capacities would be displayed during their day-to-day playtime. A nursery equipped with musical instruments was prepared and staff recorded their observations of the children's musical activities over a period of several years. As Barrett & Tafuri (2012) have noted, the results of this study revealed that young children engage in massive amounts of musical play. The study provided a rich description of the diversity of children's early music making abilities. These included:

- Young children's capacity and willingness to experiment (both vocally and instrumentally);

- Their readiness to spontaneously engage in invention individually and with others;

- A strong relationship between words and rhythm in the early songs;

- The embodied nature of much of their music making.

Taken together, this demonstrates that children are active agents in their world. They intentionally express themselves through music and engage in music making individually and socially. These activities serve as a way to actively define and redefine not only who they are, but also who they want to become via processes that shape their continuously evolving identities. In this way, they use their personal and musical agency which are vital ingredients for effective music learning. More precisely, these can be defined as: "a belief in one's capacity to engage musically, initiate musical ideas, and intentionally influence one's musical life circumstances" (Wiggins, 2016, p. 104). Agency is used to initiate instances of self-expression and musical play with other children but also between children and adults. This is used to decide whether or not to learn to sing or play a preferred song or musical piece, to create a new song or composition, to interact with a musical instrument informally or perhaps to engage in a more or less structured learning approach.

Music is integral to being human and is understood to play a vital role across all cultures as a way of expressing one's inner emotions, feelings and thoughts (Hallam, 2006). Since music is everywhere (whether we notice it or not), it becomes an everyday element that children of all ages and people absorb. Whether in the home environment, the family car, on school buses, at supermarkets, restaurants, coffee shops, dentist clinics or even hospitals, people of all ages are internalising musical output as a normal part of their daily lives. It plays a crucial role in individual and social development, and our experience of music is framed and shaped by sonic interactions within particular sociocultural contexts. As such, it is therefore influenced by individual subjectivity, maturation and biography (Welch & McPherson, 2012). Children and young people are greatly influenced by all of the previously mentioned ideas, and their musical worlds will ultimately depend on the value children, young people and their parents place on the activity, as well as the cultural modes of experiencing music and wider opportunities for musical engagement.

Musical Worlds and Musical Learning

'Musical worlds' refers to the contexts of music making where young children, children, young people and people in general use music as a means to express individual and group identities and where learning occurs. Mans (2009, p. 10) defines musical worlds as: "culturally informed systems of musical thinking and creating". The type of learning which occurs in musical worlds, also called 'contexts' in the music education literature, can be classified according to the degree of formality by which music is acquired and transmitted (see Table 1.1).

Informal learning takes place in everyday life and begins well before formal schooling. Enculturative learning transpires via cultural immersion through a variety of processes that lead to implicit understandings of the value and knowledge of musical repertoires through membership and participation in society (Campbell, 2016). For example, it is through enculturative learning that we learn language (verbal and gestural) and gender roles. These are learned, but not taught. Instead, they are acquired mostly through mechanisms outside our conscious awareness. Around the world, children grow musically in ways that are highly similar across cultures but also through the process of enculturation whereby their idiosyncratic musical engagement and music making reflects their home, family and cultural environment. Their schooling will be performed in accordance with national policies which are likewise also culturally informed.

Table 1.1 Types of musical learning contexts

Informal (Campbell, 1998, 2010)	Enculturative	When learning occurs naturally, non-consciously, and without direct instructional activity of any sort.
	Partly guided	When learning occurs outside institutionalised settings through the prompting of non-consecutive directives, by expert musicians or others less qualified all the way to novices.
Formal (Campbell, 1998, 2010)	Guided	With a teacher, in highly-structured settings such as schools. It has a predetermined curriculum and accredited assessment structure.
Non-formal (Hallam, 2017)		May take place in a school or institution, but in an informal context.

Source: Adapted from Campbell (1998, 2010, 2016); Hallam (2017)

Informally, children and young people participate in several cultural activities wherein music has a prominent role (e.g., religious rituals, sports activities where national anthems are played and sung or where there is cheering from fans through singing). They listen to music in a variety of ways: purposively, passively, actively or even unintentionally; to music that they have chosen; or music that has been chosen by others. Perhaps they will teach themselves to play a song on a keyboard using YouTube, or through the infrequent modelling of a parent, neighbour, sibling or friend. Many learn to use creative software (e.g., Garage Band) in order to create and produce their own music. Some may join a band and learn music with the help of peers or expert musicians, sometimes in more or less structured ways. Young children, children and young people also use music informally in a range of activities and settings. For instance:

- Solitary or small group improvisatory music making and play at home (Young, 2006);

- In playgrounds (at school or other settings) where traditional and popular repertoire is learned by interaction with other children (Campbell, 2010);

- Brief improvisatory utterances while listening to music or while singing either alone or with friends, including family (e.g., whistling, tapping on a table top) (Campbell, 2010);

- Listening to and participating in musical experiences in the family and wider cultural environment while nurturing musical preferences and cultural traditions (Campbell, 2010).

Research conducted on informal learning in music highlights the importance of valuing aural learning at a deeper level in music education. This has led to calls for the inclusion of aspects of informal music learning in formal music learning contexts (e.g., Davis, 2012; Green, 2008). These ideas have been taken forward by, among others, Musical Futures, a not-for-profit organisation which first began in the UK as the Paul Hamlyn Foundation Initiative. The approach is based on the use of learning methods that are employed by popular musicians and community practitioners, outside formal settings. Hence, Musical Futures is regarded as an 'informal' teaching and learning approach but which can still nevertheless be offered in formal learning environments. It takes learners' musical interests as a departing point and is highly focused on experiential learning, whereby sound comprehension/reproduction comes before study of symbolic notation. In this way, there is an intense focus on development of aural skills through playing by ear. Learning is acquired through immersion in music listening and music making, often in highly sociable group learning environments wherein learners develop a variety of cooperation and negotiation skills. Moreover, in these situations performing, composing, listening and improvising are considered as being holistically integrated within the broader context of music learning.

Formally, young children, children and young people may take part in structured musical activities where learning is guided by a teacher in accordance with the musical provision formally available at their preschool environment or school. However, even in such environments it is also likely that they will engage in non-formal music making, such as using music in play activities during break times as well as other informal learning experiences. Sometimes, they may also receive formal music tuition outside the school environment. For example, learning to play a musical instrument at a specific institution such as a conservatoire, academy or at home under the tutelage of an instrumental music teacher.

Considered together, the aforementioned formal/informal opportunities underscore the social nature of music making and music learning. Regardless of the type of learning taking place in different musical worlds or contexts, and regardless of the degree of formality by which music is acquired and transmitted, we most frequently learn from and/or with others. Even 'independent learning' utilises processes, strategies and information that has been previously learned *from* others, or via products created *by* them. These methods of acquiring musical learning align with social constructivist theories of learning, which characterise learning as a constructive process of the *individual* but which takes place in a *social* context (Lave & Wenger, 1991; Rogoff, 2003; Vygotsky, 1978). Today, the predominant views on music learning and teaching are rooted in these theories but also through insights gained by cognitive-developmental educational scholars (e.g., Bruner, 1966; Gross, 1974; Piaget, 1970; Vygotsky, 1978), and more generally speaking through socio-cultural trends (e.g., Barrett, 2005; Lave & Wenger, 1991; Schirato & Yell, 2000).

These trends and theories emphasise that knowledge is acquired as the result of the interactions between the individual and relevant others (i.e., relatives, teachers in educational contexts, and various others within specific socio-cultural realities). These interactive and dynamic processes are situated in mediated interactions between people through a continuous, reciprocal process of meaning generation (see Amsel & Byrnes, 2002; Lave & Wenger, 1991; Salomon, 1993). Relationships are established between meaning, creativity and basic human needs which in turn suggests that the main purpose of the arts is to address basic human needs such as the ability to "create". Furthermore, this is linked with a need for "mutually belonging" and communal "meaning making" (Dissanayake, 2000, p. 156).

In tandem with this, music educational processes have been acknowledged as creative acts both for teachers and learners and which require their spontaneous cooperation in order to succeed (Bannan & Woodard, 2009). This notion has also been underscored by Campbell (2010) who suggests that people engage in music making experiences as a means of making meaning and communicating their understandings of their worlds. Drawing on Merriam (1964), Campbell (2010, p. 304) states that the meanings taken from musical engagement include "emotional expression, aesthetic enjoyment, entertainment, communication, physical response, enforcement of conformity and stability of culture, and integration of societal norms and expectations". These functions of music occur through both informal, formal and non-formal instances of musical engagement.

Musical Development

Musical development necessarily takes place within the wider context of general human development. As such, it is influenced by various interwoven biological, sociological and psychological factors. One of the foundational questions in developmental psychology throughout its history as a discipline has been: how much musicality during development is biologically or genetically (i.e., inborn, inherited) determined, and how much is socially influenced (i.e., acquired through experience of and interaction with the environment). This debate is commonly known as the 'nature-nurture' problem. It has given rise to a variety of different theories focused upon the influence of biology, environment and education (in the broadest sense) and moreover, the manner in which they vary vis-à-vis the extent to which they see individual characteristics as being genetically determined or socially influenced (McDermott et al., 2016).

Nature Versus Nurture

John Locke (1632–1704) proposed that a child is born as a *tabula rasa* (namely, a "blank state"), and therefore is entirely receptive and malleable relative to the surrounding influences within its environment. Locke (1690) considered that learning alone rather than inherited characteristics can explain children's acquisition of knowledge and understanding. Another viewpoint was put forward by Jean-Jacques Rousseau (1712–1778), who proposed a 'natural' theory of development, wherein the main premise is that children are innately 'good' and require little moral guidance for normal development (Rousseau, 1762/1956). He introduced the notion of sequential stages of development, to emphasise that children grow according to "nature's plan". In marked contrast to this, Francis Galton, in his book *Hereditary Geniuses* (1869), argued that intellectual ability runs in families and proposed an inherited genetic component to intelligence. Indeed, studies conducted over the past century or so concerning the influence of genetics on intelligence and which have focused upon twins and adopted children (Bouchard & McGue, 1990; Segal et al., 2018) uncovered correlations between identical twins even if they had been separated at birth. By contrast, foster and adopted children correlated the least. Against this viewpoint are those who argue in favour of an environmental approach to human development and who suggest that with the exception of basic reflexive actions, such as sucking, all human behaviours are learned, not predetermined. They argue that with proper support, motivation and appropriate instruction any person with a normal brain and physical functions can obtain and develop the same level of learning as any other individual, regardless of the level of intellectual demand required.

Skinner (1938) was one of the main supporters and proponents of this theory which has since gone under the broad rubric of "Behaviourism". Suggesting that environmental experiences are the real determinants of human development, he argued that children pass through similar stages of development because they are exposed to *similar cultural experiences*, not for any underlying, innate biological reasons. According to Skinner, although there are innate capacities (those abilities infants are born with, existing at the moment of birth, such as sucking) infants learn through a repetitious and cumulative process of conditioning and association governed by positive or negative reinforcement. Building upon this, Albert Bandura (1986), a proponent of "Social Learning Theory", added that direct conditioning is not always necessary for learning to occur, and that behaviour reinforcement can occur in more subtle ways. For example, this can include observation and modelling that arises without explicit teaching or direct support from others.

Bandura recognised the important fact that children learn by watching others. He emphasised the important role demonstration plays in the process of skill acquisition. In so doing, he argued that learning is not only a cognitive activity, but one that occurs within and through a shared collaborative process involving a learner and at least one other person. Although recognising the importance of environmental factors in learning, Bandura also emphasises a biological component by stating that children at different ages will be able to grasp different things. Moreover, he argued that the development of thought will exert influence on the type of reinforcement and learning that occurs. He recognised that within the shaping of individual development, a strong role on thought processes coupled with social interaction were vital. Despite differences in historical perspectives (not to mention heated debates in the 'nature-nurture' debate), today there is a general consensus that all these elements crucially intertwine in terms of contributing to, and playing a part in, how humans acquire and develop particular characteristics and skills (see Hargreaves & Lamont, 2017).

Cognitive Constructivism: A Brief Overview

The main premise in cognitive developmental theories is that the child plays an active role in understanding his/her environment. Specifically, they actively seek to learn rather than simply being a passive recipient of experiences provided via the surrounding environment. Piaget (1951, 1971) observed that particular conceptual skills[1] seemed to be attainable only if the child had reached a particular stage of cognitive development. According to Piaget, children are biologically predisposed to adapt to an environment by interacting with objects and events. He named four development stages which he claimed followed a fixed order but at *individually variable* chronological ages. Consider, for example, that some types of knowledge and behaviour cannot occur until a preceding stage has been completed. He termed and defined these stages as follows:

- **Sensorimotor** (from birth to around 18 months of age): development from reflexive to voluntary action. The child differentiates him/herself from the outside world. Intellectual functioning is entirely practical at this stage.

- **Pre-operational** or **symbolic** (from around 18 months to 7 years): ego-centrism declines and the ability to take other people's perspectives into account increases. The child starts being able to use symbols such as gestures, speech, play and mental images.

- **Concrete-operational** stage (around 7 to 11 years): the child is capable of using logic, mentally apprehending mental or physical actions.

- **Formal operations** (beyond 11 years): reasoning becomes more abstract, and whole systems of belief can be constructed.

Currently, within cognitive-developmental theories as broadly considered, Piaget's conceptualisation of fixed stages of development has been refuted in light of evidence showing that behaviours and activities within and between stages are far more diverse than Piaget suggested (Flavell, 1996; Genovese, 2003). Additionally, the view individuals develop regardless of their cultural and social environment holds little weight in contemporary understandings of educational psychology. However, the underlying concept of 'constructivism', whereby children actively seek to make sense of their environment (rather than being passively shaped by it), still holds true (Hargreaves & Lamont, 2017). As does his assumption that there are qualitative changes in thought processes as children develop, such that children's problem-solving strategies are recognised to alter with age and are usually considered as central to effective learning.

While Piaget's work is strongly focused on how children respond to their learning environments, other developmental theories place more emphasis on social interactions. Vygotsky (1978) defined a "zone of proximal development" which refers to the theoretical space between what a child *currently* knows and what she/he can *potentially* know if access to appropriate models and experiences within the social environment are provided. He argues that a child's chances at performing a task more efficiently increase if the child receives and understands adult guidance or works in collaboration with others through the process of "scaffolding".

Scaffolding can be defined as a useful interaction between an adult and a child, with the aim of helping the child achieve a specific goal. Vygotsky places a heavy emphasis on social and cultural factors in the development of intelligence. Furthermore, his theory also argues that there exists a strong link between the development of language and the development of thought. This theory deeply influenced Bruner's (1973) work which combined Piaget and

Vygotsky's theories into a coherent whole. Specifically, in the form of a three-staged sequence of development in which each stage partially overlaps, termed as "modes of representation". He states that in early infancy, children use *enactive representations* which are the basis of a sensorimotor foundation for cognitive experience. Later on, they develop *iconic knowledge*, based on images and direct experiences, and finally *symbolic knowledge*, which is grounded in language and transmitted through various cultural processes.

By observing children learning in everyday life, home and community settings Rogoff (2003) concluded that child learning and development transpires through participation in various activities located within their respective socio-cultural environments. Learning and development (as considered from a perspective of participation occurring within everyday life in children's own environments) is implicit and unintentional rather than deliberate. This stands in opposition to formal learning where learning is, by definition, of a more purposive nature (Young & Ilari, 2012). In this regard, Eraut (2000) has established important definitions for *implicit*, *reactive* and *deliberative learning*. They are:

• Implicit learning: occurs with little conscious awareness and is absorbed as part of an ongoing activity;

• Reactive learning: spontaneous learning taking place in response to a current activity;

• Deliberative learning: is planned to occur at certain times and in structured ways.

By emphasising music learning and development as resulting from the interaction between a person and his/her environment, it becomes clear that 'learning' is not something 'done' to the child, young people or learners in general. Rather, in an individual's life everything can potentially function as a 'teacher', and everything can potentially provide a learning opportunity and experience. Therefore, as teachers we should acknowledge all forms of learning as equally valid and formative, including implicit, reactive and more deliberative forms of learning. Equally, we should also appreciate learning with and without a teacher, as teaching is essentially about promoting learners' learning independence. It is also clear that access to high-quality music making and educational opportunities (be it within the home environment, school and/or community), as well as a supportive family combined with motivation to put in the time and effort required to develop one's musicality and musicianship will influence the type and rate of musical development achieved.

A Humanist Approach: Learning Power Theory

Given the potential which each human has to expand and grow through the various values and personal views different learners can bring to a learning environment, humanist theories argue that the learning environment should therefore be personalised to the needs of each individual learner. The main premise in this way of thinking is that the growth of the individual over an entire lifecycle must be taken into consideration: the individuality of each learner alongside his/her cognitive and affective needs are integral to the effectiveness of any potential growth. A theory which builds directly upon this idea is Learning Power Theory (LPT) which proposes a holistic conception of learning. To do this, it bridges together socio-cultural theories of learning, research into identity formation and life narratives, as well as motivational theories and concepts from Authentic Pedagogy and quality teaching methodologies (Claxton, 2002). In this theory, learning is conceptualised as:

> an embodied and relational process through which learners regulate the flow of energy and information over time in order to navigate a learning journey to achieve a purpose of value.
>
> (Crick et al., 2015, p. 121)

This short definition of learning contains relevant insights from a wide and diverse body of respected and credible research developed over the past 20 years or so. Drawing upon this research, we can understand the main principles of LPT as follows:

- **Learning is an embodied process**: Knowledge is generated through the perception and experience of an individual within his/her world and received through bodily senses, residing not only in the mind but also the body. Over the last 30 years, such ideas have been decisive in shaping and influencing debates within cognitive sciences (e.g., Johnson, 2007; Lakoff & Johnson, 1999) and arts education (e.g., Bowman, 2000; Van der Schyff et al., 2018). Thus, a strong emphasis has been placed upon action and knowing-through-action in music education. These ideas imply that the nature and structure of our mental activities derive from real and imagined physical actions, and thus learning is a consequence of our bodily interactions with the world, in which physical actions can eventually be internalised as thought (Bruner, 1966; Piaget, 1936, 1971; Vygotsky, 1991; Burnard & Boyack, 2017).

- **Learning is a relational process**: Over the last few decades, cognitive-developmental and socio-cultural trends (e.g., Barrett, 2005; Lave & Wenger, 1991; Schirato & Yell, 2000) have emphasised that knowledge arises as the result of the interactions between the individual and pertinent others –for instance, relatives, peers and teachers in educational contexts, and transpiring within specific socio-cultural realities. Such an interactive and dynamic process is situated within a framework of mediated interactions between people in a process of continuous and reciprocal meaning generation (Amsel & Byrnes, 2002).

- **Learners are in charge of the process:** Learner regulate the flow of energy and information as an expression of their own agency. Learners intentionally engage musically, initiating musical ideas and thereby intentionally influencing their own musical life circumstances. Personal agency is therefore central.

- **Learners seek to achieve a purpose of value**: The idea of 'purpose' is crucial in this conceptualisation as the authors state that effective learning requires the identification of personal desire or purpose, in response to identifying a need or a problem that requires a solution of some sort. Articulating a purpose in learning requires that learners know something about themselves, their stories and what matters to them, and therefore purpose is associated with identity as well as with time and place (Crick et al., 2015).

Learning Power therefore involves intra-personal (that is, occurring within the individual) and inter-personal processes (namely, occurring between people). As such, it is significantly influenced by the social organisations, cultural practices and world views of the learning contexts in which learners find themselves (Crick et al., 2015). Embedded in systems theory (e.g., Bertalanffy, 1968; Luhmann, 1996),[2] Learning Power considers five social interconnected processes that enable an understanding of learning as a journey of enquiry from purpose to performance (for more see Crick & Goldspink, 2014). In this journey, teachers and educators can play a crucial role. These are:

- **Forming a learning identity and purpose**: The learner is a purposeful agent in his/her own learning process and journey, shaping complex data into personally negotiated products or outcomes. Because humans are essentially social, and since knowledge is a matter of competence, knowing becomes a matter of participating in encounters *towards* the construction of a new identity. Teachers can help to facilitate this by engaging with learners' identities and developing a sense of 'becoming'. This can be achieved through promotion of a learner's critical agency as well as a systematic nurturing of the development of *learning to learn* abilities. Over time, this process will result in genuinely independent learners.

- **Developing learning power**: Developing attitudes, dispositions and values required for engaging effectively with new learning opportunities and enabling learning to be a meaningful experience. In fact, attitudes, dispositions and values are central to empower or dis-empower learning and in fulfilling a learner's chosen purpose. At this level, seven learning dispositions have been identified. These constitute what has come to be collectively termed as 'learning power' (see Table 1.2).

- **Generating knowledge and know-how**: This refers to the ability of the learner to pro-actively engage with knowledge and information. By

Table 1.2 Learning dispositions in Learning Power Theory

Learning dispositions	Definitions
Hope and optimism	Having the optimism and hope to learn and achieve over time. Having a growth mindset and believing in one's own ability to generate new knowledge.
Critical curiosity	Wanting to get beneath the surface and find out more. Always wondering why and how?
Meaning-making	Making connections between what it is required knowledge and new information and experiences. Making meaning by linking one's own story with new learning and purposeful action.
Collaboration	Being able to work with others to collaborate and co-generate new ideas and products. Being able to listen and contribute productively to a group or team.
Belonging	Being part of a learning community be it at home, and within educational as well as other contexts. Knowing there are social resources that can be used when needed.
Creativity	Using intuition and imagination to generate new ideas and knowledge. Taking risks and playing with ideas and artefacts to reach new solutions.
Openness to learning/ mindful agency	An emotional orientation of being open and ready to invest in learning. Having flexible self-belief, as well as being willing to persist and manage any self-doubt. These are necessary pre-requisites for developing resilience in learning and developing metacognition.

Source: Adapted from Crick et al. (2015)

acquiring competence in learning how to learn, identity, purpose and learning power are needed but these alone are not necessarily enough. These personal qualities interact with learning opportunities in both formal and informal contexts. However, knowing how to structure knowledge through selecting, collecting, collating, manipulating, mapping, analysing and using data to achieve a purpose is a distinct process in itself and where using tools (e.g., pencils, paper, etc.) is an integral part of the process. At this level, the challenge teachers are faced with is to support learners in being able to make sense of the complex data they encounter and moreover finding ways of working with and utilising the data in order to achieve a meaningful purpose overall. Formal education tends to focus on generating knowledge and know-how. However, all five processes are pedagogically significant for when it comes to designing contexts for learning as well as facilitating learning (Crick & Goldspink, 2014).

- **Applying or performing learning in authentic contexts – or becoming competent**: Authentic Learning contexts allow learners to explore, discuss and meaningfully construct concepts and relationships within contexts that involve real-world problems, and which are personally relevant to the learner. In order to support learners in developing learning to learn as a specific competence, teachers need to hand over responsibility for learning to learners themselves, both in terms of knowledge construction and performance abilities. In this way, they can nurture and promote active learning.

- **Sustaining learning relationships**: Humans are social beings and learning takes place via interaction with others. Learning almost always operates in communities of practice, be they real or virtual. The quality and nature of the relationships established with others is crucial in several ways, namely: either facilitating or inhibiting the development of learning to learn but also carrying feedback which, in turn, impacts upon how identity, learning power, knowledge and the development of competence progresses. While sustaining learning relationships, it is important that teachers are aware of the different types of professional relationships they can establish with learners. They need to be ready to move between different types of relationships via effective professional judgements about when and which type of relationship to enact (see Table 1.3).

Table 1.3 Some types of professional relationships teachers can establish with their learners

Type of relationship	Definitions
Expert/novice	The teacher is considered as highly knowledgeable and the learner as new to the topic. This type of relationship can be effective in terms of communicating certain types of knowledge.
Coach/coachee	The coach supports the coachee in identifying and developing their identity, purpose and strategies in order to enact them using a structured and formal approach.
Mentor/mentee	Mentors support mentees identifying learning needs and this also supports identity and purpose development. This type of relationship tends to be of a more informal nature when compared with coaching.
Counsellor/counselee	The teacher seeks to enable the learner to negotiate a pathway through a challenging personal or social issue and directs the learner to further professional support where available and as appropriate.
Co-learners	Teachers and learners learn together while undertaking a particular task.

These modes of relationship work together to form a continuum in learning facilitation and where trust is a crucial element for the sustenance of learning relationships. Learning, as conceptualised earlier, requires that teaching moves beyond the mere transmission/reproduction of knowledge and is conceptualised as a means of facilitating learning among learners themselves as truly independent learners. Facilitation as a general approach creates opportunities for establishing a partnership with (and between) children and young people through development of shared objectives and shared achievements. In this way, dialogue is promoted as a way to explore diverse assumptions and options (Higgins, 2012). Facilitation encourages learners to take individual responsibility for contribution at all levels in the learning process: specifically, it aligns effectively with the latest principles on inclusion and participation which have been the subject of a substantial amount of research by contemporary authors and specialists within the field of community music (more on Chapter 6, Section Community Music). Taking all of the previous ideas into consideration, I therefore argue that *all* contexts of music teaching and learning would benefit from a more deliberate, consistent and purposeful use of facilitation by teachers and educators alike.

Expanding upon this, in my view Learning Power Theory offers a reliable basis through which music teachers and educators can conceptualise their teaching philosophy and approach. A teaching philosophy is a set of beliefs and values that teachers hold about learning, teaching and their role in the pedagogic process itself. Hence, it is not only of vital importance it is also used to decide on what to do, when, where and how and moreover to justify what they do as *teachers*. A teaching philosophy should emerge as the result of a teacher's sincere and considered reflection on their teaching experiences from a teacher's perspective but also from the point of view of their learners. It must be based on concepts put forward and tested by reputable research and which are conceptualised as best practice among the professional community of which they are part. LPT provides a solid, reliable 'ethos'. It forms a set of guiding beliefs for a successful and efficacious teaching philosophy as based on strong understandings of learning processes as complex systems with interconnected dimensions to which you can add your own considerations on how to model, represent and evaluate learning.

Reflective Questions

1. Why do many children and young people value music, and why are music and music learning important?				
• Define communicative musicality and its importance from communicative, social, creative and self-expression perspectives.	Aligned with CME, Level 4 Unit (U) or Area of Study (AOS) and Assessment Criteria number of ABRSM (2014) and TCL (2013, 2019)			
• Consider how music is integral to being human, an everyday element, used across cultures in various ways to express emotions, feelings, thoughts, and personal and cultural identities.	ABRSM		TCL (2013)	
	U1:	1.1.1 1.2.1	U1:	1.1
			TCL (2019)	
• Highlight the active role children have in learning and understanding their environments.			AOS2:	1.1.1 1.1.2

2. How are formal, informal and non-formal learning contexts important to young people's musical development?				
• Provide definitions of formal, informal and non-formal learning and examples.	ABRSM		TCL (2013)	
• Consider your own music learning experiences (formal, informal and non-formal) and reflect on how they have contributed to the person you are today.	U1:	1.1.2 1.2.1 1.4.2	U1:	2.1
			TCL (2019)	
			AOS2:	1.1.3
• Reflect on how you could possibly bring informal music learning experiences to your learners within formal music teaching contexts.				

3. How can children and young people engage in musical activity and learning without the need of a formal music education?				
• Focus on informal and non-formal learning contexts and their importance from a developmental perspective.	ABRSM		TCL (2013)	
	U1:	1.2.1	U1	2.1 2.2
• Acknowledge the role that others (e.g., parents, siblings, and friends) can have in supporting children and young people music learning.			TCL (2019)	
			AOS2:	2.1.2 2.1.3 2.1.4 2.1.5
• Reflect on how engagement with technology and media offers a multiplicity of multimodal ways that young children, children and young people can use for expressing, experimenting, learning and developing themselves musically in various ways, without the need for formal learning (more on this in Chapter 2).				

4. Considering children and young people as active agents in their world, intentionally expressing themselves through music and engaging in music making individually and socially. How can you as a teacher support and nurture their agency development further?				

	ABRSM		TCL (2013)	
• Define agency.				
• Define scaffolding and how it applies to what you do as a teacher.	U2:	2.1.2 2.3.1	U2:	1.2 3.1
• Reflect on the five dimensions and seven learning dispositions of Learning Power Theory, particularly regarding how you can develop each of these dimensions and dispositions in your teaching with a view to empowering your learners in their learning.			TCL (2019)	
			AOS3:	1.1.7 1.1.8
• Consider how can you ensure that the musical repertoire used in your lessons is enjoyable and connects with learners' musical preferences? How can you balance this with the need to expose learners to a variety of different repertoires?				

5. Considering the types of professional relationships teachers can establish with their learners (as in Table 1.3), what type or types of relationship do you tend to establish with your learners and why? Would it be beneficial to use other types? If so, which ones? Why? What benefits could you and your learners obtain?				

	ABRSM		TCL (2013)	
• Reflect on how the professional relationships you establish with learners impacts upon their agency, creativity, and develops curious and inquisitive mind-sets.	U2:	2.3.1	U2:	1.2 3.1
• Reflect on the impact of your current professional relationship with students, specifically on their motivation for learning and self-confidence.			TCL (2019)	
			AOS3:	1.1.7 1.1.8

Notes

1. Conceptual Skills allow an individual to visualise and understand abstract concepts and situations, in addition to developing conclusions and/or creative and successful solutions. Examples include interpersonal skills; communication; decision making; and negotiation skills.
2. Systems Theories are grounded on the central premise that individuals do not operate in isolation. Instead, they grow and develop within and through complex systems and are involved in constant and dynamic interactions with their physical and social environment. These systems include the individuals, families, communities, organisations, society and wider world. Systems theories explore how the different parts of a system interact and interconnect. It holds that each system should be considered

as consisting of several elements that enable the system to operate and function as a complete whole (Teater, 2014).

Further Reading

Campbell, P. S. (2016). Global practices. In G. E. McPherson (Ed.), *The child as musician: A handbook of musical development* (pp. 556–576). Oxford University Press.
Crick, R. D., & Goldspink, C. (2014). Learner dispositions, self-theories and student engagement. *British Journal of Educational Studies*, *62*(1), 19–35. https://doi.org/10.1080/00071005.2014.904038
Hargreaves, D., & Lamont, A. (2017). *The psychology of musical development*. Cambridge University Press. https://doi.org/10.1017/9781107281868
Malloch, S., & Trevarthen, C. (2018). The human nature of music. *Frontiers in Psychology*. https://doi.org/10.3389/fpsyg.2018.01680

References

Amsel, E., & Byrnes, J. P. (2002). Symbolic communication and cognitive development, conclusions and prospects. In E. Amsel & J. P. Byrnes (Eds.), *Language, literacy, and cognitive development: The development and consequences of symbolic communication* (pp. 239–264). Taylor & Francis.
Associated Board of the Royal Schools of Music (ABRSM) (2014). *Level 4 certificate for music educators: Assessment framework*. ABRSM.
Bandura, A. (1986). *Social foundations of thought and action: A social cognitive theory*. Prentice-Hall.
Bannan, N., & Woodard, S. (2009). Spontaneity in the musicality and music learning of children. In S. Malloch & C. Trevarthen (Eds.), *Communicative musicality, exploring the basis of human companionship* (pp. 465–494). Oxford University Press.
Barrett, M. (2005). Musical communication and children's communities of musical practice. In D. Miell, R. MacDonald, & D. J. Hargreaves (Eds.), *Musical communication* (pp. 261–280). Oxford University Press.
Barrett, M., & Tafuri, J. (2012). Creative meaning-making in infants' and young children's musical cultures. In G. McPherson & G. F. Welch (Eds.), *The Oxford handbook of music education* (pp. 296–313). Oxford University Press.
Bertalanffy, Ludwig von (1968). *General system theory: Foundations, development, applications*. George Braziller.
Bouchard, T. J., & McGue, M. (1990). Genetic and rearing environmental influences on adult personality: An analysis of adopted twins reared apart. *Journal of Personality*, *58*(1), 263–292. https://doi.org/10.1111/j.1467-6494.1990.tb00916.x
Bowman, W. D. (2000). A somatic, "here and now" semantic: Music, body, and self. *Bulletin of the Council for Research in Music Education*, *144*, 45–60.
Bruner, J. S. (1966). *Towards a theory of instruction*. Cambridge University Press.
Bruner, J. S. (1973). *The relevance of education*. Norton.
Burnard, P., & Boyack, J. (2017). Engaging interactively with children's group improvisations. In P. Burnard & R. Murphy (Eds.), *Teaching music creatively* (2nd ed., pp. 26–38). Routledge.
Campbell, P. S. (1998). *Songs in their heads: Music and its meanings in children's lives* (1st ed.). Oxford University Press

Campbell, P. S. (2010). *Songs in their heads: Music and its meanings in children's lives* (2nd ed.). Oxford University Press.

Campbell, P. S. (2016). Global practices. In G. E. McPherson (Ed.), *The child as musician: A handbook of musical development* (pp. 556–576). Oxford University Press.

Claxton, G. (2002). *Building learning power: Helping young people become better learners*. TLO Limited Bristol.

Crick, R. D., & Goldspink, C. (2014). Learner dispositions, self-theories and student engagement. *British Journal of Educational Studies*, *62*(1), 19–35. https://doi.org/10.1080/00071005.2014.904038

Crick, R. D., Huang, S., Ahmed Shafi, A., & Goldspink, C. (2015). Developing resilient agency in learning: The internal structure of learning power. *British Journal of Educational Studies*, *63(2)*, 121–160. https://doi.org/10.1080/00071005.2015.1006574

Davis, S. (2012). Instrumental ensemble learning and performance in primary and elementary schools. In Gary McPherson & G. F. Welch (Eds.), *The Oxford handbook of music education* (pp. 417–434). Oxford University Press.

Dissanayake, E. (2000). *Art and intimacy: How the arts began*. University of Washington Press.

Eraut, M. (2000). Non-formal learning and tacit knowledge in professional work. *British Journal of Educational Psychology*, *70*(1), 113–136. https://doi.org/10.1348/000709900158001

Flavell, J. H. (1996). Piaget's legacy. *Psychological Science*, *7*(4), 200–203. https://doi.org/10.1111/j.1467-9280.1996.tb00359.x

Galton, F. (1869). *Hereditary genius: An inquiry into its laws and consequences*. Macmillan Publishers.

Genovese, J. E. C. (2003). Piaget, pedagogy, and evolutionary psychology. *Evolutionary Psychology*, *1*(1), 127–137. https://doi.org/10.1177/147470490300100109

Green, L. (2008). *Music, informal learning and the school: A new classroom pedagogy*. Ashgate.

Gross, L. P. (1974). Modes of communication and the acquisition of symbolic competence. In D. R. Olson (Ed.), *Media and symbols: The forms of expression, communication, and education* (pp. 56–80). The University of Chicago Press.

Hallam, S. (2006). *Music psychology in education*. Institute of Education, University of London.

Hallam, S. (2017). Musical identity, learning, and teaching. In R. MacDonald, D. J. Hargreaves, & D. Miell (Eds.), *Handbook of musical identities* (pp. 476–492). Oxford University Press.

Hargreaves, D., & Lamont, A. (2017). *The psychology of musical development*. Cambridge University Press.

Hargreaves, D., MacDonald, R., & Miell, D. (2012). Musical identities mediate musical development. In G. E. McPherson & G. F. Welch (Eds.), *The Oxford handbook of music education* (pp. 125–142). Oxford University Press.

Higgins, L. (2012). *Community music in theory and in practice*. Oxford University Press.

Johnson, M. (2007). *The meaning of the body: Aesthetics of human understanding*. The University of Chicago Press.

Lakoff, G., & Johnson, M. (1999). *Philosophy in the flesh: The embodied mind and its challenge to western thought*. Basic Books.

Lave, J., & Wenger, E. (1991). *Situated learning: Legitimate peripheral participation.* Cambridge University Press.

Locke, J. (1690). *An essay concerning humane understanding* (Vol. 1, 1st ed.). Thomas Basset.

Luhmann, N. (1996). *Social systems.* Stanford University Press.

MacDonald, R. A. R. (2008). The universality of musical communication. In S. Zeedyk (Ed.), *Promoting social interaction with individuals with communication impairments* (pp. 39–51). Jessica Kingsley.

Malloch, S., & Trevarthen, C. (2018). The human nature of Music. *Frontiers in Psychology, 9.* https://doi.org/10.3389/fpsyg.2018.01680

Mans, M. (2009). *Living in worlds of music: A view of education and values.* Springer.

Marsh, K., & Young, S. (2016). Musical play. In G. E. McPherson (Ed.), *The child as a musician: A handbook of musical development* (2nd ed., pp. 462–484). Oxford University Press.

McDermott, J. H., Schultz, A. F., Undurraga, E. A., & Godoy, R. A. (2016). Indifference to dissonance in native Amazonians reveals cultural variation in music perception. *Nature, 535*(7613), 547–550. https://doi.org/10.1038/nature18635

Merriam, A. P. (1964). *The anthropology of music.* Northwestern University Press.

Moorhead, G. E., & Pond, D. (1978). *Music of young children.* Pillsbury Foundation.

North, A., & Hargreaves, D. (2008). *The social and applied psychology of music.* Oxford University Press.

Piaget, J. (1936). *Origins of intelligence in the child.* Routledge.

Piaget, J. (1951). *Play, dreams, and imitation.* Routledge.

Piaget, J. (1970). *Main trends in psychology.* George Allen & Unwin.

Piaget, J. (1971). *Biology and knowledge.* The University of Chicago Press.

Rogoff, B. (2003). *The cultural nature of human development.* Oxford University Press.

Rousseau, J. J. (1956). *Émile for Today. The Émile of Jean Jaques Rousseau selected* (W. Boyd translated and interpreted). Heinemann. (Original work published 1762).

Salomon, G. (1993). *Distributed cognitions.* Cambridge University Press.

Schirato, T., & Yell, S. (2000). *Communication and culture.* Allen & Unwin.

Segal, N. L., Montoya, Y. S., & Becker, E. N. (2018). Twins reared apart and twins in families: The findings behind the fascination. *Twin Research and Human Genetics, 21*(4), 295–301. https://doi.org/10.1017/thg.2018.34

Skinner, B. F. (1938). *The behavior of organisms: An experimental analysis.* Appleton-Century.

Trinity College London (TCL) (2013). *TCL level 4 certificate for music educators: Specifications.* TCL.

Trinity College London (TCL) (2019). *TCL level 4 certificate for music educators, areas of study.* TCL.

Van der Schyff, D., Schiavio, A., Walton, A., Velardo, V., & Chemero, A. (2018). Musical creativity and the embodied mind. *Music & Science, 1,* 1–18. https://doi.org/10.1177/2059204318792319

Vygotsky, L. S. (1978). *Mind and society.* Harvard University Press.

Vygotsky, L. S. (1991). Genesis of the higher mental functions. In P. Light, S. Sheldon, & M. Woodhead (Eds.), *Learning to think* (pp. 32–41). Taylor & Frances/Routledge. (Reprinted from Leontyev, A., Luria, A., & Smirnoff, A. (Eds.). (1966). *Psychological Research in the USSR* (Vol. 1). Moscow: Progress Publishers).

Welch, G. F., & McPherson, G. E. (2012). Introduction and commentary: Music education and the role of music in people's lives. In G. E. McPherson & G. F. Welch (Eds.), *The Oxford handbook of music education* (pp. 5–20). Oxford University Press.

Wiggins, J. (2016). Musical agency. In G. E. McPherson (Ed.), *The child as musician: A handbook of musical development* (2nd ed., pp. 102–121). Oxford University Press.

Young, S. (2006). Seen but not heard: Young children, improvised singing and educational practice. *Contemporary Issues in Early Childhood, 7*(3), 270–280. https://doi.org/10.2304/ciec.2006.7.3.270

Young, S., & Ilari, B. (2012). Musical participation from birth to three: Toward a global perspective. In G. E. McPherson & G. F. Welch (Eds.), *The Oxford handbook of music education* (pp. 279–295). Oxford University Press.

2 Self-Expression Through Music Shaping Musical Identities

To Guide Your Reading

- How is music used by children and young people as a means of self-expression?
- How do children and young people use music to express individual and group identities?
- How can music education help children and young people develop their skills, knowledge and understanding of music to enhance their existing musical affinities?
- Why are technologies and social networking important for children and young people's engagement with music?
- Why is it important to support children and young people's musical choices?
- In what ways can musical understanding be demonstrated?
- What are some important models of musical development and how can these be recognised in children and young people's music making and responding?
- How can these models be used to explain and rationalise planning and music teaching decisions?

Introduction

This chapter focuses on how children and young people express and develop their musicality through various forms of musical self-expression and engagement. Namely, through listening, singing, interacting and playing musical instruments but also by composing and inventing musical notation, improvising, and through movement play and dance. Musical self-expression via the previously mentioned multifaceted ways is considered from a musical development perspective in order to explain manifestations of musical development and to provide a basis through which teachers can rationalise their planning and music teaching decisions.

Musical Identities: *What* and *How*?

Represented in the ways in which children and young people engage with music in everyday life, musical identities are defined by how children and young people perceive themselves with regard to their own musical aspirations, abilities and achievements (Hargreaves & Lamont, 2017). An integral part of the work we do as teachers and educators is to promote and support the development of musical identities. However, we need to keep in mind that the musical identities *we* try to promote need to be in agreement with the self-concept and personal goals of children and young people rather than with *our own* musical identity or musical style preferences. Only by doing this can we actively promote purposeful engagement in musical learning. To succeed at this level, it is crucial to have an understanding of the various factors that contribute to shaping both learners' identities (in general) but also their musical identities. Equally important is that we realise that all different contexts of musical engagement be they formal, informal, non-formal and the many intersections between them are all important. They work together to promote the development of context specific music skills, resulting ultimately in the creation of different types and styles of musicianship (Rickard & Chin, 2017).

There are many different forms of musical engagement that children and young people use to express themselves, and which continuously contribute to shaping their identity and musical identity. These include listening to music sang by others in their immediate home environment (mother, father, siblings, caregivers, etc.); actively engaging in musical interactions spontaneously (alone and with others) or when prompted; experimenting and exploring sound production by using sound making objects, available musical instruments and through the use of technology; and, of course, composing and improvising with music. Over time, exposure to these more active or passive musical experiences (either alone or with others) and more frequently than ever mediated through media and technology, begin to mould preferences in musical self-expression, engagement and thus the shaping of a distinctly 'musical' identity.

Children's sense of self-esteem, feelings of security and self-worth and sense of self-proficiency in various areas including music develop in great part as a result of their interactions with relevant others, including teachers. Obviously, the positive encouragement of family, friends, teachers and others exert a strong influence on developing musicians, affecting their perception of themselves (Davidson & Burland, 2006). A child *successfully* learning to play a new piece of music will become more self-confident about her/his musical learning potential, and this will in turn positively affect the child's self-concept as a musician. Music teachers and educators therefore play a crucial role in facilitating the development of successful learning experiences. Needless to say, this can only be achieved through effective planning and delivery of enjoyable and successful learning experiences to each and every learner (more on this in Chapters 4, 5 and 6).

Planning and delivery of enjoyable learning experiences requires in-depth knowledge of our learners combined with an awareness of the range of social markers by which young children, children and young people express aspects of their identity. These include their age; gender; ethnicity; family and group memberships (Cooper, 2014); and participation in virtual communities which is now an integral part of modern culture (Davis, 2016). Regarding age, there is no doubt that music is a powerful badge of identity for children and young people as they use their musical preferences to associate themselves to/with others and become members of their peer group. Young people's engagement with mainly popular music is a prominent feature during adolescence: many state that in their free time, their preferred activity is listening to music (Rickard & Chin, 2017). In fact, the connection teenagers establish with music is so strong that for many, music assumes the status of one of their most important and treasured possessions (Bahanovich & Collopy, 2009).

Various other factors also have a role to play in identity and music identity formation. These include parents' expectations for their children; role allocations and family dynamic interactions within the household; and parental and child self-concepts of gender and social roles (Borthwick & Davidson, 2002; Hallam, 2005). Becoming aware of parental and socio-cultural expectations, family dynamics and child self-concepts regarding those expectations can provide us with relevant information on what *may* or *may not* musically agree with a child's self-concept and preferences. Although some work has been done by music teachers over the past decades to overcome gender stereotypes in music education contexts, and which have seen some good results (see Hall, 2005), gender related conceptions still nevertheless exert a heavy weight upon children's and young people's perceptions of themselves as musicians.

For instance, girls often see themselves as good singers, and have more positive attitudes towards music than boys, whereas boys appear to be more confident in composition (Dibben, 2002). Gender distinctions exist not only with regard to attitudes towards music making but also in relation to preferences towards learning to play certain musical instruments. Boys continue to play the electric guitar, drums and large low-pitched instruments much more often than girls (Hallam, 2017). While it is important to combat gender-based stereotypical notions in music education, at the same teachers need to set aside time to understand how far they can go when attempting to push boundaries: benefits from teaching and learning interventions will only materialise whenever they are in agreement with learners' sense of self-concept.

Ethnicity has been shown to lead to association with a certain musical culture and associated musical genres, styles, practices and group memberships (Ilari, 2017). Consequently, it is relevant that teachers are aware of how ethnicity and age may be influencing learner's associations with certain musical styles and therefore they should consider ways to develop inclusive and democratic learning environments where learners' musical backgrounds and preferences are acknowledged, respected and represented in the classroom (more on this in Chapters 4 and 5). This aspect of belonging to a group or community (including belonging to a nation) is also communicated through national anthems and country-associated musical repertoire. It also tends to be strongly reinforced by teachers in the educational and cultural environment and by set school curricula (Folkestad, 2006). Nevertheless, in multicultural contexts it is important to understand how children and young people negotiate and reconfigure their identities in new or global surroundings (Folkestad, 2017).

Engagement with technology and media in its many forms is also shaping and offering a multiplicity of multimodal ways that young children, children and young people can use for expressing, experimenting, inventing and re-inventing themselves musically. Today, these experiences are quite diversified when considered in comparison with young children and children's musical experiences prior to the advent of technology, or for those whom technology is not as yet an integral element in their everyday lives (i.e., not every child has access to an iPad and Garage Band).

In light of what has been said earlier, it is possible to understand that identity and musical identity development is a highly dynamic process, where many factors work together in a creative interplay. It is in this highly dynamic interplay that children and young people construct, negotiate and re-construct multiple identities since identity is by no means fixed or singular: rather, it continuously evolves overtime (Cooper, 2014). Each learner has a unique life trajectory which shapes who they are and who they are becoming. This is therefore a fascinating but also a highly complex and sophisticated process (Marsh & Young, 2016) wherein many factors are influencing young children, children and young people's musical idioms, preferences and constantly defining and redefining their ever-evolving identity at all levels (personal, social, musical).

Focusing upon long-term strategies to promote musical identities is a primary goal for every music teacher and should be considered in all interactions we undertake with learners. From a teaching point of view, doing this effectively requires a deep understanding of how young children, children and young people express themselves through music by listening; singing; interacting and playing musical instruments; composing and inventing music notation; improvising alone and with others; and through movement and play, moving to music and dancing. These methods of expression are discussed in more detail in the following sections.

Listening

Music listening is something young children, children and young people do alone or with others, either purposively or unintentionally, side-by-side with other activities or as an activity in its own right. They may listen to their own music making or that of others in live or recorded performances, or livestreamed through TV, radio or the internet. Or, they may listen to pre-recorded music materials (video, audio or both) which may be associated with games, video clips, films, cartoons and other material. As music is everywhere, it becomes an everyday element that children of all ages and people listen to almost everywhere: in the home environment; in the family car; on school buses; and in supermarkets, restaurants, coffee shops, dentist clinics and even hospitals.

Listening to music is certainly not a passive activity. In fact, a great deal of knowledge about music is acquired through listening and exposure to music in a form of aural osmosis, which Richard and Chin (2017) refer to as "musicianship of listening". One example is how music listening (and especially popular music listening) is done side-by-side with many different activities within the home and family environment. In this way, young children and children are influenced by their parent's musical choices and enjoy being engaged with their parents' music (Davis, 2016). Listening to radio music in the car has, for instance, been reported as a lifeline of family interaction, where discussions about musical preferences between parents and children take place, and where children become acquainted with their parents and siblings' musical preferences, while also coming to know what sorts of music parents disapprove of (Davis, 2016). These listening experiences – done in the family environment – help children to connect with parents while negotiating their own positions concerning their musical preferences.

A group of children aged 5–10 and taking part in a four-year study on informal music learning, were asked about ways in which they engaged with music. Notably, listening to music was mentioned by a high number of children before any other form of music engagement (Davis, 2016). This same study demonstrated that children have developed a wide set of musicianship skills through listening, and which included gaining foundations for compositional processes (for those interested and engaged in composing); listening with a discerning ear for specific vocal or instrumental qualities; and for music that entertained and facilitated their musical identity, be it as a singer-songwriter, performer and/or other.

Listening in many cases also includes viewing associated video clips or being in a live performance; feeling the music and identifying with it at deep level of the self; and experiencing and assimilating its associated performative behaviours and practices. For young people in particular, listening to pop music is by far their most frequent leisure activity (even more than sport), to such an extent that pop music preferences are a core aspect of their identity. Pop stars provide role models for young people's lifestyles, including patterns of friendship, hair and clothing styles, leisure interests and other aspects of behaviour (Hargreaves & Lamont, 2017). The appeal of music during this stage of development (adolescence) appears to relate to music's ability to address relevant issues at this particular stage of life. These can include the need to identify with specific sets of values and beliefs; acquiring the ability to be socially responsible and accountable for one's own behaviour; becoming emotionally independent from parents; coping with mood fluctuations; and developing relationships with peers (Campbell, 2010).

Comparisons made between listening to classical and pop music by 9–10- and 13–14-year olds, respectively in the UK and Portugal, associated the benefits of listening to pop music with enjoyment and as distinctively differing from those acquired listening to classical music. In this study, listening to classical music was associated with pleasing parents and teachers while pop music was associated with listening at home with enjoyment, and also mood and social relationships regulation (Boal-Palheiros & Hargreaves, 2001; North et al., 2000) Presently, school music in many contexts remains almost exclusively associated with Western classical music, whereas music outside of school tends to be more associated with popular music styles (Folkestad, 2005). This is the case despite popular music being present at school, having been brought in by the learners and also in many cases by teachers (Hargreaves & Lamont, 2017).

Murphy (2017) makes the point that apart from developing a musical ear, listening to music provides starting points for the development of creativity. This is accomplished through the opportunities it provides for connecting familiar musical material with unexpected musical features. He also provides indications on how to best select music for classroom listening, engage students in active listening and generate creative responses as a result. Although focusing on the context of primary school teaching, the advice and strategies provided by Murphy can be used in all contexts of music teaching and learning and will undoubtedly result in a much more enriched learning experience.

Singing

The development and progression of singing behaviours is deeply connected with age, developmental factors but also with the type of musical environment surrounding the child as well as the level of stimulation and exposure to music and music making. We shall now consider how this applies to the various groups of learners in turn, particularly with regard to spontaneous singing; production of standard songs; learning song's taught by others; self-directed learning of songs (alone and with peers); and inventing songs.

Young Children's Singing

Preschool singing is characterised by a multiplicity of singing behaviours experienced between the ages of 1–5 years, and which are intertwined with the child's playful, acquisitive, spontaneous and creative nature as they go about making sense of their "local" musical worlds (Barrett, 2012).

Young children's exposure to songs of their own cultures leads them to attempt to repeat phrases and elements, many times with the support of the mother or caregiver, and who quite often regularly sings to the child for a multiplicity of purposes. These purposes include calming, soothing and helping the child falling asleep; stimulating playful question and answer communicative interactions; expressing their own emotions and feelings; and reinforcement of cultural meanings, norms, and behaviours. This process of exposure and enculturation leads young children to engage in the production of both spontaneous (invented) and standard singing (singing of well-known songs).

Spontaneous Singing

Spontaneous singing occurs when young children utter spontaneous vocalisations which are natural, unprompted, and self-invented. These expressive vocal soundings which go beyond spoken language, may include rhythmic speech and vocalising and singing with or without an associated language or language meaning. These mostly occur in situations of free-play (Countryman et al., 2016). Given that instances of music making can sometimes sound quite different from what we, as a collective, would interpret as 'singing', they can at times be interpreted by adults as merely being 'noise' or 'speaking' (Dean, 2019).

By studying in detail, the spontaneous singing of 2–3-year-old children in a free play day-care nursery, Young (2002) was able to categorise the types of spontaneous singing she observed into six categories:

- "**Free-flow vocalising**": vocalisation without words, often occurring in solitary play and without a defined musical shape.

- "**Chanting**": short musical phrases which are repeated.

- "**Reworking of known songs**": use of fragments of known songs.

- "**Movement vocalising**": vocalisation which includes movement either of self or objects.

- "**Singing for animation**": occurring in association with dramatic play.

- "**Comic-strip type noises**": imitation of sounds, mostly in association to playing with objects.

Characteristics of spontaneous singing vary considerably in relation to development. While for children aged between 1–2 years of age spontaneous singing typically consists mostly of repetitions of a brief melodic phrase, for three-year olds it is possible to distinguish three different melodic phrases. In none of these, singing is uncommon (Welch, 2016). Age also appears relevant when considering perception and expression of emotion in singing and recent evidence suggests that recognition of emotions in music and speech develop in parallel (Vidas et al., 2018). Children aged 4–5 years old have used conventional music strategies to express happiness and sadness through their invented songs, which included the use of major/minor keys, and syncopated rhythms for happy songs or a reduced pitch range for sad songs (Adachi & Trehub, 1998; 2011). The words and themes for happy songs centred around family, friends and sweets whereas sad songs focused on negative versions of these, such as having no family.

Production of Standard Songs

Production of standard songs refers to the learning of songs which are well known to a certain group of people, including in most cases words set to music or a rhythm, although they may be sung with or without words.

Standard songs tend, to some extent, to maintain a recognisable melodic and rhythmical contour. In most cases, there are variations of the same material due to the strong element of oral tradition through which these songs are communicated. Welch's extensive research on how young children learn to sing standard songs has led him to propose a model of vocal pitch-matching development (VPMD) for young children (Welch, 2016, p. 456). This has provided numerous interesting and useful insights for teachers and educators (see Table 2.1). The model is particularly helpful for recognising the different phases that children pass with regard to pitch matching development, before reaching a stage where no significant melodic or pitch errors occur. It also highlights that pitch matching in the context of child development is a *process* rather than a given trait.

To investigate the relevance of words in learning songs, Adachi and Trehub (1998) studied children's performance of familiar songs with and without words. They concluded that pre-school children performed better when they sang *with* words whereas older children were better when singing *without* words. Therefore, it appears that words are crucial in helping younger children to learn tunes, and music teachers and educators should have this in mind when planning teaching and learning activities for this particular age group.

Table 2.1 A model of vocal pitch-matching development for learning standard songs

Phase 1	• The words of the song appear to be the initial centre of interest rather than the melody. • Singing sounds more "chant-like" and employs restricted pitch range and melodic phrases. • In infant vocal pitch exploration, descending patterns predominate.
Phase 2	• There is a growing awareness that vocal pitch can be a conscious process and that changes in vocal pitch are controllable. • Sung melodic outline begins to follow the general (macro) contours of the target melody or key constituent phrases. • Tonality is essentially phrase based. • Self-invented songs borrow elements from the child's musical culture. • Vocal pitch range used in song singing expands.
Phase 3	• Melodic shape and intervals are mostly accurate, but some changes in tonality may occur, perhaps linked to inappropriate register usage. • Overall, however, the number of different reference pitches is notably reduced.
Phase 4	• No significant melodic or pitch errors in relation to relatively simple songs from the singer's musical culture.

Source: Adapted from Welch (2016, p. 456)

Children and Young People's Singing

Children have a diverse range of singing abilities upon entry into compulsory schooling. While some children will be highly proficient in singing and be able to sing complete songs from their own cultural environments, others will be less advanced, due to less exposure to opportunities to develop their singing potential. If provided with an appropriate nurturing environment with frequent opportunities for vocal exploration and accurate imitation, it is likely that their singing ability will be nurtured and developed (Young, 2018). In relation to their singing behaviours, children and young people sing songs taught by others (e.g., at school, community choirs, learning from a tutor or family), engage in self-directed learning of songs alone and with peers (e.g., in the playground, at home, at school) and invent songs.

Learning Songs Taught by Others

Studies carried out in the US and the UK have shown that children gradually move from speech-like chanting towards singing within a limited range. This is followed by an expanded vocal pitch range with incremental skill in the ability to match pitch correctly (Rutkowski, 1997; Welch, 1998). Children learning via copying of a sung model will in general do so more effectively when using neutral syllables rather than attempting the song with its words from the outset, as this gives children an opportunity to focus on the pitches that are to be reproduced more attentively (Welch, 1998). Moreover, while children aged 5–7 were very good at learning the words of the songs, they have only started to become more pitch accurate when pitch elements of the songs were deconstructed into simpler tasks. Simplified tasks included matching individual pitches, copying short melodic fragments and echoing of melodic contours (Welch, 1998; 2016).

Singing development is age, sex and task sensitive (Welch, 2016). Pitch range gradually increases with age. Concerning gender, although boys and girls were equally successful in the simplified tasks overtime, when boys were asked to sing the complete song as a group, their pitch became less accurate. Moreover, as a group, over the three years of this longitudinal study they demonstrated little improvement in song singing. Girls as a group have advanced more in their singing development when compared with boys, and this gap reportedly increased from ages 5 to 12 (see Welch et al., 2012). Gender stereotypes may have a role to play at this level as singing in primary schools in many contexts including Australia and the UK (Hall, 2005; Joyce, 2005) has been shown to be perceived as a 'female' activity. For instance, boys tend to believe that girls are better at singing and (hence, perhaps) there are less boys involved in singing activities than girls. In relation to singing tasks, having to sing a 'school' song negatively affected boys, as they struggled as a group to keep accurate pitch.

Beyond gender differences, singing competence varies at an individual level, depending on the task. That is, while a child may be more proficient at

matching specific pitch intervals, another child may be more skilled at repro-
ducing the melodic contours of a specific musical phrase. In the later years of
childhood, only a few children are reported as singing 'out-of-tune' at the age
of 11 years, however three times more boys are 'out-of-tune' than girls (Welch,
2016). The onset of puberty will change the quality and nature of the singing
voice, for both genders and in different ways. The age for onset and rate of
voice change are highly variable and therefore unpredictable. While it is possible for a young person to pass all stages in voice change in 12 months, it is
also possible that this process could also take several years (Ashley & Mecke,
2013). It is crucial that teachers are aware of these issues in order to prescribe
appropriate singing expectations for learners by considering what they can
realistically achieve at different stages of development and in accordance with
their particular circumstances.

Self-Directed Learning of Songs Alone

Considering the ways in which a child, with the pseudonym Kit, learned to
sing popular songs of her preference, Davis (2016) reported:

> Popular music is a constant companion for Kit, and her iPod touch is
> always within reach. Her method of learning songs, even for her private
> lessons, is to figure it out by ear first. She approaches this by first sing-
> ing the lyrics repeatedly until these words are secure. In this process she
> records herself singing on her cell phone voice recorder and then evaluates
> her accuracy. . . . [her] ear is her guide.
>
> (Davis, 2016, p. 269)

In this example, it is possible to acknowledge the importance of imitation
of aural models and the use of technology in mediating self-directed learning. In another example, Davis (2016), reporting on the development of
children's singing preferences, stated that many children participants in her
study admired pop artists vocal qualities and that this admiration was strongly
linked to wanting to emulate such vocal qualities, or through recognising such
vocal qualities as being similar to theirs. She gave the example of a boy called
John who has been singing publicly since the first grade. John has a preference for Bruno Mars because his voice is always the right pitch to match his.
This researcher concluded that children and young people's musical identity
in some cases evolved through identification of vocal timbre with other pop
artists as well as their ability to perform songs that were aligned with their
sense of self.

Self-Directed Learning of Songs With Peers

There is a huge contrast between learning songs from others in formal learning
settings, learning songs alone and learning songs and making music with peers

(for example, in the playground and outside of school). Harwood and Marsh (2012) describe self-directed learning of songs with peers as having the following major characteristics:

- There is a shared learning responsibility between the child and the peer community.

- The peer community provides both necessary social support for individual attempts and verbal critique of group performances.

- Learners choose the repertoire, and such choices express and define their identity. This repertoire is also tied to gender identity.

- The distinction between listener and performer is blurred, with opportunities to participate at many levels.

- Because learning is organised by repertoire, there is no perceived progression of skill from simple to complex and no set of preparatory exercises are therefore required.

- The means of learning are observation and imitation of aural/oral models performed by more experienced peers. When a games/play breaks down, play resumes from the beginning.

- On the playground, everyone owns the music and local, communally accepted standards.

- There is a focus on creative reworking of musical material rather than a fixed product.

- Body movement is an integral part of musical performance in the playground.

- Learning 'by feel' is preferred over intellectual analysis.

This self-directed activity with social, musical and developmental purposes provide many rich pathways to musical expression, development of musicianship and social skills through interactive peer learning experiences.

Inventing Songs

Typically, children aged 5–7 have developed a range of song creation strategies and also have a clear sense of musical form and ways to express emotion in their invented songs. They are also adept at borrowing elements from their immediate musical cultures (Welch, 2016). Their invented songs include (Davies, 1994):

- **Narrative songs**: often of a chant-like nature, containing repeated figures and features.

- **Songs with conventional features**: usually with well-defined opening and closure, repetition of elements, elements and phrases that are borrowed from the child's immediate culture and which may be transformed in varied ways.

Intertwined with inventing songs are also composing, invention of musical notation and improvisation, which nowadays have become massively facilitated by the use of technology. More detail on this, including on young people creative development, is included in the following sections. Spontaneous singing and invention occur within a socio-cultural frame of reference that children intentionally and purposefully adopt and adapt to "protest, plead, command, tell stories, annoy and tease" (Bjorkvold, 1989, p. 216). By doing so they actively generate and communicate the idiosyncratic understandings they have of their respective worlds.

Interacting and Playing Musical Instruments

More so now than ever, inexpensive musical instruments and sound making objects and devices are available to children, and they enjoy engaging with these when and where they are available. These may include electronic and acoustic devices such as toy pianos; electronic keyboards and guitars; ukuleles; acoustic guitars; recorders; a variety of percussion instruments and several apps which enable the use of touchscreen devices for playing digital keyboards; and various other digital instruments. Regardless of such availability, the surrounding culture and environment exert a strong influence on the type of music young children, children and young people may play in spontaneous or structured interactions as well as the types of instruments available, and the learning settings they may be exposed to. These can include:

- Self-directed learning;

- Structured learning with a teacher;

- Semi-structured learning perhaps guided by relatives or friends;

- Learning to play by ear or using a system of music notation;

- Engaging spontaneously in music making using improvisation or performing standard repertoire composed by others;

- Playing in group or solo.

In this section we will consider how young children, children and young people interact with musical instruments, their motivations for instrumental music learning and the important role teachers have with regard to supporting learners developing metacognitive and practice skills, the goal of which is to produce self-regulated learners.

Young Children

What may (at a first) apparently look like production of random and sporadic sounds by young children when spontaneously playing musical instruments is actually produced by structured and organised body movements and gestures which tend to result in regular rhythmic groupings and sequences. This point was emphasised in a study conducted by Delalande and Cornara (2010) with children aged between 10 months to 3 years and which explored the musical dimension of sounds produced by children in their exploration of instruments and sound making objects. This work revealed that the children's first approach to these instruments and objects was multi-sensory in nature. That is, exploration was audio-visual-motor and tactile.

Furthermore, in the aforementioned study young children approached instruments and sound making objects in various ways, for instance: banging the strings of a guitar with metal spoons; rubbing the strings with their hands or with spoons; or simply pulling them. Each gesture produced a different sound and these different sounds provoked curiosity and attention in the children. After producing several different sounds, young children became more interested in one, or a few, of those sounds and explored them further. This would culminate in the building of events and sequences, repeating them with some changes and combining them with other sounds. Young children's choices appeared to deeply relate with their own tastes, culture, characteristics of the instruments and their interactions with others.

More than mere sound production and exploration, three-year-olds, interacting with a chromatic metallophone displayed an awareness of form and capacity to structure musical ideas through the use of repetition and variation of melodic ideas (Mialaret, 1997). In alignment with Delalande's findings (2010), this research also suggests that young children's exploratory behaviour with instruments is both expressive and reflective of their developing understanding of the music of their culture.

Parental behaviour when engaging with singing and musical instruments also has an important role to play in young children's engagement with musical instruments. Tafuri (2008) asked parents to keep a diary of their children's engagement with singing and musical instruments. The study revealed that children were attracted to the musical instruments available at home. For instance, from 6 months onwards 97% of the children were very alert to the presence of instruments and if parents played them, they also wanted to do the same. Although singing may include in many cases body movements, playing a musical instrument involves movements that can in many cases be more substantial, such as banging and shaking, and the extent and depth of these movements allow both young children and children to interpret and express sound in ways that are deeply "felt by the body" (Tafuri, 2017, p. 210).

Children and Young People: Motivations for Instrumental Music Learning

The reason why some children move from the playful phase of engagement with musical instruments to wanting to learn to play specific instruments depends on the extent to which engaging with music satisfies internal motives and provides personal fulfilment (Hallam & Bautista, 2012). Interaction with musical instruments (including singing):

- Provides opportunities for self-expression of one's own identity and emotions, curiosity and self-actualisation;

- Induces feelings and responses, including exploration of aggressive drives through the use and development of required motor skills combined with some opportunities for exhibitionism;

- Fuels a desire for achievement and, progress and self-confidence in one's own potential.

Some children are intrinsically interested in engaging and learning to play a particular instrument because of the type of sound it produces, or the way the instrument looks and/or feels (McPherson et al., 2016). However, instrument size, weight and the physical strength required to play dictate that while some instruments may be appropriate for young children (e.g., a keyboard, smaller sized string instruments, etc.), others such as brass and woodwind are more appropriate to be started around 6 or 7 years of age. Extrinsic reasons for wanting to learn to play a specific instrument may include a willingness to join in with friends who are learning it already; emulation of a person they admire (be it a relative that plays the instrument, a friend, or a famous artist); and encouragement from a parent, teacher or relevant other (McPherson et al., 2016).

A study dedicated to understanding beginning instrumentalists during the first three years of their learning has provided rich insights into children's own perspectives on factors that have motivated them to start learning an instrument (Evans & McPherson, 2015). In summary:

- Many 7–8-year-old beginners stated that they thought learning to play a musical instrument would be fun, enjoyable and exciting, judging from having observed performances by musical ensembles at school and in community settings but also having friends and siblings also involved in instrumental learning.

- Those who had a strong musical ensemble presence in school and community environment(s) were more likely to persist after three years of learning.

- The choice of instrument, from the children's perspective was influenced by what they considered as easy instruments to play; if they liked the looks of the instrument; whether they considered it was an appropriate size for them; and whether their friends were playing the same instrument.

- There was gender stereotyping with regard to instrument selection. Boys tended to choose instruments such as trumpets and trombones and girls instruments like flutes and clarinet.

- Children had clear notions about their capacity for successfully mastering each instrument, which were often influenced by gender stereotypes.

- Children were able to differentiate between the importance of being good at music, whether they considered that their learning would be useful in the short and long term and the amount of effort required for improvement. In the end, they would choose what they believed they could succeed at.

As seen from the previous points, and as concluded by the authors of this study, children's motivations to learn to play musical instruments are intimately related to the beliefs they have about the activity, the expectations they have with regard to attaining success in such learning and the value they attach to the activity.

Development of Metacognitive and Practice Skills

While engaging in instrumental music learning, children and young people develop 'learning to learn' skills, namely, 'metacognitive skills' as it is known within the music psychology and education literature. Metacognitive skills are an essential element for developing the needed expertise to learn to play musical instruments, be it in a self-directed learning situation or when learning in formal settings. These include the ability to plan, monitor and evaluate one's own learning, particularly during practising in more systematic ways or during a playful engagement. At this level, O'Neill and McPherson (2002) discuss two fundamental learning orientations:

- **Adaptive mastery-oriented learners**: keep working hard even in the advent of failure and enjoy putting in the required effort to achieve their goals, remaining focused on achievement, regardless of the difficulties that may come their way.

- **Maladaptive helpless-oriented learners**: tend to struggle with defining feasible goals for themselves. When they feel that nothing can be done to improve or solve the specific challenge they are having, they tend to avoid the challenge and have low levels of persistence.

Teachers have an important role when it comes to guiding learners into regular learning and practice. Time and effort put into practice alongside choosing effective practice strategies are important factors in instrumental music skill development. Doing so effectively requires an understanding of 'what practice really is' and 'what it means' for the learner. There will be a plethora of different learner experiences at this level, and it's important to understand each learner's viewpoint directly through regular talks and discussions with them. This is important since practice does not only refer to the ways in which children select, organise, integrate and rehearse new knowledge and skills, on their own, or as per how teachers have asked them to practice. It also encompasses the wide range of thoughts and behaviours that children engage with, and which influence their motivation and how they feel with regard to their practice and learning (McPherson et al., 2016). Motivating learners to practice requires understanding these thoughts and behaviours and how they can be used to support and guide learners to experience practice sessions which are both enjoyable and fulfilling.

During their practice, children may play the repertoire and material they are required to learn by their teacher. They may as well spend time playing pieces they have already mastered, which they often do for the sake of the pleasure of the musical experience alone rather than with any refining purposes. It is important that children and young people are allowed to do this since rote learning and practice can breed resentment and even push children to quit music education altogether. Time might as well be spent trying to figure out songs or music they are interested in – this has wide ranging benefits from a musicianship development perspective but also in the promotion of independent learning skills and personal fulfilment.

Whenever children are aiming to figure out a part of a piece of music with which they are struggling with (be it in playing musical instruments or singing) they prefer to go back and play/sing from the beginning rather than breaking music down into smaller parts that can be worked at and reworked until accomplished (Davis, 2016; Harwood & Marsh, 2012). Seemingly, this is because they don't like to stop the flow, have a preference for repetitive learning and like to engage with familiar material. This doesn't mean that teachers should not break things down and focus upon providing learning and practice strategies where learning can be optimised. However, it highlights that teachers should appreciate the importance of repetition and therefore the need for engagement with at least some familiar material. However, they must also balance the need to polish and perfect the learning of new material as well as inculcate effective practice strategies to accomplish this. In her book *Developing Successful Practising*, MacMillan (2010) provides practical insights at this level including suggestions for engaging parents in the process. Apart from the best ways to practice towards mastering the learning of repertoire, scales and technical work, suggestions are also given on how to develop both sight reading and playing from memory skills.

The Importance of Developing Self-Regulated Learners

Children and young people who undertake to commit to a longer-term of learning, namely continuing playing and learning to play musical instruments until adulthood and beyond, are more likely to continue their involvement with the instrument than those who express a short-term view. This has been demonstrated in a recent longitudinal study by Evans and McPherson (2017). This relationship was mediated by the amount of practice that they did. Researchers explained these results in light of self-determination theory which states that people's well-being thrives whenever their behaviour is personally regulated rather than by others. Self-regulation is directed towards the fulfilment of three basic psychological needs. These are:

- **Competence**: the desire for effectiveness in one's activities;

- **Relatedness**: the need to feel that you are a part of something and accepted by other people and groups;

- **Autonomy**: the need to feel that one is in control of one's own life and activities rather than being directed by others (such as a parent or a school teacher).

Therefore, when teaching children and young people it is vital that teachers promote independent learning skills, strive to develop intrinsic motivation and allow the learner to be in the 'driver's seat' as much as possible with regard to their learning journey. If, on the other hand, they are continuously working towards teachers', a school's or parents' goals, their motivation will be greatly diminished. Self-expression through music in the forms of singing or playing a musical instrument needs to be *meaningful*: it is something children and young people do for themselves, be it alone or with others. If the experience loses its embedded and vital element of self-expression, it will only be a matter a time before children and young people engaged in formal instrumental music learning decide to quit.

It is also important to remember that instrumental musical learning factors, such as age-related developments in co-ordination, bodily strength and dexterity play an integral role in music education achievement. Access to high quality educational opportunities, a supportive family and the motivation to put in the time and effort required to acquire instrumental skills are also equally important. Clearly, teachers therefore have a very important role in and responsibility towards, the development of learners' instinctual, creative abilities.

Composing and Inventing Musical Notation

In this section we will explore how young children, children and young people engage in the creative process of musical composition, including invention of musical notation and how technology can mediate creative musical self-expression through composition. Creating a musical composition is an act of self-expression: it is a highly creative endeavour which requires imagination in exploring musical meanings in topics and things which may not be considered otherwise. Creativity in music can be defined as "the development of a musical output that is novel for the individual(s) and useful for their situated musical practice" (Odena, 2018).

Young children, children and young people are naturally predisposed to creativity. According to Glover (2000), children aged 4–14, greatly enjoyed not only the opportunity to engage in the creative process of musical composition but also thinking and talking about their musical composition work. In doing so, they have necessarily considered form and structure. Another study where 137 compositions of children in Australia aged 5–12 were analysed, revealed that repetition was used by children as a structural device and demonstrated that children in this age spectrum have developed their own musical ideas through processes which included abstraction, inversion and transferral (Barrett, 1996).

Creativity is not, however, simply or linearly dependant on musical education and training. This has been shown via comparisons made between the compositional work of two 8-year-old boys, one with formal music training and the other with no formal training. The boy who did not have formal musical training composed a piece for bass and metallophone. It included a clear tonal centre, pulse and meter, with changing meter and harmony; tempo changes such as ritardando to mark closure; and several performance effects. The composition of the other boy, who had had some musical training, was described by the researchers as being quite repetitive, with little development, exploration or experimentation of musical ideas (Barrett, 1996).

What can be concluded from the comparative study stated earlier is that although the untrained boy did not have formal music training, his informal music learning experiences and enculturation experiences had certainly contributed to his level of development in terms of creativity and expressiveness. Sadly, the boy in formal music training was unable to showcase more exploration and experimentation of musical ideas. This leads me to question, therefore, how effectively are music teachers introducing these concepts in their teaching and giving learners the freedom and confidence required to explore them further? How do they establish informal learning in the everyday lives of their learners? How do they generate motivation for learning that leads their learners to engage with music learning and creative development outside the boundaries of the contact hours they have with their learners? I strongly believe that creativity can be nurtured, developed and promoted through a 'rich music education'. However, for this to occur such 'rich music education' needs to be defined and conceptualised in ways where developing creativity becomes an essential and crucial priority in each educational interaction (more in Chapter 6).

The earlier point is also strongly reinforced by Burnard and Murphy (2017) in their edited book *Teaching Music Creatively*, as well as Odena's (2018) *Musical Creativity Revisited*. While the former provides practical strategies for developing musical creativity in primary school contexts, the latter focuses on secondary school contexts and cross-community settings. Many of the ideas in these books provide important building blocks for the design of pedagogies vis-à-vis creative collaboration which are easily transferable and applicable to other music teaching and learning contexts, be it in group or in one-to-one settings.

Inventing Musical Notation

Young children, children and young people might feel inclined to notate their work, especially if their musical culture is one where music notation has a role to play in the modes of music making. Young children and children may do so spontaneously in an attempt to represent the sound and sequence of events of their own musical compositions. This act may be influenced by observing a family member or concert musicians using a musical score when performing, or for example through musical play when attempting to organise a group performance where others are involved.

In accounts of children's invented notations, researchers identified several commonalities in the ways in which children notate. When inventing notations for their own works, children draw on a broad range of symbols borrowed from other domains, including letters; words; numbers; directional signs; icons; pictographs; and music notation signs. Margaret Barrett, who has dedicated a substantial amount of her research to studying how children develop notation for their musical work, has categorised young children's (aged 4–5 years old) invented notations as follows (Barrett, 2005, pp. 127–131):

- "**Exploration**": random drawings or scribbles, with little discernible relationship to the sound event.

- "**Notation of instrument**": sketches of the instrument.

- "**Notation of instrument with modification**": sketches of the instrument that include modifications of size and/or shading to indicate a musical parameter such as dynamics or pitch.

- "**Notation of gesture/enactive**": imitation on paper of the actions used to produce the sound.

- "**Abstract/symbolic notation**": use of lines, circles, dots and triangular shapes to represent discrete sounds, with one-to-one correspondence between sound and symbol.

- "**Adopted symbols**": for example, attempts to write the lyrics, pictographs or drawings of the lyrical content of songs.

- "**Conventional notation**": borrowed from other domains, such as letters, numbers, words, directional signs and icons.

Barrett also states that when children notate their work, they don't seem to move progressively through hierarchically distinct stages where prior strategies are abandoned in favour of newly acquired strategies. Rather, they appear to move back and forth in terms of the type of notational strategies used (Barrett, 2005). In common with conventional music notation, invented notation provides a way of recording, conceiving, conserving, communicating and constructing musical meaning. In turn, this provides valuable insights into how children perceive, conceive and construct their musical worlds vis-à-vis their musical development.

Similarly to learning the conventions of grammar, punctuation and spelling, there are also stages in transforming invented notations into more conventional forms of notation that can be meaningful and understood by others (Upitis, 2017). Moving to such a stage should only be done when the child recognises a 'need' to notate in ways that are more accessible to others and has a clear intention of participation in forms of musical discourse where music is communicated and conceived through conventional music notation. Teachers should also keep in mind the rule of 'sound before symbol', which ultimately implies that musical notation, be it invented or conventional, *is not* an essential element for music participation to occur. Ultimately, the process of inventing notation for their own compositions by any learner is a creative endeavour and should be considered as such and therefore promoted by teachers as a form of self-expression.

Through analysis of more than 700 compositions by children aged 3–15, Swanwick and Tillman (1986) arrived at descriptions of their typical music compositional behaviour, offering one of the first attempts to categorise children's composing activities. The model consists of a musical development sequence based on the concepts of mastery, imitation, imaginative play and meta-cognition. It is grounded in the work of Moog and Piaget. Providing insights with regard to the development and progression of compositional behaviour, this framework was generated at a time when child development was heavily conceptualised in age-related stages and phases. It contains a total of eight developmental stages, each associated with typical age ranges. Each are succinctly described as follows:

- **"Sensory"** (0–3 years): exploration and experimentation with the timbre of sound and extremes of dynamic levels (i.e., loud versus soft). Improved responses are not organised, and pulse is unsteady.

- **"Manipulative"** (4–5 years): starts to acquire progressive control of instrumental techniques and steadier pulse. Improvised responses are typically long and repetitive.

- **"Personal expressiveness"** (4–6 years): personal expressiveness appears in singing first and later in instrumental improvisations, seen by changes in dynamics and speed. There is little consideration of structure.

- **"Vernacular"** (5–6 years, well established by ages 7–8 years): repetition of melodic and rhythmic patterns and some musical conventions start to appear, such as phrases of two or more measures.

- **"Speculative"** (apparent in 10-year olds): Experimentation and willingness to explore structure.

- **"Idiomatic"** (13–14 years): structural features become more controlled, use of contrast. Pop influences can be evident at this time.

- **"Symbolic"** (unlikely before age of 15): Strong identification with their own music and an ability to reflect on the compositional process and experience.

- **"Systematic"** (from 15 onwards): conscious use of stylistic principles, organised musical materials with expansion of musical possibilities in a systematic manner.

Although enabling thought about musical development through consideration of natural development and maturation processes of children interacting with others in their own cultural environments, the idea of development as 'progression' is integral to this model.

   This model has been criticised by many (e.g., Hargreaves & Lamont, 2017) for its:

- Emphasis on age-related change. Please note that the idea of development as 'progression' corresponding to specific age ranges has been refuted by current trends of musical development research (see Philpott & Spruce, 2012);

- Generalisation from composing behaviour to wider musical development;

- Implicit hierarchy of valuing conceptual understanding over sound exploration.

Teachers should therefore refrain from categorising children into age-related stages as each child is unique and develops at a different pace. In addition, opportunities for exploration of musical creativity within the environment will have a strong influence on how development occurs. In that regard, the experience of exploration of sound and music making needs to be given full emphasis, as in itself, it demonstrates and reveals musical understandings. Furthermore, while the model enables discussion on the development of compositional behaviours, this development should not be extrapolated to other areas of music making since it is not transferable.

Technology Mediating Creative Musical Self-Expression
Through Composition

Technology offers a multiplicity of tools for engaging with and further developing musical creativity through music composition. Digital Audio Workstations (DAW) in most cases allow for recording, editing, mixing and mastering audio files. This can range from simple music material to advanced professional material. Using DAW, learners can engage creatively in playing with sound, without necessarily needing to use conventional musical notation. They experiment with artificial sounds while also bringing pre-recorded sounds *from* their environment *into* their compositions and learn to edit and mix different sound elements in synchronous or related time. This can result in a finalised learner-authored product that can be exported and played back using a variety of devices. A movie entitled *We Are Your Friends* (2015) (co-produced by Tim Bevan and Eric Fellner, financed by StudioCanal) illustrates this in the context of DJ-ing.

Exploring electronic instruments and manipulating music elements can be done by using MIDI and sequencers available within DAW platforms and by using devices that can communicate with each other, for instance: audio plugins; electronic keyboards; or surfaces with sliders, knobs and buttons. The DAW user can experiment using a keyboard, mouse and MIDI controllers. By using MIDI files and sequences, learners can manipulate and learn about the various musical elements via direct experimentation. This can include (but is by no means limited to) changing instrumentation; altering tempo; transposing the material; and using various special effects. The internet also allows for compositional work to be undertaken, either alone or via groups. This way of working opens up opportunities to foster collaborative music projects where learners can compose and perform with others around the world in real time, using high-speed internet access. This is nothing short of revolutionary: indeed, in this rapidly evolving domain you may have as much to learn from your learners as they do from you.

There are many examples of successful utilisation of music technology in music education classrooms. One is a project carried out by Dillon and Brown (2010), who worked with two secondary schools to produce compositions and recorded performances of songs covering the topic of 'bullying'. Learners worked in a lab using iMac computers, in groups of three to four learners and used pen and paper to write lyrics and consider song structure. The project ran for six weeks, with learners meeting for two hours each week. Learners identified and deconstructed the structure of rap songs, and by using software called *Jam2Jam*, they improvised music material over the rap song. After the music was complete, they looked for images (or created posters) to be included in their performance, and they performed their work for parents and peers at an evening performance.

Dillon and Brown (2010) report that the project provided mature musical and lyrical development and that this was facilitated by the use of improvisational and recording technology. The project also offered a connection to other areas of the curriculum, such as a literacy, while addressing an issue of social relevance, all the while adding a sense of achievement and ownership to learners in a highly creative process. The focus was on the creative process itself, and the technology became 'invisible' in the process. Learning *how to use* the technology should not take priority over an experience. Rather, *the tool should become one with the user* in the act of expressive music making. This example demonstrates the importance of social meaning, alongside the inherent meanings defined by the process of song writing production and performance (Dillon & Brown, 2010).

More recently, the findings of an international EU funded project aimed at encouraging children's creative music making through the use of reflexive music technology,[1] revealed that the children in the study developed creativity and improvisation skills as a result of engagement with the MIROR (MIROR-IMPRO and MIROR-COMPO)[2] improvisation and composition programmes.

Nevertheless, the role of a supportive adult helping the children to understand how to navigate and explore the software, but also providing encouragement and feedback, was crucial for such development to occur (Rowe et al., 2017).

Music technology, when used appropriately, allows for promotion and exploration of children's creative potential and provides a plethora of ways for self-expression thereby allowing learners to have their voices heard. It also promotes inclusion, participation and critical reflection which can ultimately lead to the development of learner agency. Furthermore, learners are motivated to use new digital technologies, and these technologies are the way forward for musicians in the twenty-first century. Ensuring that learners obtain the high-quality learning experience they are entitled to necessarily implies preparing them for life, and more specifically in the case of music education, there is no way for this mission to be fully accomplished in today's world without the use of technology in the music classroom.

Improvising: Alone and With Others

Improvisation is a spontaneous creative endeavour where music is created 'in the moment'. It requires input from the improviser's existing musical knowledge as acquired through practice and experience but also the ability to trust oneself and others involved. In group improvisation, this dynamic interchange is based on cooperation, turn taking and interaction for the purposes of collaborative music making. Different players assume different roles at different points in time. Many musical cultures across the world have improvisation at their heart, particularly those outside the Western classical music tradition. Reading music from notation has been prioritised in music education in the West, and this has impacted negatively upon musicians educated under this formal system of music education in terms of developing their improvisatory potential. This has had strong repercussions for the education these teachers and educators provide to their learners: it tends to be much less focused on improvisatory music making and more on notation-based music making and performance.

Flohr (1985) studied the improvisatory abilities of children on a xylophone, and concluded that children's ability to use structure gradually developed across their age range in accordance with their level of musical understanding. He proposed a three-stage model for how children develop skills in musical improvisation, and which has many similarities with Swanwick and Tillman's (1986) model mentioned in the previous section. It is as follows:

- **"Motor energy"** (2–4 year of age): children play notes of mostly equal duration and repeat pitches frequently.

- **"Experimentation"** (4–6 years): children experiment widely.

- **"Formal properties"** (6–8 years): children use structural elements such as tonality and repetition.

In another study, melodic improvisations of 62 children aged 7–9 years were analysed: each child improvised three melodies per year on a pentatonic xylophone. The results have shown that children's improvised material increasingly utilised antecedent-consequent phrases and a higher usage of repeated melodic and rhythmic motives in the ages of 7–8 and considerably less so for 8–9-year olds. There was also a strong sense of pulse (Brophy, 2005). Keyboard melodic improvisations of 6–11-year olds revealed three stages in the development of hierarchical structures of tonal music (Paananen, 2007). They are:

- First, children focused either on deep structures (tonality or meter) or melodic-rhythmic surface structures.

- Second, deep and surface structures start becoming co-ordinated.

- Third, deep and surface structures are fully integrated.

Koutsoupidou and Hargreaves (2009) considered how improvisation affects the development of children's creative thinking in music. They focused on two groups of children with each submitting to a different form of intervention. One group of children (aged 6 years old) was given music lessons for a period of 6 months. The lessons included a wide range of improvisation activities during which they improvised through their voices, musical instruments and also their bodies. The other group of children received music lessons (also for 6 months) and of a didactic nature; that is 'teacher-centred' but did not include any improvisation. The results revealed that improvisation played a significant role on the development of creative thinking. These findings testify to the importance of inclusion of instances of improvisation and musical creative development work in all strands of music teaching and learning. This includes even 'traditional' lessons which tend to be about learning repertoire composed by others.

Children and young people engage in improvisatory practice for song writing and use technology to record and assess their freshly improvised work. This, of course, aids in developing their musical identity (Davis, 2016). They were seen to use processes used by popular musicians during practice, wherein learning integrates listening, performing, improvisation and composing throughout the process. Combined, each of these components emphasise individual creativity (Green, 2008). This type of improvisatory behaviour and learning takes place either when they engage in music making alone or in friendship groups but also through self-directed, peer-directed and group learning. There is a high element of imitation of musical material and attempts to copy music by ear, and which many times results in improvised material which can then be used for a new song for a new album or various other purposes.

Burnard and Boyack (2017) emphasise the importance of teachers and students being improvisers together, namely, creating music together with students in real time. They also state that apart from the improvisatory moments, teachers should provide space and time for reflection and talking with students about the improvised elements after they have occurred. If you are considering ways to further develop or start including improvisation in your teaching, I recommend reading the reference cited earlier. Furthermore, if you are considering the use of interactive technology for developing improvisation as a means of creative musical expression, please consult Rowe, Triantafyllaki and Pachet's (Eds.) (2017) book, *Children's Creative Music-making with Reflexive Interactive Technology: Adventures in Improvising and Composing.*

Movement Play, Moving to Music and Dancing

Movement is an instinctual reaction to music and is inseparable from music. It is a powerful means of self-expression and a powerful tool for learning music in its own right. It is integral to all the ways in which children (and people in general) express themselves through music, be it in addition to listening, singing, instrumental music performance, composing or improvising. For this reason, a number of pedagogical approaches to formal music learning use movement and gesturing as an integral pedagogical tool in music learning (e.g., Jaques-Dalcroze, 1921; Kodály, 1965; Orff & Keetman, 1950).

In particular, young children engage in massive amounts of musical play. This includes a high degree of imitation, experimentation and prompting interaction with others. Their body is the main source of knowledge as they learn "by feel" rather than through specific stepwise methodologies (Barrett & Tafuri, 2012; Harwood & Marsh, 2012, p. 329). A study of 2–3-year olds undertaking improvised singing in a nursery environment demonstrated that children frequently enacted rhythmic whole-body movements which included stomping, bouncing, running and galloping. As the author states, these were "voiced in rhythms matching their bodily movements exactly" (Young, 2006, p. 274). In relation to when recorded music is played, research studies have consistently shown that children typically respond with movement (Young, ibid.). Common traits among these movements observed for 3-year-olds included performance of simple bounding or twirling repetitive movements and which matched musical aspects such as tempo, intensity and other musical elements. An interesting finding from this research was that effective adult modelling of young children's movements was only achieved whenever the adult matched the children's movement style and natural tempo.

The positive benefits of movement and music on young children's behaviour have been demonstrated in a study conducted by Lobo and Winsler (2006). These investigators randomly assigned pre-schoolers to a dance and music intervention using two different conditions: 1) a group of children received equivalent amounts of time with an interventionist doing only free play; and 2) another group received a creative dance and music programme. Teachers and parents, who were not aware of the group to which their children were assigned, were asked to independently rate children's social and behavioural competence before the programme started and after the 12-week intervention. The results have shown that children in the creative dance and music program achieved significantly greater gains in social competence and demonstrated noticeable improvements in behaviour when compared to those in the other group. The authors were unable to say for sure whether it was dance/movement, music or both in combination that may have played a role in these findings.

Physical engagement with music enables a deeper intellectual and emotional experience and demonstrates what young children, children and young people are hearing and musically thinking (Campbell, 2010). It also provides them with an "enhanced form of listening", a more "concentrated sense of the music" (Davis, 2016, p. 273) and an opportunity for participation through rhythmic engagement. The process necessarily involves decision making as to when and how to move, as governed by tempo and patterns of a repetitive nature in which they add a depth of knowledge acquired in all sorts of other experiences to their enactment of movement. For instance, reports of children moving/dancing to popular music have shown that the children's experience with the song (both visually through music video) aurally enabled them to bring a depth of bodily understanding (Campbell, 2010). Moreover, dancing also provided a space for play acting, with some children being observed acting in the role of a guitar player, another instrumentalist or the singer of the song as if they were the performer (Davis, 2016).

Synchronisation in time creates a strong sense of togetherness (Overy & Molnar-Szakacs, 2009) and a space for the development and creation of both individual and collective identities (Davis, 2016). Recently, the concept of movement identity has been introduced and defined as "ways in which patterns of moving associated with different contextual situations including dance genres, become part of the identity of the individual" (Karkou & Joseph, 2017, p. 236). Similarly to musical identities, movement identities are shaped by interactions with others: new dances and movements as well as expectations are equally important to all other aspects of musical identity. In his book *Play, Sing and Dance* (2013), Doug Goodkin provides useful ideas for contemporary application of the Orff approach, which focuses upon the importance of movement play and singing in learning. If you are looking for ideas on how to use movement play in your teaching, I highly recommend this book.

Reflective Questions

1. How music is used by children and young people as a means of self-expression?				
• Outline the various ways children and young people express themselves through music. • Consider the benefits of such musical self-expression. • Reflect on how music teachers and educators can further promote and support children and young people's musical self-expression.	Aligned with CME, Level 4 Unit (U) or Area of Study (AOS) and Assessment Criteria number of ABRSM (2014) and TCL (2013, 2019)			
	ABRSM		TCL (2013)	
	U1:	1.1.2 1.2.2 1.3.2	U1:	2.1 2.2
			TCL (2019)	
			AOS2:	1.1.1 1.1.2 2.1.1 3.1.1
2. How children and young people use music to express individual and group identities				
• Consider your learners and reflect on the range of social markers by which children and young people express aspects of their identity using music. • Highlight how children and young people may use music in different ways for expressing individual and group identities and consider what importance music assumes for them in their everyday lives. • Consider how, as a teacher, do you promote the development of musical identities which agree with your learners' self-concepts? What else can you do at this level? How?				
	ABRSM		TCL (2013)	
	U1:	1.1.2	U1:	2.1 2.2
			TCL (2019)	
			AOS2:	3.1.1

3. Why technologies and social networking are important to young people's engagement with music?				
• Consider the level of exposure your learners may have to technology and social networking. • Expand on how technology can be used to promote musical creativity and self-expression. • Reflect on how do you currently use technology in your teaching? Is there scope for further developments at this level in your teaching for the benefit of your learners regarding the use of technology?				
	ABRSM		TCL (2013)	
	U1:	1.2.2	U1:	2.2
			TCL (2019)	
			AOS2:	2.1.4

4. Describe some models of musical development, and reflect on how these can be recognised in children and young people's music making and responding? How can these models inform planning and teaching decisions?				
• Consider models of musical development which are particularly applicable in your own teaching context and examine how they may inform your planning and teaching. • Keep in mind that musical progression is more important than age related change, therefore models with fixed ages attached to certain stages need to be used with caution. In addition, models proposed are specific for the contexts where they were created, and therefore are not transferable to other areas of musical development.				
	ABRSM		TCL (2013)	
	U2:	2.1.1	U1:	2.1 2.2
			TCL (2019)	
			AOS2:	3.1.2

5. Describe the many ways in which musical understanding is demonstrated and how participation in music and music education support the development of musical understanding?				
• Reflect on the various ways through which children and young people express themselves through music and consider how they provide demonstration of musical understanding. • Consider how can you support learners' creativity development (with or without the use of technology) and connect this with developing aspects of musicianship (i.e., knowledge and skills). • Provide related examples obtained through your teaching or musical learning.	ABRSM		TCL (2013)	
	U1:	1.2.2	U1:	3.2
			TCL (2019)	
			AOS2:	3.1.3 3.1.4

Notes

1. Reflexive music technology consists of systems that imitate the behaviour of its user, through continuously learning from the user's behaviour. This allows analysis of how the user may play melodies or specific rhythms as performed, for example, on a keyboard and for models to be built on the user's specific style. This way the user can further explore their own style and take learning insights on his/her approach from a different and more reflexive perspective.
2. MIROR (MIROR-IMPRO and MIROR-COMPO) are interconnected software programmes which allow users to consider, freely examine, backtrack and reflect upon their own style to create novel generation of compositions. The style is first generated by the user's previous interactions with the software. After this, the software system proposes phrases, structures or themes, which are always in the style of the user, thereby allowing users to create novel compositions or improvisations based on previous dialogues with the MIROR-IMPRO system.

Further Reading

Burnard, P., & Murphy, R. (Eds) (2017). *Teaching music creatively*. Routledge.

Davis, S. G. (2016). Children, popular music, and identity. In G. E. McPherson (Ed.), *The child as musician* (pp. 265–283). Oxford University Press. https://doi.org/10.1093/acprof:oso/9780198744443.003.0014

Goodkin, D. (2013). *Play, sing, dance: An introduction to Orff Schulwerk*. Schott.

Hallam, S., & Bautista, A. (2012). Processes of instrumental learning: The development of musical expertise. In G. McPherson & G. F. Welch (Eds.), *The Oxford handbook of music education* (pp. 658–676). Oxford University Press.

MacMillan, J. (2010). *Successful practising: A handbook for pupils, parents, and music teachers*. Jenny MacMillan.

Odena, O. (2018). *Musical creativity revisited: Educational foundations, practices and research*. Routledge.

Rickard, N. S., & Chin, T. (2017). Defining the musical identity of "non-musicians". In R. A. MacDonald, D. J. Hargreaves, & D. E. Miell (Eds.), *Handbook of musical identities* (pp. 288–303). Oxford University Press.

Rowe, V., Triantafyllaki, A., & Pachet, F. (2017). *Children's creative music-making with reflexive interactive technology: Adventures in improvising and composing*. Routledge.

References

Adachi, M., & Trehub, S. E. (1998). Children's expression of emotion in song. *Psychology of Music, 26*, 133–153.

Adachi, M., & Trehub, S. E. (2011). Canadian and Japanese preschoolers' creation of happy and sad songs. *Psychomusicology: Music, Mind and Brain, 21*(1–2), 69–82. https://doi.org/10.1037/h0094005

Ashley, M., & Mecke, A. C. (2013). 'Boys are apt to change their voice at about fourteen years of age': An historical background to the debate about longevity in boy treble singers. *Reviews of Research in Human Learning and Music, 1*, epub201. https://doi.org/10.6022/journal.rrhlm.2013001

Associated Board of the Royal Schools of Music (ABRSM) (2014). *Level 4 certificate for music educators: Assessment framework*. ABRSM.

Bahanovich, D., & Collopy, D. P. (2009). *Music experience and behaviour in young people, national survey*. British Music Rights.

Barrett, M. S. (1996). Children's aesthetic decision-making: An analysis of children's musical discourse as composers. *International Journal of Music Education, 28*(1), 37–62. https://doi.org/10.1177/025576149602800104

Barrett, M. S. (2005). Musical communication and children's communities of musical practice. In D. Miell, R. MacDonald, & D. J. Hargreaves (Eds.), *Musical communication* (pp. 261–280). Oxford University Press.

Barrett, M. S. (2012). Commentary: Music learning and teaching in infancy and early childhood. In G. E. McPherson & G. F. Welch (Eds.), *The Oxford handbook of music education* (pp. 226–228). Oxford University Press. https://doi.org/10.1093/oxfordhb/9780199730810.013.0013

Barrett, M., & Tafuri, J. (2012). Creative meaning-making in infants' and young children's musical cultures. In G. E. McPherson & G. F. Welch (Eds.), *The Oxford handbook of music education* (pp. 296–313). Oxford University Press.

Bjorkvold, J. (1989). *The muse within* (W. H. Halverson, Trans.). Harper Collins.

Boal-Palheiros, G. M., & Hargreaves, D. J. (2001). Listening to music at home and at school. *British Journal of Music Education, 18*(02), 103–118. https://doi.org/10.1017/S0265051701000213

Borthwick, S. J., & Davidson, J. (2002). Developing a child's identity as a musician: A "family" script perspective. In R. MacDonald, D. Miell, & D. J. Hargreaves (Eds.), *Musical identities* (pp. 60–78). Oxford University Press.

Brophy, T. S. (2005). A longitudinal study of selected characteristics of children's melodic improvisations. *Journal of Research in Music Education, 53*(2), 120–133. https://doi.org/10.2307/3345513

Burnard, P., & Boyack, J. (2017). Engaging interactively with children's group improvisations. In P. Burnard & R. Murphy (Eds.), *Teaching music creatively* (2nd ed., pp. 26–38). Routledge.

Campbell, P. S. (2010). *Songs in their heads: Music and its meanings in children's lives* (2nd ed.). Oxford University Press.

Cooper, V. (2014). Children's developing identity. In M. Reed & R. Walker (Eds.), *A critical companion to early childhood* (pp. 281–296). Sage.

Countryman, J., Gabriel, M., & Thompson, K. (2016). Children's spontaneous vocalisations during play: Aesthetic dimensions. *Music Education Research, 18*(1), 1–19. https://doi.org/10.1080/14613808.2015.1019440

Davidson, J. W., & Burland, K. (2006). Musician identity formation. In G. E. McPherson (Ed.), *The child as a musician. A handbook of musical development* (pp. 475–490). Oxford University Press.

Davies, C. (1994). The listening teacher: An approach to the collection and study of invented songs of children aged 5–7. In H. Lees (Ed.), *Musical connections: Tradition and change* (pp. 120–127). International Society for Music Education.

Davis, S. G. (2016). Children, popular music, and identity. In G. E. McPherson (Ed.), *The child as musician* (pp. 265–283). Oxford University Press. https://doi.org/10.1093/acprof:oso/9780198744443.003.0014

Dean, B. (2019). Spontaneous singing and musical agency in the everyday home: Lives of three- and four-year-old children. In S. Young & B. Ilari (Eds.), *Music in early childhood: Multi-disciplinary perspectives and inter-disciplinary exchanges* (pp. 103–118). Springer. https://doi.org/10.1007/978-3-030-17791-1_7

Delalande, F., & Cornara, S. (2010). Sound explorations from the ages of 10 to 37 months: The ontogenesis of musical conducts. *Music Education Research, 12*(3), 257–268. https://doi.org/10.1080/14613808.2010.504812

Dibben, N. (2002). Gender identity and music. In R. MacDonald, D. Hargreaves, & D. Miell (Eds.), *Musical identities* (pp. 117–133). Oxford University Press.

Dillon, S. C., & Brown, A. R. (2010). *Access to meaningful relationships through virtual instruments and ensembles.* Proceedings of the ISME Commission for Community Music Activity: CMA XII Harmonizing the Diversity That Is Community Music Activity. www.researchgate.net/publication/38183704_Access_to_meaningful_relationships_through_virtual_instruments_and_ensembles

Evans, P., & McPherson, G. E. (2015). Identity and practice: The motivational benefits of a long-term musical identity. *Psychology of Music, 43*(3), 407–422. https://doi.org/10.1177/0305735613514471

Evans, P., & McPherson, G. E. (2017). Processes of musical identity consolidation during adolescence. In R. A. R. MacDonald, D. J. Hargreaves, & D. Miell (Eds.), *Handbook of musical identities* (pp. 213–231). Oxford University Press.

Flohr, J. W. (1985). Young children's improvisations: Emerging creative thought. *Creative Child & Adult Quarterly, 10*(2), 79–85.

Folkestad, G. (2005). Here, there and everywhere: Music education research in a globalised world. *Music Education Research, 7*(3), 279–287. https://doi.org/10.1080/14613800500324390

Folkestad, G. (2006). Formal and informal learning situations or practices vs formal and informal ways of learning. *British Journal of Music Education, 23*(2), 135–145.

Folkestad, G. (2017). Post-national identities in music: Acting in a global intertextual musical arena. In R. MacDonald, D. J. Hargreaves, & D. Miell (Eds.), *Handbook of musical identities.* Oxford University Press. https://doi.org/10.1093/acprof:oso/9780199679485.001.0001

Glover, J. (2000). *Children composing 4–14.* Routledge.

Goodkin, D. (2013). *Play, sing, dance: An introduction to Orff Schulwerk.* Schott.

Green, L. (2008). *Music, informal learning and the school: A new classroom pedagogy.* Ashgate.

Hall, C. (2005). Gender and boys' singing in early childhood. *British Journal of Music Education, 22*(1), 5–20. https://doi.org/10.1017/S0265051704005960

Hallam, S. (2005). *Enhancing motivation and learning throughout the lifespan.* Institute of Education, University of London.

Hallam, S. (2017). Musical identity, learning, and teaching. In R. MacDonald, D. J. Hargreaves, & D. Miell (Eds.), *Handbook of musical identities* (pp. 476–492). Oxford University Press.

Hallam, S., & Bautista, A. (2012). Processes of instrumental learning: The development of musical expertise. In G. E. McPherson & G. F. Welch (Eds.), *The Oxford handbook of music education* (pp. 658–676). Oxford University Press.

Hargreaves, D., & Lamont, A. (2017). *The psychology of musical development.* Cambridge University Press.

Harwood, E., & Marsh, K. (2012). Children's ways of learning inside and outside the classroom. In G. E. McPherson & G. F. Welch (Eds.), *The Oxford handbook of music education* (pp. 322–340). Oxford University Press.

Ilari, B. (2017). Children's ethnic identities, cultural diversity, and music education. In Raymond MacDonald, D. J. Hargreaves, & D. Miell (Eds.), *Handbook of musical identities.* Oxford University Press. https://doi.org/10.1093/acprof:oso/97801996 79485.001.0001

Jaques-Dalcroze, E. (1921). Rhythm, music and education. *Journal of Education, 94*(12), 319–319. https://doi.org/10.1177/002205742109401204

Joyce, H. (2005). *The effects of sex, age and environment on attitudes to singing in key stage 2* [Unpublished master's dissertation, University of London].

Karkou, V., & Joseph, J. (2017). The moving and movement identities of adolescents. In R. MacDonald, D. J. Hargreaves, & D. Miell (Eds.), *Handbook of musical identities* (pp. 232–244). Oxford University Press. https://doi.org/10.1093/acprof: oso/9780199679485.003.0013

Kodály, Z. (1965). *Let us sing correctly.* Boosey & Hawkes.

Koutsoupidou, T., & Hargreaves, D. J. (2009). An experimental study of the effects of improvisation on the development of children's creative thinking in music. *Psychology of Music, 37*(3), 251–278. https://doi.org/10.1177/0305735608097246

Lobo, Y. B., & Winsler, A. (2006). The effects of a creative dance and movement program on the social competence of head start preschoolers. *Social Development, 15*(3), 501–519. https://doi.org/10.1111/j.1467-9507.2006.00353.x

MacMillan, J. (2010). *Successful practising: A handbook for pupils, parents, and music teachers.* Jenny MacMillan.

Marsh, K., & Young, S. (2016). Musical play. In G. E. McPherson (Ed.), *The child as a musician: A handbook of musical development* (2nd ed., pp. 462–484). Oxford University Press.

McPherson, G. E., Davidson, J., & Evans, P. (2016). Playing an instrument. In G. E. McPherson (Ed.), *The child as a musician. A handbook of musical development* (2nd ed., pp. 401–421). Oxford University Press.

Mialaret, J. P. (1997). *Explorations musicales instrumentales chez le jeune enfant.* Presses Universitaires de France.

Murphy, R. (2017). Enhancing creativity through listening to music. In P. Burnard & R. Murphy (Eds.), *Teaching music creatively* (2nd ed., pp. 104–117). Routledge.

North, A. C., Hargreaves, D. J., & O'Neill, S. A. (2000). The importance of music to adolescents. *British Journal of Educational Psychology*, *70*(2), 255–272. https://doi.org/10.1348/000709900158083

Odena, O. (2018). *Musical creativity revisited: Educational foundations, practices and research*. Routledge.

O'Neill, S., & McPherson, G. E. (2002). Motivation. In R. Parncutt & G. E. McPherson (Eds.), *The science and psychology of music performance. Creative strategies for teaching and learning* (pp. 31–46). Oxford University Press.

Orff, C., & Keetman, G. (1950). *Musik für Kinder I*. Schott.

Overy, K., & Molnar-Szakacs, I. (2009). Being together in time: Musical experience and the mirror neuron system. *Music Perception*, *26*(5), 489–504.

Paananen, P. A. (2007). Melodic improvisation at the age of 6–11 years: Development of pitch and rhythm. *Musicae Scientiae*, *11*(1), 89–119. https://doi.org/10.1177/102986490701100104

Philpott, C., & Spruce, G. (Eds.). (2012). *Debates in music teaching*. Routledge.

Rickard, N. S., & Chin, T. (2017). Defining the musical identity of "non-musicians". In R. A. MacDonald, D. J. Hargreaves, & D. E. Miell (Eds.), *Handbook of musical identities* (pp. 288–303). Oxford University Press. www.oxfordscholarship.com/view/10.1093/acprof:oso/9780199679485.001.0001/acprof-9780199679485-chapter-16

Rowe, V., Triantafyllaki, A., & Pachet, F. (2017). *Children's creative music-making with reflexive interactive technology: Adventures in improvising and composing*. Routledge.

Rutkowski, J. (1997). The nature of children's singing voices: Characteristics and assessment. In B. A. Roberts (Ed.), *The phenomenon of singing* (pp. 201–209). Memorial University Press.

Swanwick, K., & Tillman, J. (1986). The sequence of musical development: A study of children's composition. *British Journal of Music Education*, *3*(3), 305–339. https://doi.org/10.1017/S0265051700000814

Tafuri, J. (2008). *Infant musicality: New research for educators and parents*. Ashgate.

Tafuri, J. (2017). Building musical self-identity in early infancy. In R. MacDonald, D. J. Hargreaves, & D. Miell (Eds.), *Handbook of musical identities* (pp. 197–212). Oxford University Press. https://doi.org/10.1093/acprof:oso/9780199679485.003.0011

Trinity College London (TCL) (2013). *TCL level 4 certificate for music educators: Specifications*. TCL.

Trinity College London (TCL) (2019). *TCL level 4 certificate for music educators, areas of study*. TCL.

Upitis, R. (2017). Celebrating children's invented notations. In P. Burnard & R. Murphy (Eds.), *Teaching music creatively* (pp. 118–134). Routledge.

Vidas, D., Dingle, G. A., & Nelson, N. L. (2018). Children's recognition of emotion in music and speech. *Music & Science*, *1*, 1–10. https://doi.org/10.1177/2059204318762650

Welch, G. F. (1998). Early childhood musical development. *Research Studies in Music Education*, *11*(1), 27–41. https://doi.org/10.1177/1321103X9801100104

Welch, G. F. (2016). Singing and vocal development. In G. E. McPherson (Ed.), *The child as a musician. A handbook of musical development* (2nd ed., pp. 441–461). Oxford University Press. https://doi.org/10.1093/acprof:oso/9780198530329.003.0016

Welch, G. F., Saunders, J., Papageorgi, I., & Himonides, E. (2012). Sex, gender and singing development: Making a positive difference to boys' singing through a national programme in England. In S. Harrison, G. F. Welch, & A. Adler (Eds.), *Perspectives on males and singing* (pp. 27–43). Springer Netherlands. https://doi.org/10.1007/978-94-007-2660-4_3

Young, S. (2002). Young children's spontaneous vocalizations in free play: Observations of two-to three- year-olds in a day care setting. *Bulletin of the Council for Research in Music Education, 152*, 43–53.

Young, S. (2006). Seen but not heard: Young children, improvised singing and educational practice. *Contemporary Issues in Early Childhood, 7*(3), 270–280. https://doi.org/10.2304/ciec.2006.7.3.270

Young, S. (2018). *Critical new perspectives in early childhood music: Young children engaging and learning through music*. Routledge.

3 Multidimensional Benefits of Music

To Guide Your Reading

- How can participation in music education promote social and intellectual development, creativity as well as emotional and physical well-being?
- How can participation in music and music making benefit children and young people in other aspects of learning?

Introduction

Music offers a unique platform for personal development. This chapter provides a review on the wide-ranging benefits resulting from musical experiences and musical learning. It does so via four intertwined dimensions: 1) communicational, social and personal development; 2) perceptual, cognitive and intellectual; 3) creativity development; and 4) emotional and physical well-being. While making the case that music making and learning bring a panoply of benefits at various levels, it is also emphasised that the level of benefits materialised is contingent upon a variety of factors. These include the type, quality and duration of activities; the value placed on the musical activity by young children, children, young people and those surrounding them (e.g., parents, cultural contexts, educational environment etc.); and, of course, the extent to which music making and engagement aligns with their self-concept and personal goals.

Communicational, Social and Personal Development

Music has been shown to provide extensive benefits when it comes to promoting self-expression and interactions with others. Evidently, it therefore has strong implications regarding communicational, social and personal development. Engagement with music can create a positive self-attitude, self-image and self-awareness due to accomplishment and recognition (Abeles & Sanders, 2007; Burton et al., 2000; Costa-Giomi, 1999). By providing a platform for self-expression, music encourages not only children but people in general to perform in front of others. This can in turn facilitate group work, and promote several benefits which are both social and therapeutic in nature (Harland et al., 2000).

Group music participation helps to create an increased awareness of others: as such, it leads to the development of social cohesion within the class or group but also better social adjustment and well-being in general. These benefits are then transferable to various other settings (Harland et al., 2000). Parents and teachers have reported first-hand on the benefits they have witnessed in children who engage in musical participation. These include a sense of accomplishment; learning to be disciplined; an appreciation of music; maturing relationships; self-confidence; a sense of belonging; the development of responsibility; teamwork; and enhanced physical co-ordination (Brown, 1980; Hallam & Prince, 2000).

Music-based extra-curricular activities (including rehearsing and performing in school shows) has contributed to: the development of self-confidence; making friendships with like-minded people; the development of a sense of belonging; group commitment; increased social networking skills; confidence in presenting in front of others; and cooperativity (Abeles & Sanders, 2007). Working in small groups for the previously mentioned purposes has been shown to help learners develop trust as well as negotiation and teamworking skills (Davidson & Good, 2002). Although all of the aforementioned have repercussions at a personal level, listening to music as a singular activity (whether alone or in a group) has also been shown to help young people: regulate their moods; release tension; maintain a sense of belonging and community; pass time; and draw their attention away from worrying issues (Tarrant et al., 2000). Hence, we can see that music is a key element in the lives of young children, children and young people. Functioning through communicative and social musical interactions, it evidently has strong repercussions on communicational, social and personal development for all involved.

Perceptual, Cognitive and Intellectual

There has been widespread interest concerning the effects of music on perceptual, cognitive and intellectual development, particularly over the last 30 years or so. This has resulted in a wide body of literature emerging which encompasses many different aspects. Here, I shall briefly consider the development of perceptual and language skills, literacy and numerical skills, as well as intellectual and general attainment through music.

Music Develops Enhanced Perceptual and Language Skills

In the brain, the systems that process speech and music are shared. Therefore, musical processing mechanisms directly impact upon the perception of language, in particular the processing of pitch patterns in language. This is due to shared use of auditory patterns with musical training and which thereby develops the ability to perceive and distinguish between various auditory patterns, including phonemes (the units of sound in a word) (Gaab et al., 2005; Moreno et al., 2009). This has been regarded as critical in developing phonological awareness, and consequently contributing to learning to read successfully. For instance, young children have shown improved phonemic awareness after regularly attending a 30 minutes per week music session over a period of four months (see Gromko, 2005). Children aged 5–7 years old also showed improved auditory discrimination a year after commencing instrumental music playing (mostly piano) (Forgeard et al., 2008; Norton et al., 2005). Engagement with music enhances the development of perceptual processing systems. In turn, this helps with perceiving and identifying speech sounds and patterns. Where earlier engagement and prolonged participation have been observed, this has showcased even greater impact.

Music Aids the Development of Literacy Skills

Learning to discriminate between sound patterns and associating them with specific visual symbols (such as those used in music cultures where notation is used) has been shown to contribute to the development of phonological awareness and improved reading skills (Gromko, 2005). Butzlaff (2000) conducted a meta-analysis of 24 studies focusing on how music aids literacy skills and found a relationship between music training and standardised measures of reading proficiency. However, there were some differences across these studies. Butzlaff (ibid.) explains these may have resulted from the use of different types of music learning activities and children's prior musical development. The development of reading skills is deeply affected by children's rhythmic listening abilities as well as their levels of attention control. A study focusing on 7–9-year olds (who experienced reading difficulties) used a 10 minute music intervention training per week for six weeks. It consisted of physical and rhythmical entrainment via clapping, stamping, and singing in time to a piece of music while following simple musical notation. These children showed significant improvement in their reading comprehension skills as result of this music training (Long, 2007). Moreover, childhood music training has been shown to develop enhanced listening skills and attentional control (Strait et al., 2015).

Lorenzo et al. (2014) examined the effect of formal musical training on language development in 3- to 4-year-old children. The experimental group received formal music classes for 20 minutes, three times a week at minimum, over a period of two years. Control group[1] children did not receive formal music classes. These music classes emphasised the exploration of all music elements in quality musical activities that incorporated singing, playing instruments, improvising and exploring movement. Child observation records were used to assess child development, and these were administered six times during the course of the study. Results indicated that continued formal music education enhances early childhood language development. Similar findings are also reported elsewhere (e.g., Herrera et al., 2011; Jentschke & Koelsch, 2009).

Music Aids Intellectual Development

Intellectual development and intelligence are global constructs traversing many different and separate cognitive abilities. The American Psychological Association Dictionary, edited by VandenBos (2007), describes intelligence as: "a person's ability to understand complex ideas, to adapt to the environment, to learn from experience, and to engage in reasoning and decision-making in all sorts of situations (both new and familiar)". Intelligence, therefore, can be considered as the total of all mental competencies. Moreover, since there is no single centre for intelligence in the brain, researchers examining the effects of music on intellectual development and intelligence have focused upon considering different, specific processes (Hodges & Gruhn, 2012). Some of these processes include spatial-temporal reasoning[2]; brain size; mental speed; processing efficiency[3]; and memory skills. Research has demonstrated that music experiences and learning can influence these processes and that the effects experienced are highly dependent on the nature of the musical tasks, the duration and intensity of the involvement (Hallam, 2010).

In a pioneering study which generated much controversy upon its publication in 1993, Frances Rauscher, Gordon Shaw, and Catherine Ky investigated the effects of listening to music composed by Mozart. They used the *Sonata for Two Pianos in D major, K. 448* in comparison to listening to verbal relaxation instructions, and also silence. They asserted that they had found a temporary enhancement of spatial-reasoning lasting between 10 to 15 minutes after participants had listened to the music. This enhancement was measured by paper-cutting and folding tasks. One may be reasonably cynical in this instance. While Rauscher et al. (1993) only showed an increase in "spatial intelligence", the results were popularly interpreted as an increase in general IQ. This misconception, and the fact that the music used in the study was by Mozart, had an obvious appeal to those who valued this music. This resulted in the "Mozart effect" being widely reported upon within popular culture. The finding has since led nurseries to start playing classical music to children and in the southern state of Georgia in the United States. Newborn babies were offered a free classical CD shortly after the study came out.

Other research has confirmed that active engagement with music positively impacts upon visual-spatial intelligence. This has been demonstrated by a review of 15 studies, where a link between music instruction lasting for two years led to a significant improvement in spatial-temporal reasoning (Hetland, 2000). Children aged 4–6, submitted to a 75 minutes per week, parent-involved music curriculum for 30 weeks, have scored substantially better in the Stanford-Binet Bead Memory subtest[4] in comparison with others who did not undertake this programme (Bilhartz et al., 1999). In addition, pronounced effects of music training on the Intelligent Quotient (IQ) were shown by Schellenberg (2004). In a controlled study, he randomly assigned a sample of 144 children to two different types of music lessons (keyboard or voice), or to control groups that received drama lessons (or no lessons) for a year. IQ was measured before and after the lessons. The results were clear: children in the music groups showed greater increases in full-scale IQ. Although the effect was relatively small, it was nonetheless generalised across IQ subtests, index scores, and a standardised measure of academic achievement.

The previous results suggest that music training stimulates specific brain changes in school-aged children. Findings from neuroscience have also highlighted structural and procedural differences occurring in the brain as a result of music learning experiences. These were more likely to occur and to be more pronounced in those who have undertaken intense music learning before the age of 7 (Hodges & Gruhn, 2012). For instance, musicians were found to have greater volumes of grey matter in comparison with control groups, and functioning across widely distributed areas such as the motor, auditory and visuospatial systems (Bermudez & Zatorre, 2005).

Altogether, this research demonstrates that music has a marked effect in the development of *some* mental capacities and consequently generates numerous interconnected repercussions in terms of intellectual development. However, since intelligence is a multidimensional construct which involves the combined total of mental capacities and competencies, and since these can't be studied simultaneously, caution must be exercised with regard to making assumptions that music listening or training necessarily will result in people becoming 'smarter'. Additionally, more nuanced understandings regarding the types of musical activity that can indeed bring about intellectual development, and specifically at what *levels* of intellectual development this occurs, are required. As Hallam (2010) has adroitly noted, some studies have employed broader music education plans and strategies while others have focused upon instrumental tuition. A synergistic analysis between these approaches would likely offer the most propitious insights in any future studies.

Music Aids General Attainment

Academic attainment is dependent upon the development of literacy and numerical skills, as well as the overall level of motivation young children, children and young people have towards learning in general. Motivation is highly impacted upon by learners' self-perception of ability, self-efficacy and personal aspirations (Hallam, 2005). Musical engagement has a role to play in literacy (as discussed earlier) and possibly numerical development. This is likely due to similarities in music and mathematics, specifically the existence of patterns and proportions as well as the stimulation of corresponding cognitive activities in both domains (Sanders, 2018).

Moreover, when musical engagement is conducive to increasing positive perceptions of self-proficiency, this may transfer across to other areas of the curriculum and consequently result in improved general attainment levels (Hallam, 2005). Although a relationship *has* been established between music and general attainment levels, other factors such as having a supportive environment and parental support cannot be ruled out as mitigating and/or contributory factors in this relationship (Yang, 2015). Given the sheer potential for numerous, individual cases combining and intertwining varying numbers of aforementioned factors, it is wise not to jump to dramatic, and over-generalised, conclusions in describing the nature of the relationship between them. In other words, simply listening to Mozart does not a child prodigy make.

Creativity

Music education has also been shown to positively impact upon creativity among children and young people. A group of 3–4-year olds who had taken part in a singing and musical group play activities, twice a week for three years, showed enhanced abstract thought and creativity (Kalmár, 1982). Children involved in daily music instruction of 30 minutes for a year showed increased perceptual motor skills[5] and creativity in relation to control groups (Wolff, 1979). young people engaged in music learning have also scored higher on creativity indices (Hamann et al., 1991). However, as demonstrated by Koutsoupidou and Hargreaves (2009) in order for this to materialise, music engagement experiences need to offer opportunities for the development of creativity through various means. These include: the inclusion of improvisation; composition; and development of a sense of personal expression in musical performance based on creative and critical thinking.

Emotional and Physical Well-Being

Community and school-based musical experiences have, in general, been shown to increase health and well-being (Welch & Ockelford, 2010) and also enjoyment in school and social connectivity (Abeles & Sanders, 2007). Following this, Ruud (2017) argues for the importance of musical identity in fostering emotional health. She states that if we consider health as a construct in which the quality of life is an integral part, then music can function as a "cultural immunogen – that is, a self-technology that protects, and maintains our health and quality of life" (Ruud, 2017, p. 589). Based on her own research work, this author states that music is:

- A provider of vitality: that is, emotional stimulation, regulation and expression.
- A tool for developing agency and empowerment.
- A resource in creating a sense of belonging.
- A means of achieving meaning and coherence in life.

(Ruud, 2017, pp. 593–594)

Research evidence is emerging concerning the benefits of emotions which are musically expressed, regulated and induced with specific regards to health and well-being in the context of everyday life (e.g., McDonald et al., 2012).

Music engagement and participation contributes to social interaction and communication, both of which are basic human needs. Meaningful engagement provides: a sense of purpose; motivation; self-confidence and self-esteem; arousal; and energy with a consequent sense of enhanced personal, emotional and physical well-being. Furthermore, it helps with physical relaxation and the releasing of physical and emotional tensions. In this way, stress can be alleviated, and music can therefore provide a sense of happiness, enjoyment and help to develop uplifting moods. Going further, music making stimulates cognitive functions such as the ability to concentrate, maintaining attention while practising and performing and it also stimulates memory. In music making, use of the body and body movement of *some* sort is necessarily required, depending on the activity (i.e., playing piano versus singing, dancing or playing a brass instrument). This conveys a concomitant sense of physicality which can be experienced as a form of exercise (Keikha et al., 2012). Regular practice results in increased physical co-ordination, toning of relevant muscles as well as improved breathing, improved eye-sight co-ordination and a variety of other benefits.

Reflective Questions

1. Explain how music can benefit children and young people by enhancing their communicational, social, personal and intellectual development?				
• Consider how engagement with music can create a positive self-attitude and increased self-esteem. • Highlight the benefits of group music participation and of music-based and extra-curricular activities.	Aligned with CME, Level 4 Unit (U) or Area of Study (AOS) and Assessment Criteria number of ABRSM (2014) and TCL (2013, 2019)			
	ABRSM		TCL (2013)	
	U1:	1.3.1	U1:	3.1 3.2
			TCL (2019)	
			AOS2:	3.1.5
2. Explain how music can benefit children and young people by enhancing their creativity?				
• Reflect on the nature of musical engagement which can promote the development of creativity. • Provide examples of what you do/could do as a teacher to promote development of creativity in your lessons.				
	ABRSM		TCL (2013)	
	U1:	1.3.2	U1:	3.2
			TCL (2019)	
			AOS2:	3.1.5
3. Explain how music can benefit children and young people by enhancing their physical and emotional well-being?				
• Consider how musically expressed emotions can promote health and well-being. • Highlight how the use of body and how body movement can contribute to physical well-being.				
	ABRSM		TCL (2013)	
	U1:	1.3.1 1.3.2	U1:	3.1
			TCL (2019)	
			AOS2:	3.1.5

Notes

1. Control group is a group used in scientific experiments which is isolated from the rest of the experiment and other groups submitted to experimental interventions. It is aimed at testing the independent variables in a study. In this way, it becomes possible to compare results among all groups in the study (including the control group) and ascribe or rule out findings of the intervention pertaining to the variables in study.

2. Spatial-temporal reasoning refers to the ability to conceptualise and realise the three-dimensional relationships of objects in space, recognising their interconnections and manipulating them.
3. Processing efficiency refers to aspects of mental processing which include mental processing speed, working memory and selective attention, among others.
4. Stanford-Binet Bead Memory sub-test is part of an assessment tool designed to assess the level of intelligence across several ages and ability levels where the level of difficulty is adjusted for the age ability and the person being assessed. It assesses intelligence in five areas: fluid reasoning; knowledge; quantitative reasoning; visual-spatial reasoning; and working memory. These tests use verbal and non-verbal methods to accommodate young children and non-readers. In particular, the bead stringing task involves having to string a certain number of beads in a certain set amount of time.
5. Perceptual motor skills are developed through the child's interaction with the environment, through the combined and intertwined use and development of senses and motor skills. In the process visual, auditory, sensory and tactile abilities develop and combine with emerging motor skills, resulting in enhanced perceptual motor skills.

Further Reading

Hodges, D., & Gruhn, W. (2012). Implications of neurosciences and brain research for music teaching and learning. In G. E. McPherson & G. F. Welch (Eds.), *The Oxford handbook of music education* (pp. 205–223). Oxford University Press.

McDonald, R., Kreutz, G., & Mitchell, L. (2012). What is music, health and wellbeing and why is it important? In R. McDonald, G. Kreutz, & L. Mitchell (Eds.), *Music, health and wellbeing* (pp. 3–11). Oxford University Press.

Ruud, E. (2017). Music, identity and health. In R. MacDonald, D. J. Hargreaves, & D. Miell (Eds.), *Handbook of Musical Identities* (pp. 589–601). Oxford University Press.

References

Abeles, H., & Sanders, E. (2007). *Year V assessment report, New Jersey symphony orchestra's early strings program.* Center for Arts Education Research, Columbia University.

Associated Board of the Royal Schools of Music (ABRSM) (2014). *Level 4 certificate for music educators: Assessment framework.* ABRSM.

Bermudez, J., & Zatorre, R. (2005). Differences in gray matter between musicians and nonmusicians. *Annals of the New York Academy of Sciences, 1060,* 395–399.

Bilhartz, T. D., Bruhn, R. A., & Olson, J. E. (1999). The effect of early music training on child cognitive development. *Journal of Applied Developmental Psychology, 20*(4), 615–636. https://doi.org/10.1016/S0193-3973(99)00033-7

Brown, J. D. (1980). *Identifying problems facing the school band movement.* Gemeinhardt.

Burton, J. M., Horowitz, R., & Abeles, H. (2000). Learning in and through the arts: The question of transfer. *Studies in Art Education, 41*(3), 228–257. https://doi.org/10.2307/1320379

Butzlaff, R. (2000). Can music be used to teach reading? *Journal of Aesthetic Education, 34*(3/4), 167–178. https://doi.org/10.2307/3333642

Costa-Giomi, E. (1999). The effects of three years of piano instruction on children's cognitive development. *Journal of Research in Music Education, 47*(3), 198–212. https://doi.org/10.2307/3345779

Davidson, J., & Good, J. (2002). Social and musical co-ordination between members of a string quartet: An exploratory study. *Psychology of Music, 30*(2), 186–201.

Forgeard, M., Winner, E., Norton, A., & Schlaug, G. (2008). Practicing a musical instrument in childhood is associated with enhanced verbal ability and nonverbal reasoning. *PLoS ONE, 3*(10), e3566. https://doi.org/10.1371/journal.pone.0003566

Gaab, N., Tallal, P., Kim, H., Lakshminarayanan, K., Archie, J. J., Glover, G. H., & Gabrieli, J. D. E. (2005). Neural correlates of rapid spectrotemporal processing in musicians and nonmusicians. *Annals of the New York Academy of Sciences, 1060*(1), 82–88. https://doi.org/10.1196/annals.1360.040

Gromko, J. E. (2005). The effect of music instruction on phonemic awareness in beginning readers. *Journal of Research in Music Education, 53*(3), 199–209. https://doi.org/10.1177/002242940505300302

Hallam, S. (2005). *Enhancing motivation and learning throughout the lifespan.* Institute of Education, University of London.

Hallam, S. (2010). The power of music: Its impact on the intellectual, personal and social development of children and young people. In S. Hallam & A. Creech (Eds.) *Music education in the 21st century in the United Kingdom: Achievements, analysis and aspirations* (pp. 2–17). Institute of Education.

Hallam, S., & Prince, V. (2000). *Research into instrumental music services.* Department of Education and Employment (DfEE).

Hamann, D., Bourassa, R., & Aderman, M. (1991). Arts experiences and creativity scores of high school students. *Contributions to Music Education, 14*, 35–47.

Harland, J., Kinder, K., Lord, P., Stott, A., Schagen, I., & Haynes, J. (2000). *Arts education in secondary schools: Effects and effectiveness.* National Foundation for Educational Research (NFER)/The Arts Council of England, Royal Society for the Encouragement of the Arts, Manufacture and Commerce (RSA).

Herrera, L., Lorenzo, O., Defior, S., Fernandez-Smith, G., & Costa-Giomi, E. (2011). Effects of phonological and musical training on the reading readiness of native- and foreign-Spanish-speaking children. *Psychology of Music, 39*(1), 68–81. https://doi.org/10.1177/0305735610361995

Hetland, L. (2000). Learning to make music enhances spatial reasoning. *Journal of Aesthetic Education, 34*(3/4), 179–238. https://doi.org/10.2307/3333643

Hodges, D., & Gruhn, W. (2012). Implications of neurosciences and brain research for music teaching and learning. In G. E. McPherson & G. F. Welch (Eds.), *The Oxford handbook of music education* (pp. 205–223). Oxford University Press.

Jentschke, S., & Koelsch, S. (2009). Musical training modulates the development of syntax processing in children. *NeuroImage, 47*(2), 735–744. https://doi.org/10.1016/j.neuroimage.2009.04.090

Kalmár, M. (1982). The effects of music education based on Kodaly's directives in nursery school children: From a psychologist's point of view. *Psychology of Music, Spec Iss*, 63–68.

Keikha, A., Jenabadi, H., & Mirshekar, H. (2012). The effects of music on increasing motor skills and auditory memory in mental retarded children aged 15–10 with 65–75IQ (case study). *Modern Applied Science, 6*(4), 106–111. https://doi.org/10.5539/mas.v6n4p106

Koutsoupidou, T., & Hargreaves, D. J. (2009). An experimental study of the effects of improvisation on the development of children's creative thinking in music. *Psychology of Music*, *37*(3), 251–278. https://doi.org/10.1177/0305735608097246

Long, M. (2007). *The effect of a music intervention on the temporal organisation of reading skills* [Unpublished PhD thesis, University of London].

Lorenzo, O., Herrera, L., Hernández-Candelas, M., & Badea, M. (2014). Influence of music training on language development. A longitudinal study. *Procedia – Social and Behavioral Sciences*, *128*, 527–530. https://doi.org/10.1016/j.sbspro.2014.03.200

McDonald, R., Kreutz, G., & Mitchell, L. (2012). What is music, health and wellbeing and why is it important? In R. McDonald, G. Kreutz, & L. Mitchell (Eds.), *Music, health and wellbeing* (pp. 3–11). Oxford University Press.

Moreno, S., Marques, C., Santos, A., Santos, M., Castro, S. L., & Besson, M. (2009). Musical training influences linguistic abilities in 8-year-old children: More evidence for brain plasticity. *Cerebral Cortex*, *19*(3), 712–723. https://doi.org/10.1093/cercor/bhn120

Norton, A., Winner, E., Cronin, K., Overy, K., Lee, D. J., & Schlaug, G. (2005). Are there pre-existing neural, cognitive, or motoric markers for musical ability? *Brain and Cognition*, *59*(2), 124–134. https://doi.org/10.1016/j.bandc.2005.05.009

Rauscher, F. H., Shaw, G. L., & Ky, C. N. (1993). Music and spatial task performance. *Nature*, *365*(6447), 611–631. https://doi.org/10.1038/365611a0

Ruud, E. (2017). Music, identity and health. In R. MacDonald, D. J. Hargreaves, & D. Miell (Eds.), *Handbook of musical identities* (pp. 589–601). Oxford University Press. https://doi.org/10.1093/acprof:oso/9780199679485.001.0001

Sanders, E. M. (2018). *Music learning and mathematics achievement: A real-world study in English primary schools* [Unpublished PhD thesis, University of Cambridge].

Schellenberg, E. G. (2004). Music lessons enhance IQ. *Psychological Science*, *15*(8), 511–514. https://doi.org/10.1111/j.0956-7976.2004.00711.x

Strait, D. L., Slater, J., O'Connell, S., & Kraus, N. (2015). Music training relates to the development of neural mechanisms of selective auditory attention. *Developmental Cognitive Neuroscience*, *12*, 94–104. https://doi.org/10.1016/j.dcn.2015.01.001

Tarrant, M., North, A. C., & Hargreaves, D. J. (2000). English and American adolescents' reasons for listening to music. *Psychology of Music*, *28*(2), 166–173. https://doi.org/10.1177/0305735600282005

Trinity College London (TCL) (2013). *TCL level 4 certificate for music educators: Specifications*. TCL.

Trinity College London (TCL) (2019). *TCL level 4 certificate for music educators, areas of study*. TCL.

VandenBos, G. R. (2007). Intelligence. In G. R. VandenBos (Ed.), *APA dictionary of psychology*. American Psychological Association. https://dictionary.apa.org/intelligence

Welch, G. F., & Ockelford, A. (2010). Music for all. In S. Hallam & A. Creech (Eds.), *Music education in the 21st century in the United Kingdom: Achievements, analysis and aspirations* (pp. 36–52). Institute of Education, University of London, Bedford Way Papers.

Wolff, K. (1979). The non-musical outcomes of music education: A review of the literature. *Bulletin of the Council for Research in Music Education*, *55*, 1–27.

Yang, P. (2015). The impact of music on educational attainment. *Journal of Cultural Economics*, *39*(4), 369–396. https://doi.org/10.1007/s10824-015-9240-y

Section II

Planning, Leading and Assessing Musical Learning

4 Preparing for the Development of Inclusive Learning Environments

To Guide Your Reading

- What is meant by inclusion, equality and diversity in the context of music education?
- What barriers to musical learning and common assumptions can unintentionally create barriers?
- What are learning styles and what implications do they have for music teaching?
- How can you identify and support those with learning difficulties?
- How can you identify and support prodigies and very gifted children?
- How should you respond to diverse learning needs and aspirations?
- How can you deal with cultural diversity in music teaching contexts and use music to address discrimination and promote equality, diversity and inclusion?
- How can teachers promote the development of motivation towards musical engagement and learning?
- How can teachers promote children and young people's positive behaviour and be able to prevent, manage and respond to inappropriate behaviour?

Introduction

The main purpose of this chapter is to provide music teachers with up-to-date knowledge that they can use to develop inclusive learning environments. Therefore, definitions of inclusion, equality and diversity open the chapter, and this is followed by a brief overview of barriers to music learning. Given that children and young people are diverse learners, the subsequent sections focus upon differences in learning styles; difficulties with learning; working with very gifted children; and teaching in culturally diverse contexts. This is followed by a short review on the topic of motivation, where the important role that teachers have in promoting and developing learners' motivation and development of musical identities in every lesson is considered. The chapter concludes with a section on promoting positive behaviour, where types and reasons for inappropriate behaviour are discussed and procedures are identified for promoting positive behaviour and dealing with challenging behaviour.

Inclusion, Equality and Diversity

If there is one idea that music teachers can agree upon, it would be the notion that our main mission is to enhance *every* learner's growth as a musician and enabling *each* learner to achieve their potential. This main idea guides everything we do (Kaikkonen, 2016). Translating this from an ideal to an integral element fully embedded in our day-to-day teaching, however, necessarily requires an understanding of what inclusive learning environments truly are while also identifying barriers to learning and devising ways for widening participation and learning. Regardless of where you teach and the teaching setting you find yourself in, your learners will certainly be from different social, family and cultural milieus. They are unique individuals with their own learning preferences, motivations, and specific life situations, conditions and circumstances all of which combine to influence how they approach and engage with learning.

In addition to individual uniqueness, educational environments have become more and more diverse in recent decades as a result of migration, globalisation, technological advancements, media and inclusion of learners with varying levels of abilities in the same classroom (e.g., prodigies, average learners and learners with learning difficulties and disabilities). Developing inclusive learning environments starts with a recognition that different learners have different learning needs. This will be true when they embark on their learning journey but also as time, learning and development progresses. UNESCO's guidelines on inclusion (2009) and arts education (2006) explicitly allude to the rights of diverse groups of children within mainstream, comprehensive education. This covers cultural experiences and arts education, and it defines inclusion as:

> a process addressing and responding to the diversity of needs of all children, youth and adults through increasing participation in learning, cultures and communities, and reducing and eliminating exclusion within and from education. It involves changes and modifications in content, approaches, structures and strategies with a common vision that covers all children of the appropriate age range and a conviction that it is the responsibility of the regular system to educate all children.
>
> (UNESCO, 2009, pp. 8–9)

From this perspective, inclusion is an approach to ensure inclusive learning environments for all learners. Inclusive learning environments in music and beyond are focused upon:

- Respect for equality and diversity;

- Enabling participation, while considering and removing barriers to learning and of access to learning experiences;

- The design and delivery of learning processes that meaningfully engage learners with the curriculum while also enabling them to achieve their potential.

This directly links to the concepts of equality and diversity. Equality recognises the right that each a person has to being afforded an equal opportunity to develop their talents. More specifically, equality in this context is about ensuring individuals are treated fairly and equally, regardless of their race, gender, age, disability, religion, sexual orientation and/or other protected characteristics. In the context of education, this does not necessarily mean being treated identically in all instances. Rather, the idea is to offer learner-centred approaches which are tailored to individual learning needs and with consideration of learning styles, motivations and aims. Diversity is about accepting differences between people and recognising and respecting these differences to create an all-inclusive atmosphere. Such differences may include race; gender; age; disability; religion; and/or sexual orientation.

Children are also diverse learners, and from a teaching and learning perspective the following differences should be considered: differences in learning needs; learning styles; and motivation and preferences. In the context of education, acknowledgment and appreciation that each individual is unique, embracing acceptance and valuing difference are the stepping stones towards the creation of an environment where learners can thrive together. Hence, we must understand and appreciate that individual characteristics make people unique and not 'different' in a negative way. This requires understanding learner's particular circumstances, life contexts and particular situations and conditions which may affect their learning (either temporarily or on a permanent basis). Armed with such insights, we can optimise their learning.

While diversity brings richness to the teaching and learning environment, it also brings a level of unpredictability with regard to challenges that may surface in real-time classroom teaching and learning. As teachers, we need to be ready to accept that there will be times where we will be placed outside of our comfort zone and we need to be ready to find solutions. Solutions can be found by adopting a humble and flexible approach, one where we are open to learning on an everyday basis from our learners and proactively engaging in continuous professional development and consulting and working collaboratively with others. This could be achieved with special needs assistants, other professionals in the fields of education and health, parents, as well as seeking advice from more experienced teachers and other professionals. As a process, a constant cyclical approach to identifying barriers to access and participation in music learning and music making is needed. It must be considered side-by-side with identifying strategies to help learners overcome barriers while always assessing the effectiveness of actions taken.

Identifying Barriers to Music Learning

Barriers to accessing music education are both context and culture specific. Therefore, it is impossible to provide an exhaustive list of all possible barriers. However, and generally speaking, barriers to accessing music education can be grouped into the following categories (Kaikkonen, 2016):

- School system and society;

- Intrapersonal;

- Informational;

- Physical learning environment;

- Informational and physical combined.

School System and Society

Financial constraints can cause barriers to learning in school systems and societies at many different levels. For instance, there may be low or simply not enough funding available for allowing access to music education for all both in and outside school environments. Family related financial constraints can mean families are unable to pay for lessons, purchase music instruments, or obtain further extra learning support, particularly whenever educational music provision is not freely offered at school. Competition for funding between music and other school subjects, in association with conceptions where music is wrongly deemed as 'less important', leaves music being put forward as an optional subject, or as a paid optional subject in many educational contexts.

Lack of qualified or experienced and knowledgeable teachers who can provide the high-quality music learning that learners are entitled to can result in the absence of, or more regularly, low-quality music education provision which doesn't engage learners in meaningful learning. Another problematic and common issue are time pressures in the school curriculum, where music is either not offered or offered in proportionally less time in comparison to other school subjects.

Inflexible curricula are another huge issue impacting upon how teachers and learners work together and where it can remain difficult or impossible to develop a learner-centred approach. Obviously, this directly impacts upon learners' motivation, and particularly whenever a curriculum doesn't allow room for manoeuvre vis-a-vis considerations of learners' learning styles and specific circumstances which may affect information accessibility. These can include learning difficulties; disabilities; giftedness; and cultural diversity (including integration of children from ethnic minority groups, immigrants and refugees).

Socio-cultural conceptions operate across many fronts. This includes misleading conceptions that musicians need to be talented and gifted, which thereby leads to many learners disengaging as they may not be aware of the sustained development work that is required to reach a higher skill level. In short, they assume they don't have what it takes. The value that parents, teachers and school administration ascribe to music and music education (both implicitly and explicitly) also has strong repercussions on whether children and young people will engage in music learning, under what circumstances and for how long.

Intrapersonal Barriers

Learner's lack of confidence and self-belief in their music potential affects engagement and motivation, resulting in many learners giving up musical learning and music making. This lack of confidence is in many cases caused by lack of parental and teachers' encouragement. Other intrapersonal barriers relate to cases where learners have specific conditions where their communication skills may be affected, and where teachers are not aware of what may work best for that particular learner nor of best practice on how to promote learning for learners with those conditions. Furthermore, teachers may not have the necessary interpersonal skills to cater for learners from diverse backgrounds, different skill levels or having various learning needs which can also constitute a barrier to their learners' learning.

Informational Barriers

Informational barriers concern how information is communicated and perceived. For instance, in cases where the communication in the learning environment takes place in a language that a child or young person can't understand or is not proficient in (as is the case with recently arrived immigrants or refugees). Concurrently, situations can arise where educational provision doesn't consider specific learner abilities and preferences with regard to receiving and perceiving information via the senses, nor considers self-expression and expressions of knowledge which use means other than the ones used by the 'norm'. For example, when music teachers use Western classical music notation in cases where learners could benefit much more from using Figurenotes notation[1]; or an absence of resources for learners with needs related to hearing. These examples are also in many cases directly related to a lack of resources in the physical learning environment.

Physical Learning Environment Barriers

These can include logistical and geographical barriers as well as resources needed for learning to take place. For instance: living far away from a school or learning institution and not having access to transportation at all, or on a regular basis; lack of an appropriate venue and room for establishing a safe and welcoming music learning environment for music education activities to take place; a lack of resources (at the institution or at the learner's home environment), such as lack of music instruments; a lack or complete absence of other resources such as assistive technology for engaging learners with specific conditions; and a lack of access to technology which can promote musical engagement and participation.

Informational and Physical Barriers

Technology is nowadays making possible the creation of brand-new instruments to suit musicians' particular needs and skills (see the work of organisations such as Drake Music and OpenUp Music). This includes applications such as mobile devices, Soundbeam, Brainfingers and instruments such as MagicFlute, Skoog and much more. Lack of access to such customised instruments for learners with specific needs is therefore a barrier to music learning and music making for some learners. Technological advances continue to bring forward tools for engaging learners with their peers and the world surrounding them (Watts et al., 2016). While all of the previously mentioned platforms are highly encouraging, there is still considerable groundwork to be done to ensure access for all in accordance with their specific needs.

Learning Styles

Children learn in different ways from one another and over time will develop their own preferred learning styles. While some children prefer to work in groups, others prefer working alone. Some are maybe highly organised and enjoy structured ways of learning, others may prefer to learn in flexible and unstructured ways. In music education, some children may have a preference for learning to play or sing a specific tune when visual information is provided (i.e., a display of the melody line through specific symbols or notation); others may prefer instead to listen to the tune repeatedly, while others may prefer actively trying it out in a process of trial and error. It is likely that all these ways of learning will need to be used at some point by both teachers and learners alike when attempting to learn to play or sing a new tune. However, the term "learning style" specifically refers to an individual's preferred means of acquiring knowledge and skills, including their preferred ways in which to think, process information and demonstrate learning (Pritchard, 2018).

It is important to emphasise that learning styles are not fixed. People can, and often do expand upon their ability to learn using less preferred or dominant styles. Furthermore, there are many different dimensions affecting learning styles, and every person will have a mixture of learning styles. Factors which can influence individual learning styles preferences can include personality, levels of exposure to certain ways of learning and doing, culture and so on. Altogether, this makes it very difficult to logically categorise and ascribe a single learning style to a particular learner, or to even create learning styles categorisations. This is evident by the many different learning style categorisations we can speak of. These include:

- **Cognitive processes** (e.g., Gardner, 1983; Sternberg, 1998)[2]: focused on how preferred styles of thinking, perceiving, remembering and problem-solving influence one's approach to learning.

- **Personality** (e.g., Grasha, 1996; Myers, 1962)[3]: considers how personality or psychological types are part of an individual's distinct character, either inborn or resulting from environmental influences and how these can influence a person's approach to learning.

- **Experiential** (e.g., Kolb, 1984; Freire, 1970; Mezirow, 2011)[4]: assesses how experience, as an integrally important component of the learning process, informs learning and the ways in which learners approach learning.

- **Perceptual learning modalities** (e.g., Fleming & Baume, 2006; Reid, 1987)[5]: examines the way information is extracted from the environment by perceptual or sensory input of information through aural (or auditory), visual and kinaesthetic (or tactile) senses and how these influence preferred learning approaches.

In all learning, the earlier aspects will be utilised in different combinations and to different depths and extents. Music learning and music making are multidimensional and require (among other things) the ability to remember and in many instances to read, produce or perform music-related information. This includes melodies and other progressions of tones or pitches, associated rhythms, dynamics, intonation and nuances. Music and musical related information will be perceived and communicated to learners in a wide variety of ways, which can include visual; aural (auditory); verbal; and physical means either individually or in a communal, social way when learning and making music. Your learners may have developed preferred ways for perceiving information in their music learning, which you may have already identified.

Understanding learners approaches to learning requires holistic consideration of learners' preferences with regard to the cognitive processes they use, how their personality influences their learning, the types of learning experiences they thrive in and their preferred perceptual learning modalities. There are many factors which interplay in this process and no single learning style categorisation focuses on all these processes simultaneously. In consideration of all the learning styles categorisations within the literature, Gardner's (1983) description combines aspects to do with certain cognitive processes, experiences and perceptual learning modalities. He emphasised that people are not ruled by or limited to only one type of intelligence, but instead possess a mixture of various intelligences. His theory of Multiple Intelligences outlines a range of learning abilities and preferences based on different types of intelligence as follows:

- Linguistic: learning by using language.

- Logical-Mathematical: learning by using logic and rational thinking.

- Spatial-Visual: learning through seeing and imagining.

- Bodily-Kinaesthetic: learning through movement and touch.

- Musical: learning through rhythm and music.

- Interpersonal: learning through social contact.

- Intrapersonal: learning through reflection, on their own.

Gardner's theory of multiple intelligences as applied to learning styles offers a possible framework which can be applied to consider learners' learning styles in a variety of music educational contexts, while also realising strategies for teaching music to learners with certain preferences (see Table 4.1).

These dimensions of learning, intelligences or learning styles interact to various degrees and it is generally accepted that the use of a mixture of learning styles contributes to an efficient and more secure musical learning modality overall (e.g., Johansen, 2005; Proctor, 2001). Furthermore, all styles are equally important and there is no right or wrong mix: it is entirely contingent upon the learner in question. Still, you will want to be aware that if you continuously encourage a certain particular approach to learning, some of your learners will learn more (particularly so those who have a preference for such an approach) while others will learn less effectively. Although learners may have preferred learning styles, it is essential to use a variety of different teaching approaches and to challenge learners to adopt different learning styles and strategies for learning. Research using brain-imaging techniques has shown that in using different learning styles, different parts of the brain are involved, and that using more parts of the brain during learning generally results in learners being able to remember more of what was learned (see Owens & Tanner, 2017). Moreover, collaborative methods of teaching and learning seem to be the most effective.

It is by continuously observing how learners evolve, act and react while they learn, that over time it becomes possible to understand that some learners may have a preference for a particular approach to their music making as well as for their learning, retaining, assimilating musical knowledge and expressing themselves musically. It is also through observation and interaction with learners that teachers can realise that learners' learning styles may have changed. Recognising and identifying that different learners have preferred learning styles, necessarily requires that teachers develop and implement teaching approaches that cater to a variety of different learning preferences in the classroom.

Table 4.1 Learning styles categories, definitions and implications for music learning and teaching

Learning style (Gardner, 1983)	Main characteristics	Some strategies for music teaching
Visual (spatial)	Learners learn more efficiently when presented with images, pictures and spatial understanding.	Use visual recognition and mapping techniques such as: let learners circle patterns; help making visible certain elements such as the white and black note shapes, use colourful and purposeful teaching aids with diagrams and shapes. Also helpful to map changes of notes and directions.
Aural (auditory-musical)	Learners prefer using auditory sound-based elements, which may include music in their learning.	Teach patterns using aural repetition, focusing on the sounds of steps as well as the tonic-dominant of alternating measures; play a sound sequence while extending the same pattern with more sounds from the top to the bottom of the keyboard by ear; singing changes of the bottom and top parts in pieces with several layers, comparing those sounds to the direction shown in the parts. This can help to 'teach' by ear and correct notes while aiding learners to listen.
Verbal (linguistic)	Learners prefer to reason, solve problems, and learning using language.	Give learners verbal and sound-based explanations, using similar strategies as those proposed for aural learners
Physical (kinaesthetic)	Learners prefer using their body, hands and sense of touch.	In instrumental music learning, feeling how far the hands can be next to each other or far apart, and emphasising the movement needed to execute certain passages; playing patterns of skip and step on every white key in an octave, feeling how the same fingers patterns are played each time and introducing movement in musical learning tasks to grasp rhythm regularity and direction.
Logical (mathematical)	Learners prefer using logic, reasoning and systematic thinking.	Explain the logic behind concepts, using strong reasoning. Provide logical strategies with sequential steps to help learners follow the logic, keeping them tuned into and engaged in discovering or contributing to the next step.
Social (interpersonal)	Learners have a preference for learning in groups or with other people.	Design music learning activities where learners have opportunities to work and make music together, such as ensemble groups aimed at discovering specific elements relevant to their learning, using active and peer learning teaching strategies.

(*Continued*)

Table 4.1 (Continued)

Learning style (Gardner, 1983)	Main characteristics	Some strategies for music teaching
Solitary (intrapersonal)	Learners prefer to work alone and use self-study.	Design creative music learning activities and work projects where learners can work on their own. Individual musical composition and/or music production activities can be used at this level and so can the learning of a musical instrument, where practise is often a solitary endeavour.

Source: Adapted from Gardner (1983)

Difficulties With Learning

While a 'normal' trajectory in learning (in terms of intellectual development) might be expected as part of the development and maturation process, it does not apply to all learners. However, it is possible to make a distinction between what might be classed as relatively uncomplicated learning versus learning that is problematic and difficult. Regardless of what stage we might be at in our lives, or what academic success we might have achieved, we will all certainly be able to identify areas in which we find learning extremely challenging. This may result from a combination of different factors such as learning styles, preferences towards certain subject areas or aspects within a particular area or other elements. Also, as learners of one sort or another, we will all likely have experienced at some point in our lives learning difficulties related to some endeavour. Those of us experiencing general or widespread learning difficulties may find learning of any sort extremely difficult.

As teachers, it is crucial that we understand our learners and the difficulties they might be experiencing at a deeper level. We must also recognise certain particularities and manifestations of their specific conditions in order to know how best to deal with them and maximise their learning and learning experiences. Learning difficulties can be general or specific and within each of these modes be mild, moderate or severe.

General Learning Difficulties

Pritchard (2018) states that manifestations of general learning difficulties can include:

- Low attainment for all (or most) school subjects, including in baseline assessments;
- Difficulty in developing and acquiring literacy and numeracy skills;
- Difficulty dealing with abstract information and in generalising concepts;

- Difficulties which are associated with all the previously mentioned issues, particularly in speech, language, emotional and social development.

The model of learning disabilities most used is still based largely upon a cognitive approach to learning, whereby four stages of information processing employed in learning are identified and learners' difficulties in these stages are correspondingly categorised. The stages are input, integration, memory and output. The information provided here on each of these stages has been adapted from Pritchard (2018).

'Input' refers to the process of receiving, taking in and recording information perceived via the senses. The most used senses required to learn music are sight, hearing, touch and the kinaesthetic/proprioceptive sense. Examples of input impairment(s) include:

- Visual perception impairment. This can include difficulties with perceiving shape, position, orientation, size and colour of objects and symbols such as music notes in the score and letter based textual information. These can appear distorted, or learners may not be able to identify them as different or distinct.

- Auditory perception impairment can lead to difficulties in hearing music or the teacher's voice accurately, or result in parts of the teaching not being heard fully or partially, or problems with the subtle discrimination of certain sounds which may be altered or even lost.

- Tactile receptors located in the joints, tendons and muscles and limbs form part of the proprioceptive system. The proprioceptive system provides us with information about the position of our body and our movements. The visual system has deep links with the proprioceptive system, and this is why some children with visual impairments have difficulty knowing where their bodies are located in space. Tactile information gathered through active exploration such as vibration, pressure, proprioception, pain and temperature is sent to the brain from the receptors along the neural pathways. Problems in the tactile receptors, brain, neural pathways among others can cause different types of impairment in the sense of touch and proprioceptive system.

Integration refers to interpretation and categorisation of information in a sequential manner while being able to link it to previous learning. An example of integration impairment could be difficulties with sequencing information in the correct order, for example the sequence of numbers or months in the year. In music, this can translate to intense difficulties in singing or performing parts of a certain musical work with the notes in the correct sequence and also difficulty memorising parts of the music in a particular sequence or generalising musical concepts to other areas of understanding.

Memory encompasses the storage of information for later retrieval and use. Differences between linguistic memory and musical memory led researchers to theorise that musical memory may be encoded differently from language-based memory. In either case, memory difficulties most commonly include problems with short-term memory, and less frequently, with long-term memory. Short-term memory problems imply that more repetitions of new learning material may be required for learning to really take root. Musicians and learners of music commonly use a simultaneous array of memory types including visual, auditory, kinaesthetic and conceptional/analytical. Conditions which result in impairment of perceptual information through any or some of these perceptual modalities can affect learner's short- and long-term musical memory to various degrees.

Finally, output refers to a stage where actions are taken, be it in the form of language or action (movement, gesture, music making, etc.), or both, as a result of processing stored information. Impairment at this level includes language difficulties, including the spoken word and sound making as well as writing and drawing. It can also include problems with muscular activity which may affect the way a child expresses him/herself in various ways (i.e., gesturally). Language difficulties can manifest themselves by having difficulty answering questions posed by others due to either difficulty recalling information required or difficulty in processing thoughts and placing them into clear spoken language. Motor skills impairment can be either fine (e.g., difficulty with colouring, drawing and writing) or gross (general clumsiness, difficulties with running and undertaking tasks which require good co-ordination).

Specific Learning Difficulties

Specific learning difficulties have specific manifestations and symptoms associated with specific conditions and impact upon individual learners with various degrees of intensity (Lavoie, 2007). Given the wide variety of specific learning difficulties and their intricacies from the point of view of teaching and learning, it would be beyond the scope of this book to provide detailed information on each condition. However, general information is provided at the CW Resource 1 on some of the most common conditions, including dyslexia; dyspraxia; autism; Asperger's syndrome; and other disorders. The information provided is given only as a starting point as you will nevertheless still have to:

- Understand exactly how a certain condition(s) specifically impact upon the learning of your learner(s) since each individual is affected in different ways.

- Identify what a specific learner is good at.

- Develop learner-centred teaching and learning methods, informed by up-to-date information on the particular conditions which affect different learners in your remit and monitor learners' progress in relation to this.

To conclude this section, from a teaching point of view, it is important that teachers recognise manifestations of learning difficulties and gain insights into how best to promote and support learners in the learning process. This can be done by consulting more knowledgeable colleagues and seeking reliable information from credible sources. Although, as part of our role as teachers we need to be alert to identify situations where a child is struggling with learning, while alerting other colleagues and parents of the problem, it is also important to have in mind that we are absolutely ***not*** entitled to make any diagnostics. While we can suggest to parents that a child be seen by other professionals with medical, psychological and special education needs expertise, we should ***not*** refer to names of conditions or attempt to diagnose or label ***any*** child with a condition. Even after a diagnose is made by appropriate professionals, a teacher's main focus should always unconditionally be to focus on learners' abilities and what they bring to the classroom, what they can do, and how they contribute or can contribute, while simultaneously putting in place support aimed at further development, in a safe learning environment, and where each learner feels welcomed and valued.

Very Gifted Children

Generally speaking, very gifted children learn very quickly and are able to apply new knowledge (declarative[6] and procedural[7]) to a variety of different situations. (McPherson & Lehmann, 2012). Their learning occurs earlier than expected for the child's age, and the child is deemed able "to do something that is usually attributed to adults" (Shavinina, 2009, p. 233). The main difference between a prodigy and a very gifted child is that the prodigy is capable of demonstrating their exceptional talent before the age of 10 (McPherson & Lehmann, 2012). Although some of the talent possessed by prodigies and the very gifted may be inborn (Simonton, 2017), environmental and developmental factors have been shown to have an important and conducive role in their talent development process.

Advocating for the importance of environmental factors in giftedness, Gagné (2004) proposed a model of skill, expertise and talent development, centred around the following elements:

- The opportunities to learn that a person has access to, including the content and structure of such learning;

- The investment made with regard to time spent learning, monetary resources available for continuing to participate in high quality learning and the overall energy devoted to learning and development;

- The progress made in learning over a sustained period of time and the speed at which learning takes place.

Often, very gifted children are first identified by their parents, who tend to nurture the child's talent further through specialised tuition, either provided by parents themselves (if they are musicians and feel capable of supporting their child's learning), by a specialist teacher or via a specialised institution. Usually, considerable investment is made by families before the child is considered 'exceptional' as compared to same age peers. It is noteworthy that many exceptional musicians come from within musician's families. Sometimes the child's exceptional ability might be identified by teachers or relevant others involved in the child's education.

Unfortunately, reports by very gifted highlight that their childhood was often traumatic as they were pushed by others in their environment to do intense hard work and demonstrate exceptional ability in certain areas. Realising the complexities around prodigies and very gifted children, UNESCO (2010) acknowledged that early achievers require special care and their special needs need to be met. Considering these needs, McPherson and Lehmann (2012) provide a number of relevant recommendations for both parents and teachers which focus upon the following key topics:

- **Parents and teachers main focus of attention should be at all times to support children's psychological needs**. This is the same for all children regardless of the child being very gifted or not. The emphasis on this point is important, however, as often the psychological needs of the very talented were/are overlooked.

- **Very gifted children will require the support of parents and teachers during sensitive periods.** These can occur either during periods of intense and rapid learning or when they encounter difficulties or have less motivation. An environment where they have developed a solid and positive 'connection' with parents and teachers is extremely important for their progress. The environment should be non-threatening, welcoming and acknowledging progress made while also providing opportunities to showcase acquisition of new skills. The child should feel appreciated and also be given freedom of choice with regard to how they engage with learning. In this way they will feel in control of their own learning journey. This will encourage responsibility and initiative, which in turn will help coping with difficulties along the way.

- Given that rapid music learning occurs in association to intense intellectual curiosity and emotional connection with aspects related to their learning it is important to **nurture their curiosity and nurture positive emotional connections with other aspects of learning**.

- **Parents and teachers should continuously work together collaboratively in order to establish how each can better support the child.** Roles and responsibilities should be clear, and meetings should be held at certain points in time to evaluate whether their support as agreed is fit for purpose, or whether adjustments may be needed. The support in place should be commensurate with child's age and developmental needs.

- **Teachers need to recognise periods of rapid learning and periods of less rapid learning and quickly shift the balance between providing challenges and providing support accordingly.** Both feelings that 'it is too easy' and 'it is too difficult' can contribute to learner loss of motivation. Knowing what works better for the learner is key and being a flexible teacher with regard to providing support when so required and positively challenging the learner to the point where it will take him/her to the next level is relevant.

- **Involve the child in decision making and goal setting.** Involving the child in discussions about expectations and in setting goals communicates respect and will convey to the child a sense of also being in the 'driver's seat' with regard to their own development. In setting goals, teachers need to refrain from pursuing parents' or teachers' own unfulfilled desires or aspirations. Goal setting should consider both long- and short-term goals and each be negotiated with the child and based on the child's developmental needs, preferences and be realistically achievable. In addition, love, care and attention should never be contingent on child's obedience or levels of success.

- **Consider the child from a holistic point of view, in terms of strengths, weaknesses, interests and personality, and offer opportunities for development of strengths and weaknesses.** Very gifted children have a set of unique strengths, and may have asynchronous development in other domains such as language, socialisation skills, motor development and so on. Catering for their development requires a holistic approach which celebrates their uniqueness and prepares them for life in the real world.

- **Seek help.** It is important to seek the advice and help of more experienced colleagues and assess if your own proficiency level and knowledge base is such that the learner will benefit from learning with you or if, at any stage of the process, you should recommend a more experienced or proficient colleague instead.

- **Promote a healthy balance between practice, rest and socialising.** As a teacher it is important that you support and promote learning at all times. This notion is often misunderstood by teachers as being that you should 'promote *work* and *practise* at all or most times'. However, this actually is highly counterproductive and will, over time, result in mental and physical burnout, negatively impact upon motivation, cause stress and endanger the learning progress that you mostly want to promote. In promoting learning as a teacher, you need to promote a fine balance between work, rest and socialising. While you are supporting a child to develop as a musician, have in mind that this can only be done in the first place by developing the person first, while catering to their basic human needs, and then as a musician.

- **Anticipate, find and deal appropriately with changes in motivation, learning style and attitude.** Anticipating factors that can affect motivation, learning style and attitude will help either in preventing factors that cause harm at these levels, or at least enable you to put in place strategies to mitigate its effect. Taking the time to genuinely know the child as a person is crucial. Therefore, understanding human development and the specific challenges prodigies and the very talented are more likely to experience is useful. For example, possible stresses related with participating in a high level competition; possible parental and/or institutional pressure to continuously impress and deliver; and intense practice, either promoted by others or the child continuously pushing him/herself to the limit. It is important that teachers and relevant others help learners in realising the tremendous journey of success they have had (even if didn't materialise in acquiring one of the first three places in a given competition). At the same time, space needs to be given to the learner to decide what direction they wish to take in relation to their career; support their decisions and guide them accordingly.

Very gifted children have an inner drive to learn which is not necessarily connected with wanting to be famous, become rich or with a view of making a professional career out of their talents. Additionally, different stages of the learning journey require different teaching and learning approaches and it is extremely important that the child is engaged in the decision-making process, provided with appropriate guidance and support, but are also led to take responsibility for their actions. Side-by-side with developing children musically and nurturing their talent, a teacher's focus should equally be upon helping them to develop the needed autonomy to become adults who have the willingness and ability to shape their lives.

Cultural Diversity

Teachers also play an important role as cultural agents. They need to be aware of the important role they hold in designing and facilitating meaningful intercultural exchanges wherein learners feel valued and develop a sense of belonging and appreciation towards others, and where equality and celebration of diversity genuinely materialise.

Culture can be loosely defined as the knowledge, beliefs, morals, religion, laws, arts and other elements acquired by humans as members of a society. Different groups in society have different traditions, beliefs and ways for expressing themselves as individuals and as members of their own society or societies. You will have, most probably, heard of terms such as 'high culture', 'popular culture', 'subculture' and 'counterculture'. While the term high culture refers to the cultural patterns that identify and distinguish a society's elite, popular culture concerns patterns that are highly widespread within a society's population. The term sub-culture encompasses cultural patterns that set apart a group or a segment of a society's population. Counter-culture pertains to cultural patterns that oppose those more widely accepted within a given society. Whereas all societies have what can be called as high, popular, sub, and counter-cultures, the balance between these is quickly shifting as a result of migration, people displacement, globalisation and access to digital technologies.

Within society, there are ethnic majority and minority groups. Majority groups quite often hold the power in that specific society and ethnic minority groups are victims of an unequal power distribution (Nadal & Rivera, 2008). While some minority groups were and are formed as a result of past or recent migration waves (e.g., Hispanic migration to the US, Polish migrants in the UK), others consist of local populations which gained minority status over time (e.g., the indigenous people of the US, Aborigines in Australia and Canada and Gipsy or Irish Travellers in Ireland). Although issues of power in society, migration and refugee influx extensively contribute to cultural diversity in the classroom, other relevant factors in this interplay include globalisation and access to the internet and digital technologies, which have enabled a fast-paced flow and exchange of information, transcending physical and geographical barriers.

We live in a world where it is now possible to interact with people from all cultures and learn more about their beliefs systems, laws, rituals, food and the way they express themselves through various art forms, including through music, both physically and virtually. Likewise, through the internet and mass media (e.g., TV, films, documentaries, shows) we encounter different ways of living and being, and become aware of cultural differences and diversity. Through repeated experiences such as these, we come across cultural elements from other societies that perhaps we can't understand (fully or partially) and other elements that we resist due to conflicting beliefs and value systems. At times we can individually (or as groups) discover cultural aspects that we enjoy, and appropriate them, making them part of who we are (i.e., use it for expressing our identities or to inculcate new dimensions to who we are). This dynamic interplay is complex and multifaceted: at times it is referred to by terms such as 'intercultural', 'multicultural', 'cross-cultural' and 'transcultural'. Although at times these terms are used interchangeably, they refer to different things. Mckinlay (2017) provides useful definitions for these terms, that teachers should consider when designing teaching and learning. They are:

- **Cross-cultural**: involves comparison of two or more cultures, for example for the purposes of cross-cultural musical analysis. The 'comparison' element involved here can promote a binary way of considering 'us' and 'them', which can potentially be divisive and promote exclusion.

- **Transcultural**: considers cultures as dynamic and fluid. While acknowledging that there is tension between similar and different cultural elements, it looks at how cultures become intertwined or combined, and how cultural barriers are broken in the process.

- **Multicultural**: refers to two or more cultures coexisting with each other, through exposure, contact and experience with different cultures, but in which the cultures involved retain their own cultural identities.

- **Intercultural**: allows for an "in-between" and "on the borders" encounter between cultures (McKinlay, 2017, p. 173). That is, through decentring dominant ways of being, knowing and doing, and where individuals involved in intercultural experiences position themselves in places of difference and diversity and imbibe insights which can transform their ways of thinking, being and doing.

Music educational contexts can be considered as a "contact zone", which hold the potential of representing a "third cultural space" (McKinlay, 2017, p. 174). The "contact zone" is a space where two or more cultures meet, where commonalities are found and where clashes occur. In the process, interactive and potentially transformative inter-exchanges lead to new understandings being formed. The "third space" is at the intersection of the cultural inter-exchanges and is a creative space for new possibilities. This creative element allows for the creation of a 'new culture' where those actively involved in the process share the new meanings created, and hence the name 'third' space because it allows individuals to enter unchartered territory in terms of their own cultural backgrounds, and to therefore go beyond the cultures involved and create new meanings.

Therefore, as McKinlay (2017) points out, when considering educational contexts as "contact zones" with the potential for a "third space" to be created, it is vital that teachers:

- **Be aware and mindful of their own musical cultural background** (as members of a specific society and having been educated in a certain musical tradition). Teachers need to reflect on possible personal tensions between teaching music they know, feel comfortable with and perhaps have a preference for, versus the ethical imperative of representing the diversity of musical backgrounds of learners in the class. Hence, teachers need to continuously ask themselves questions such as: what balance of representation of music from different cultures should I provide? What sort of representations am I conveying by using this or not using that repertoire? By using this or that system of musical notation what representation of music do I pass on to learners? What forms of musical expression do I promote in my classroom? What other forms of musical expression could be promoted?

- **Reflect on their own understandings of other musical cultures**, considering not only the musical knowledge they may or may not have. But also, their assumptions about other musical cultures, and what might have created those assumptions. The reflection should include questions such as: can I get rid of prior assumptions I may have developed towards music of a certain culture? If so, how? How can I present this and a variety of other music I am not familiar with, and do so with respect and dignity? If at this point in time I am unable to do so, what are the alternative solutions? Would it be possible and adequate to allow the learners in class from those musical backgrounds to take ownership of representing music from their own cultural context in class?

- **Be open minded, flexible and constantly engage in learning**. Instead of showcasing themselves as 'the expert in music' in the classroom, it would be highly beneficial that teachers have humility and present themselves as learners, whenever they are confronted with something new to learn. A teacher who is humble and open minded in experiencing other forms of musical expression and who is happy to learn with and from his/her own learners will become highly respected by learners.

- **Gather as much information as possible about the learners, before and during the teaching and learning process**. Particularly in the context of diversity, teachers should find out answers to questions such as: are all learners in class proficient in the spoken language and musical idioms used? If not, what can the school (and I as a teacher) do to ensure all learners are provided equal access to the content in ways they can understand? How should the mixture of cultural backgrounds impact my lesson planning, delivery and assessment? In the case of immigrants, newly arrived children will often feel isolated, disengaged and inadequate (Howell, 2011). As Ilari (2017) states, the quality of their experiences in the new homeland is directly related to the "ethos of reception" (p. 535–536). The "ethos of reception" stands for the attitudes, beliefs, opportunities and affordances held by members of the new country in relation to immigration and their particular group. Schools as a whole and teachers need to reflect on what their "ethos of reception" is and how are they helping children to feel welcomed and supporting them to thrive.

- **Learn more about themselves as teachers and individuals**. Questions to consider include: how do you see yourself as a teacher? What teacher do you want to be? Who are you in reality? How do your learners see you and what opinion to they hold of you? Furthermore, what is your role in society as a teacher/music teacher? Different teachers will have different answers to this. Collectively, I would say that as teachers we strive to provide meaningful and positive learning experiences, and we want to serve as role models for our learners by the way we enact our teaching, rights and responsibilities in society. From this perspective, we can realise the importance of providing musical representations of cultures that contribute to acceptance of differences, racial tolerance and appreciation of other cultures, while also providing classroom environments where children develop empathy and are respectful of and cooperative with each other.

- **Consider what type of "contact zone" and "third space" you will facilitate**. This requires establishing from the outset not only what will be done but also and foremost, what the purpose is. Points to consider: what level of cultural interplay are you aiming for and why (i.e., cross-cultural, transcultural, multicultural, intercultural)? How can it be achieved? Are the resources needed available? How will it be received by learners, their parents, and the institution and what are the possible implications? (In case of doubt, discuss your ideas with other colleagues, line manager and possibly school management).

Music has been shown to be an excellent vehicle for self-expression and very useful in the process of integration of children from ethnic minorities, immigrants and refugees (Marsh, 2012). However, music on its own will not generate the previously stated effects. Ultimately, it is up to us as teachers to promote, instil and enact a positive safe environment where all are valued, respected and acknowledged. It is vital that we work towards this ethical imperative, by structuring positive interactions in the classroom, which in turn foster mutual respect and understanding.

Motivation for Learning

Motivation for learning is what drives learning forward both during and beyond the lessons. It is defined as a process through which goal directed behaviour is promoted and sustained (Schunk et al., 2014). Since beliefs, values, needs and identity explain much of human behaviour, research on motivation has mostly been focused on these constructs.

Intelligence and Beliefs About Personal Ability

Learners have beliefs about their abilities and these beliefs guide much of their thinking and behaviour. Research carried out by Dweck and Molden (2005) has shown that learners' beliefs, with regard to their intelligence and ability, revolve around one of these two types of mindsets:

- Fixed mindset: intelligence and ability are seen as a trait that they cannot develop.

- Growth mindset: intelligence and ability are something that they can improve with further learning and effort.

When people experience a setback, they respond in accordance with their beliefs. Children with a fixed mindset are unlikely to pursue attempts aimed at improvement and overcoming challenges. Those with a growth mindset are likely to seek solutions to solve the problems they might be experiencing, develop strategies for learning and consider their efforts as integral to the learning process. Fixed and growth mindsets are instilled through 'what' and 'how' parents and teachers communicate to young children, children and young people. For instance, if after a music performance a child is provided the following comments, then the fixed mindset maybe promoted: 'well done, you are very talented, you have a natural gift for music'. Conversely, feedback given which emphasises *the effort made* to achieve a good performance are desirable since they will promote a growth mindset. For example: 'you have progressed so much and played really well today; you must have practised really hard and it paid off'. It is striking to realise that the inculcation of fixed mindsets with regard to music is such a widespread phenomenon with tremendous negative consequences.

Value Placed on Music

Values are beliefs that guide our decision making (Evans, 2016). Achievement is dependent on the value individuals place on the various choices they consider available to them – this became known as subjective-task value within the literature. Subjective-task values are formed at a relatively early stage in life (around 7 years old) and are deeply influenced by the value placed in music and the communicated messages on how good children are at music by adults surrounding them (parents, teachers, culture). Early negative experiences in music can have long, lasting and at times irreversible consequences (Evans, 2016). Therefore, the quality of early music interventions and experiences which communicate music as useful, important and as a worthwhile investment are vital.

Findings from research somehow put in question the quality of formal music education in inculcating the value of music in children. Subjective-task value has been shown to decline faster for music than for other school subjects in various countries (i.e., Finland, Korea, Mexico, Hong Kong, China, Brazil, Israel and the US) (McPherson & O'Neill, 2010). Furthermore, learners' confidence in their abilities in music as compared to other school subjects was ranked the lowest in Hong Kong, Mexico, Israel and the US. This international trend suggests that the value learners attach to music as a subject gradually decreases and this appears to go hand in hand with how able they see themselves as being of doing well (McPherson & O'Neill, 2010).

Subjective-task value has four dimensions (Eccles, 2005). They are:

- **Attainment value**: tasks have value when they closely align with the individual's sense of self. The sense of self is influenced by what children perceive is socially important in their environment and is implicitly and explicitly communicated by their parents, the cultural expectations held about them and their gender roles.

- **Intrinsic interest value**: this refers to the enjoyment and interest learners experience when engaged in music making, practice and learning, and is influenced by personality, the level of challenge required in effectively doing the required task(s) and the level at which the task stimulates curiosity and provides opportunities for attaining competence.

- **Utility value**: this can be defined as the degree to which a task is useful in attaining an important goal for oneself. Refers to the means to an end, and therefore can be considered as extrinsic motivation. The motivating factor is the goal and not the undertaking of the tasks for the sake of its enjoyment. For example, a child may engage in learning a musical instrument because he/she wishes to join a band or orchestra – and this is then the main goal that the child works towards.

- **Perceived cost**: relates to the amount of effort required to do and learn to do the task, including mental and physical effort, social cost (less time spent with friends due to rehearsals or practice required) and possible associated stress or anxiety involved (such as possible performance anxiety).

When music becomes an optional subject at school, interest in music has been found to be a significant factor in elective choice. In considering why learners didn't choose music as a school subject when it became an optional subject, reasons included low music competence beliefs; music was unimportant to them; learners preferred to use their time in social involvement with friends rather than practising; the culture of the school; and having to juggle family values/obligations with either music, sports or academic achievement (Waters et al., 2014). This highlights the importance of promoting the value of music and music making as an integral aspect in learners' lives and of who they are as individual people. Or to put it more simply, the importance of developing musical identities.

Developing a Musical Identity: A Decisive Factor
in Developing Motivation

Identity evolves from understandings of what one is good at, in tandem with a set of values, beliefs and attitudes a person holds about the world. At a relational level, interactions and relationships established with others bring about understandings of who they are in terms of the established connections, relative to their similarities and differences. At a collective level, identity involves considering aspects in which one differs from the collective and what sets them apart from others, resulting in identifying with specific groups in society and having distinct musical preferences.

Research suggests that establishing a long-term musical identity from the early stages of music engagement and learning is an important way to regulate motivation towards music (Evans, 2016). A longitudinal study showed that children's self-belief of how long they would be engaged in instrumental music tuition, appeared to have geared them up to put in the necessary amount of work, effort and commitment in order to achieving their (perceived) goals (Evans & McPherson, 2015; McPherson, 2001). Namely, self-belief can function much like a self-fulfilling prophecy. In the study, children who expressed long term commitment and practiced more, achieved higher results; however, those who practiced more but expressed short time commitment did no better than children who practiced less. Practice had to be accompanied by a long-term commitment, and this long-term commitment predicts persistence and achievement. This means that the long-term identity goal regulates behaviour towards achieving such goal. Therefore, supporting learners in developing a musical identity should be of the utmost priority for music teachers and educators.

Music Fulfilling Psychological Human Needs

Concerning motivation, it is also important to consider the extent to which music contributes to fulfilling psychological needs and how this ultimately leads to a fulfilling life and therefore leads learners to persist in music learning. Self-determination theory's (SDT) main argument is that people are naturally inclined towards experiences that purposefully advance their psychological health and fulfil their basic human psychological needs. As Deci and Ryan (2000) note, these needs can be summarised into three main categories:

*   **Competence**: the need to feel effective in one's interactions with the environment.

*   **Relatedness**: the need to feel a sense of belongingness in relation to the social environment.

*   **Autonomy**: the need to feel as though one's behaviour is aligned with and regulated by one's sense of self and identity.

When these needs are satisfied, people sense that their behaviour is regulated by themselves (internal regulation) rather than by someone else or something in their external environment. This internal regulation whereby a person feels in charge of one's own actions can be associated with intrinsic motivation. Contrarily, when the motive driving the behaviour is external to the individual (e.g., in the form of rewards), then it is more closely associated with extrinsic motivation.

Promoting and Developing Motivation

Teachers have a decisive role in promoting, developing and nurturing learners' motivation in each encounter with learners. Therefore, they must make each and every lesson count. In what follows are some guidelines proposed by Renwick and Reeves (2012), to assist you in developing motivation in your learners:

*   Nurture inner motivation by appealing as much as possible to learners' intrinsic motivation by focusing on intrinsic interests in the music in itself. Explain why the requested tasks are required while also instilling curiosity and setting challenges and providing material that is difficult but within reach.

*   Use informational rather than controlling language when communicating with learners. Ensure you provide a variety of different learning activities appropriate for the learner's level and ensure you explain why you are proposing these activities so that the learner creates an understanding of progress and their overall long term learning goals.

- Acknowledge and accept learners' affect and behaviour, instead of considering it as problematic from the outset. For example, don't assume that a learner not engaging with practice is necessarily not interested in music or music making. Instead, nurture practice during the lessons, let learners know what they have achieved in the lesson while practicing with you, and emphasise that once they practise at home they will achieve much more, as demonstrated by what they have just achieved in the lesson.

- Don't use external motivators such as rewards and punishments in relation to music practice as these have been shown to undermine intrinsic motivation.

In addition to the prior points, I also suggest the following:

- Don't undermine the power you can have in your day-to-day interactions with others in changing the culture around you and in creating a mindset where music is considered as an important, interesting and worthwhile subject to invest in.

- Consider the role that parents and relevant others have in motivating or demotivating your learners. An essential part of your role is to educate parents and relevant others on what they can do to support their children's musical learning, including the 'dos' and 'don'ts' with regard to motivation. In conjunction with this, emphasise why music is important and the benefits that their children will gain (both in the short and long term) through engaging with music. This is the case as the *motivator* also needs to have solid and strong reasons to get *motivated* in order to be able to *motivate* their children.

- Continuously examine and reflect upon how the music lessons you provide are actively developing your learners' sense of competence, relatedness and autonomy? Ask yourself: what can you do effectively in each and every lesson at this level? The questions in Table 4.2 may assist you at this level.

Promoting Positive Behaviour

Generally speaking, behaviour can be defined as the way in which one acts or conducts oneself both personally and towards others. Positive behaviour leads to high quality learning experiences, building positive attitudes and motivation towards learning. These experiences in turn, are linked to current and later success with regard to social skill development, education and employment. Promoting positive behaviour requires the use of positive approaches to encourage appropriate behaviour, and comes through setting positive rules which state clearly what children and young people should do rather than what they should not, with boundaries clearly stated.

Table 4.2 Developing psychological health and fulfilling basic human psychological needs through music teaching

Developing a sense of . . .	Some questions for reflection
Competence	• What can I as a teacher do/ should I be doing to effectively communicate with my learners and make them feel welcomed, valued and appreciated? • What do I do to ensure my learners leave each lesson with a good understanding of the concepts being communicated? • What do I do to ensure my learners feel able and confident in their learning and in their skill development?
Relatedness	• How can I help my learners develop a sense of belonging in their class and learning group? • Would collaborative and creative group work help at this level? • If one-to-one lessons, what opportunities do I provide for my learners to meet, listen to each other's output and make music together?
Autonomy	• Do my learners self-identify with the music they are learning? • If not, why not? And what can be done about it?

Source: Adapted from Deci & Ryan (2000)

A calm and consistent approach which encourages children and young people to make their own choices with regard to their behaviour, while also providing them with a clear understanding of the consequences of surpassing boundaries should be used at all times. At this level, it is relevant to engage children and young people as much as possible in devising the basic rules. When they are involved in the process, they are much more likely to achieve a good understanding of the rules while at the same time feeling part of a group where their views are expressed, welcomed and respected. This feeling of being 'included' and 'having had a say' will lead to greater willingness to comply, and the rules jointly created can then be displayed on the wall in an age appropriate format, and signed by all involved, in the form of a contract.

Behaviour displayed by an individual, cannot be regarded in isolation. It is part of a much wider context that includes the child's immediate (home) and wider environment (e.g., school, socio-cultural context etc.), and which strongly influences how they (and indeed we) behave. Likewise, a culture where positive behaviour is continuously promoted by all involved (i.e., children, young people, parents, teachers, teaching assistants, etc.) will likely teach how (and inspire children and young people) to enact positive behaviours in educational contexts and beyond. This will ultimately result in inclusive environments being nurtured and developed, based on respect and empathy. Teachers and educators have a crucial role to play at this level.

Respect and empathy are interlinked and to a great extent depend on one another. While respect can be defined as "accepting others for what they are, not being rude to them, or lowering their confidence and self-esteem in any way" (Gravells & Simpson, 2014, p. 32), empathy is the ability to understand and share feelings with others. Given the importance of respect and empathy in educational environments, its occurrence cannot be left to chance. Rather, they need to be designed from the outset through promotion of a culture that lives up to these values sincerely and regularly and where behaviour is considered both as an individual and collective responsibility. This is often done through the establishment of guidelines and procedures, commonly referred to as 'behaviour policy' or 'promoting positive behaviour policy'. Policies aimed at promoting positive behaviour will vary from institution to institution and should include guidance on the following:

- Procedures that staff can follow for promoting positive behaviour;

- Guidance on how to deal with inappropriate behaviour;

- Descriptions of what the expectations are with regard to behaviour, boundaries and consequences to be implemented if those boundaries are transgressed;

- Guidance on preventing bullying;

- How staff should deal with conflict and inappropriate behaviour;

- Rewards and sanctions;

- Referrals.

Understanding the reasons behind disruptive behaviour is crucial for finding solutions for the problem and there are many reasons why it can occur. It may be that the child or young person is not fully aware of what is expected in terms of behaviour. Or perhaps the learner is not grasping (for one reason or another) what the teacher is explaining, or is unable to keep focused for the time required to complete the task. It could just as well be the opposite, where the learner is bored and not being challenged enough. In addition, inappropriate behaviour can occur as a symptom indicating that something is not quite right with the learner. He or she could be a victim of abuse, including bullying, or sudden changes in the child's immediate environment are affecting the child's day-to-day sense of safety and usual routines (divorce, health related problems etc.). Generally speaking, inappropriate behaviours can be categorised under the following three main categories (Meggitt, 2011):

- Attention-seeking behaviours.

- Physical and verbal aggression towards others (abusive language; homophobic, racist and sexist language; aggressive behaviours which can culminate on fighting, hitting or biting others; intimidation of others; deliberate property damage).

- Self-destructive and self-harming behaviours (e.g., being in possession of, or taking alcohol or illegal substances, such as drugs; intentionally damaging or injuring their own body – self-harming, which could be life threatening). Self-harming is usually a way of coping with, or expressing, overwhelming emotional distress.

However, these are not mutually exclusive, and have several variations within each category. Teachers should keep a record of occurrences of inappropriate behaviour detailing what has happened, when and how. It should also consider the learning activities taking place at the time, and environmental, individual and social circumstances that could have led to the incident. These records will help uncover patterns or triggers which can then be dealt with.

Procedures for Promoting Positive Behaviour

There are a number of behaviours teachers, educators, staff and other adults need to enact in order to promote positive behaviour among children and young people. These include:

- Being a role model. Enacting at all times the type of behaviour expected from the children and young people. This sets out a positive example of behaviour which can and will be emulated by them.

- Always show respect towards everyone, including children, young people, their parents, other members of staff and colleagues. Respect is communicated not only by the words you choose to use in your day-to-day communicative interactions but also through your body language, facial expressions and the way you take the time to actively listen to others.

- Listen to the points of view of others, while valuing their opinions and not imposing your own.

- Express appreciation by praising those who have demonstrated positive and appropriate behaviour.

- Create an environment where children and young people are well aware of the rules, have participated in creating the rules themselves (depending on their age) and accepted to abide by them.

- Set limits and boundaries, ensuring children and young people know what behaviour is expected from them and what is not acceptable.

- Enact a calm approach at all times, even when boundaries have been crossed.

- Provide easy to follow explanations or alternative solutions for those who may be struggling to keep up with the boundaries.

Dealing With Inappropriate Behaviour

When dealing with inappropriate behaviour:

- Keep calm at all times.

- Do not ignore the behaviour; address it immediately (with exceptions for attention seeking behaviour, more on this later), taking into consideration factual information.

- Do not make negative remarks or comments about the child or children involved in front of children or young people and others.

- Ensure you listen to all involved when there is controversy or conflict.

- Be fair and consistent.

- If you have made a mistake in your dealings or in your judgement, apologise.

Children displaying attention-seeking behaviour attempt to gain attention from others through disruptive, aggressive or even excessively pleasing behaviour. In this case, it can be helpful to emphasise turn-taking as children need to learn to wait for their turn. However, for this to work, the child should be given attention after having waited for his/her turn. If the attention-seeking behaviour is not excessive to the point that it affects other children, it is best to ignore it, so that other children don't take that it is okay to behave in such a way. At the same time, you should provide attention and praise to another child who is behaving appropriately. Another strategy is to distract the child from the attention seeking behaviour in itself, for example, by providing an alternative learning activity that the child can immerse himself into. If the behaviour doesn't change (or keeps reoccurring) consider verbally or non-verbally expressing your disapproval (for instance, through shaking your head and frowning), and if still no improvement, then apply a sanction (Meggitt, 2011) (more on sanctions ahead).

Physical aggression is a manifestation of difficult emotions and feelings which the child is unable to control at a specific point in time. This will result in stress and anxiety in other children, and also the aggressor and teachers. In all situations involving aggression, the teacher's priority should be to remain calm, respectful and ensure the safety of all involved. The teacher's course of action in these situations includes to offer care, comfort and first aid (if needed) to the child who was hurt, and to remove the aggressor to an identified place away from the incident, verbally stating that it is wrong to do what he/she has done. This period of time-out is crucial for providing an opportunity for the aggressor to calm down and for reassuring the other children in the room. However, in order for a time-out strategy to be effective, it needs to be followed by a conversation with the child to explain why the behaviour was unacceptable and which offers alternatives on how the child or young person might have behaved instead. Circumstances of physical aggression require that teachers quickly assess the safety of the learning space for all learners, themselves and other staff. If the aggressor constitutes a danger to others in the room, removal of the aggressor in the first instance then becomes an absolute priority, and your school/institution's specific protocol must be followed.

Unacceptable language occurs mostly as a result of a child or young person being exposed to swearing and name calling in another environment and not being aware that is not acceptable to do so from one environment to another. In other instances, children and young people may use words, terms of expressions they know are not appropriate with the purposes of seeking attention. Name calling and swearing need to be tackled head-on, particularly if the language used is discriminatory in relation to race, religion, appearance, gender, family background and other pertinent categories. Teachers need to emphasise that the words the child or young person are using cannot be used in your work context (i.e., school, teaching studio, etc.). The emphasis on the word 'here' is important as teachers cannot either enforce that the words which were used will not be used elsewhere, and neither can they criticise parents or families. Teachers need to make it clear to children that resorting to swearing and name calling is unacceptable, and that the words used are hurtful. They should be made to understand that we are all different individuals and all entitled to respect and appreciation for who we are.

Self-harm is a manifestation of emotional difficulties and distress that requires expert intervention. Self-harm includes behaviours such as scratching or tearing the skin causing sores and scarring; pulling out hair in various places of the body, including the eyelashes; cutting or burning skin areas; taking tablets and medicines which are not prescribed; using alcohol or illegal substances; and making a suicide attempt. Those suffering from depression, eating disorders, taking illegal drugs or alcohol or who have serious mental health problems are at greater risk of displaying these behaviours (Dunn et al., 2006). Self-harming tends to be kept a secret, and children and young people involved in it often refuse to wear short sleeves due to scarring on their arms.

Children and young people who self-harm tend to be secretive about it, become less communicative with others or appear to be more easily irritable. Once a teacher suspects a child or young person may be self-harming, the first step is to assess the level of emergency of the situation. Emergency services should be contacted immediately if the injury is life-threatening. If the child or young person is suicidal and taken to hospital, emergency protocols for treatment and care will be implemented in accordance with institutional and national protocols and policies. If a teacher is made aware that a learner is self-harming but is not in need of urgent medical attention, then advice on the subsequent course of action should be sought from designated child protection officers at the institution, managers and other colleagues in senior positions. Child protection policy guidelines should be followed at all times.

Expectations/Rules and Boundaries

The expectations with regard to behaviour need to be clearly set out in the policy and be appropriate and realistic for children's age, stage of development and specific needs of the educational setting. In general, they should focus on respect; fairness; the need for taking turns; playing in a safe manner; and not bullying others. Rules refer to the behaviours being encouraged and will include consideration on physical, social and communicational aspects of behaviour. In setting rules, consistency is a key factor and exists to ensure that there is a described process in the policy detailing how children and young people will be assisted both in understanding and learning to enact them. Boundaries, on the other hand, are intimately related to consequences as they refer to the limits within which behaviour is adequate, and the clear consequences which will transpire for surpassing the stated boundaries must be spelt out (Meggitt, 2011).

Rewards and Sanctions

The use of rewards is based on the idea that children rewarded for enacting positive behaviour will likely want to repeat that same behaviour, with other children looking on also feeling inclined to do so. Rewards can include verbal praise (such as 'well done'); a smile of approval; an individual or group certificate or award; stickers; and sharing success by telling parents and other staff.

While rewards can be helpful and may work in the short term, there are also problems associated with using them exclusively. For instance, some children might behave in certain ways purely in order to receive the reward rather than with an understanding of the need to be considerate towards themselves and others. In fact, rewards can undermine lifelong learning, particularly when excessively used. Teachers also need to consider the type of reward carefully: it must be age appropriate and not conflicting with the children's health and parents' rules. I completely discourage the use of sweets or any type of eatable or drinkable rewards for a number of health-related reasons, including the potential for allergic and other types of reactions. Moreover, some ingredients could be incompatible with the family's religious beliefs and, more prosaically, the fact that most of these products are not compatible with the promotion of good health habits.

Sanctions can be defined as a course of action used whenever necessary in order to have people comply with a rule or behave in a particular way (Payne, 2015). In the context of promoting positive behaviour, its main purpose is to prevent inappropriate behaviour. However, they should at all times protect both the child's self-esteem and the relationship between teacher and learner. Children should always be given a warning prior to the enforcing of consequences and sanctions being issued. It is good practice to have a chat in private with the child or children in question to investigate reasons for the behaviour which might demonstrate mitigating circumstances. During this, the teacher can reiterate the rules and check for understanding, and give them a chance to cooperate. An example of sanctions for a five-year-old could be five minutes withdrawal from the group's musical activity (to ensure fairness, it should be timed with a timer). Or, depending on the gravity of the behaviour and age of the child, it could be a referral to the senior members of staff, detention or changing of seats in class. Time out has been frequently used as a sanction. It consists of the child's removal from the activity occurring at that point in time and insisting that the child undertakes a quiet activity for a given period of time, while sitting in a safe place.

When to Refer Inappropriate Behaviour to Others

Behaviour which is linked to the child or young person's age and development and presents itself as a temporary issue, and which can be managed in the educational setting, does not require referral. However, the following behaviours should be referred to other professionals using the procedures in place at your educational institution:

- Behaviours that don't match the child's stage of development;
- Physically aggressive behaviours;
- Bullying;
- Self-harming.

Prior to any referral, it is important to discuss with senior colleagues, particularly your line manager, the course of action to be taken and to have conversations with colleagues involved in the teaching and care of the child or young person in question. You should also keep written notes of meetings with colleagues and any incidents which have occurred. These written records will not only help to assess the scale of the situation, but can also provide relevant information to other professionals who may become involved in the case as a result of the referral made, for instance educational psychologists, paediatricians, health visitors, play therapists, child psychiatrists, etc.

Ultimately, environments where well-established promotion of positive behaviour policies exist, and which are suitable for the context, are more likely to lead to positive behaviour being enacted from all involved, both grown-ups and youngsters. This will enable children and young people to establish friendships, settle well into the educational environment and learning process, all the while knowing how to behave appropriately in a range of different situations, and also understand what the boundaries are and why they are needed. These environments help children and young people to develop self-esteem, a sense of self-worth and feelings of empathy towards others. These are essential in positive human development, including in becoming active members of society. Hence, you should not think that your efforts as a teacher in this regard are unimportant: a good teacher who earns respect through fair discipline can shape the direction of children for the rest of their lives.

Reflective Questions

1. Explain what is meant by inclusion, diversity, and equality and how can music making help promote these elements?				
• Define each of these terms. • Explain how you enact these concepts in your teaching. • Reflect on how music making, and music educational contexts can be optimised to help promote these elements.	Aligned with CME, Level 4 Unit (U) or Area of Study (AOS) and Assessment Criteria number of ABRSM (2014) and TCL (2013, 2019)			
	ABRSM		**TCL (2013)**	
	U5:	5.1.1 5.1.2	U5:	1.1 1.2
			TCL (2019)	
			AOS2:	4.1.1 4.1.2 4.1.3 4.1.5

2. Outline current legislation and codes of practice in relation to inclusion, diversity and equality and how these apply and impact on own context.				
• Consider referring to the legislation mentioned in this chapter. • Also refer to specific legislation (or, lack of it) on this topic in your own country and specific context of your work. • Reflect on how such legislation or the absence of it, impacts what you do as a teacher in your current context.				
	ABRSM		**TCL (2013)**	
	U5:	5.1.3	U5:	1.3
			TCL (2019)	
			AOS2:	4.1.4

3. Identify barriers for music learning, including common assumptions about musical learning which may create barriers for individuals.				
• Highlight barriers grouped into different categories. • Look at your own context of professional practice and consider what barriers there might be and your role in helping to overcome them.				
	ABRSM		**TCL (2013)**	
	U5:	5.2.4	U5:	2.1 2.2 2.3 2.4
			TCL (2019)	
			AOS2:	4.1.6 4.1.7 4.1.8 4.1.9
			AOS3:	1.1.6 2.1.3 3.1.4

4. How do you motivate, support and challenge ALL young people to make music confidently, expressively, fluently, with an understanding of style, genre and tradition, while also responding to diverse learning needs and aspirations?				

• Reflect on how you work with students with diverse learning needs and aspirations and how you motivate them to learn confidently.				
	ABRSM		**TCL (2013)**	
	U5:	5.2.1	U5:	3.1 3.2 3.3
• Provide some examples of your work at this level.			TCL (2019)	
• What aspects do you need to consider and what actions do you/can you take to promote and enact inclusive musical learning in your working context?			AOS2:	4.1.5 4.1.7 4.19

5. How can you promote positive behaviour, and manage inappropriate or challenging behaviour in children and young people?				

• Refer to the policy and procedures on promoting positive behaviour, at your own school, institution, studio or particular setting, considering the benefits of setting out expectations and boundaries.				
	ABRSM		**TCL (2013)**	
	U4:	All learning outcomes for this unit	U4:	All learning outcomes for this unit
• Explain how the policy and procedures referred above, support children and young people to feel safe, be empowered to make positive contributions, and help them develop social and emotional skills.			TCL (2019)	
			AOS3:	1.1.10 2.1.8
• Outline the categories of behaviour, or challenging behaviours, that should be referred to others and to whom.				
			AOS4:	All the learning outcomes included in point 4

Notes

1. Figurenotes is a system of notation where colours and shapes are used in a concrete way to provide information pertaining to things such as pitches, notes duration, rests, flats, sharps, key signature and so on. Basically, it conveys the same information conveyed by conventional music notation and is useful for children who have difficulty understanding abstract concepts.
2. Cognitive processes: examples of learning styles categorisations include the Theory of Multiple Intelligences, Gardner (1983); Mental Self-Government (Sternberg, 1998).
3. Personality: related learning styles categorisations, examples include the Learner Learning Styles Inventory Scales (Grasha, 1996); *The Myers-Briggs Type Indicator* (1962) and subsequent versions.
4. Experiential: related learning styles categorisations, examples include Experiential Learning theories proposed by Freire (1970), Kolb (1984) and Mezirow (2011).
5. Perceptual learning modalities learning styles categorisations include Reid's (1987) and Fleming and Baume (2006).
6. Declarative knowledge is often referred to as 'knowing that' in contrast to 'knowing how'. It refers to being aware of and understanding factual information.
7. Procedural knowledge is often referred to as 'knowing how'. It usually relates to knowing how to do things that involve certain body movements or how to use objects, such as riding a bike or playing a musical instrument. This type of knowledge is acquired through practice and repetition and becomes unconscious over time.

Further Reading

Evans, P. (2016). Motivation. In G. E. McPherson (Ed.), *The child as a musician. A handbook of musical development* (2nd ed., pp. 325–339). Oxford University Press.

Kaikkonen, M. (2016). Music for all: Everyone has the potential to learn music. In D. V. Blair & K. A. McCord (Eds.), *Exceptional music pedagogy for children with exceptionalities* (pp. 1–15). Oxford University Press.

McKinlay, E. (2017). Teaching music interculturally: Posing questions, creating possibilities. In P. Burnard & R. Murphy (Eds.), *Teaching music creatively* (pp. 170–182). Routledge.

McPherson, G. E., & Lehmann, A. (2012). Exceptional musical abilities: Musical prodigies. In G. E. McPherson & G. F. Welch (Eds.), *The Oxford handbook of music education* (Vol. 2, pp. 40–50). Oxford University Press.

Pritchard, A. (2018). *Ways of learning* (4th ed.). Routledge.

Watts, E. H., Kimberly, M., & Blair, D. V. (2016). Assistive technology to support students in accessing the music curriculum. In D. V. Blair & K. McCord (Eds.), *Exceptional music pedagogy for children with exceptionalities* (pp. 85–104). Oxford University Press.

References

Associated Board of the Royal Schools of Music (ABRSM) (2014). *Level 4 certificate for music educators: Assessment framework*. ABRSM.

Deci, E. L., Koestner, R., & Ryan, R. M. (2001). Extrinsic rewards and intrinsic motivation in education: Reconsidered once again. *Review of Educational Research, 71*(1), 1–27. https://doi.org/10.3102/00346543071001001

Deci, E. L., & Ryan, R. M. (2000). The "what" and "why" of goal pursuits: Human needs and the self-determination of Behavior. *Psychological Inquiry, 11*(4), 227–268. https://doi.org/10.1207/S15327965PLI1104_01

Dunn, E. C., Neighbors, C., & Larimer, M. E. (2006). Motivational enhancement therapy and self-help treatment for binge eaters. *Psychology of Addictive Behaviors, 20*(1), 44–52. https://doi.org/10.1037/0893-164X.20.1.44

Dweck, C. S., & Molden, D. C. (2005). Self-theories: Their impact on competence motivation and acquisition. In A. J. Elliot & C. S. Dweck (Eds.), *Handbook of competence and motivation* (pp. 122–140). The Guildford Press.

Eccles, J. S. (2005). Subjective task value and the Eccles et al. model of achievement-related choices. In A. J. Elliot & C. S. Dweck (Eds.), *Handbook of competence and motivation* (pp. 105–121). The Guildford Press.

Evans, P. (2016). Motivation. In G. McPherson (Ed.), *The child as a musician. A handbook of musical development* (2nd ed., pp. 325–339). Oxford University Press.

Evans, P., & McPherson, G. E. (2015). Identity and practice: The motivational benefits of a long-term musical identity. *Psychology of Music, 43*(3), 407–422. https://doi.org/10.1177/0305735613514471

Fleming, N., & Baume, D. (2006) Learning styles again: VARKing up the right tree! *Educational Developments, SEDA, 7*(4), 4–7.

Freire, P. (1970). *Pedagogy of the oppressed.* Seabury Press.

Gagné, F. (2004). Transforming gifts into talents: The DMGT as a developmental theory. *High Ability Studies, 15*, 119–147.

Gardner, H. (1983). *Frames of mind: The theory of multiple intelligences.* Basic Books.

Grasha, A. (1996). *Teaching with style: A practical guide to enhancing learning by understanding teaching and learning style.* Pittsburgh Alliance Publishers

Gravells, A., & Simpson, S. (2014). *The certificate in education and training.* Sage, Learning Matters.

Howell, G. (2011). Do they know they're composing': Music making and understanding among newly arrived immigrant and refugee children. *International Journal of Community Music, 4*(1), 47–58. https://doi.org/10.1386/ijcm.4.1.47_1

Ilari, B. (2017). Children's ethnic identities, cultural diversity, and music education. In R. MacDonald, D. J. Hargreaves, & D. Miell (Eds.), *Handbook of musical identities.* Oxford University Press. https://doi.org/10.1093/acprof:oso/9780199679485.001.0001

Johansen, K. (2005). What do you think about when you play? *American Music Teacher, 55*(1), 31–33.

Kaikkonen, M. (2016). Music for all: Everyone has the potential to learn music. In D. V. Blair & K. A. McCord (Eds.), *Exceptional music pedagogy for children with exceptionalities* (pp. 1–15). Oxford University Press.

Kolb, D. A. (1984). *Experiential learning: Experience as the source of learning and development* (Vol. 1). Prentice-Hall.

Lavoie, R. (2007). *The motivation breakthrough: Six secrets to turning on the tuned-out child.* Atria Paperback.

Marsh, K. (2012). "The beat will make you be courage": The role of a secondary school music program in supporting young refugees and newly arrived immigrants in Australia. *Research Studies in Music Education, 34*(2), 93–111. https://doi.org/10.1177/1321103X12466138

McKinlay, E. (2017). Teaching music interculturally: Posing questions, creating possibilities. In P. Burnard & R. Murphy (Eds.), *Teaching music creatively* (pp. 170–182). Routledge.

McPherson, G. E. (2001). Commitment and practice: Key ingredients for achievement during the early stages of learning a musical instrument. *Bulletin of the Council for Research in Music Education, 147*(1), 122–127.

McPherson, G. E., & Lehmann, A. (2012). Exceptional musical abilities: Musical prodigies. In G. E. McPherson & G. F. Welch (Eds.), *The Oxford handbook of music education* (Vol. 2, pp. 40–50). Oxford University Press.

McPherson, G. E., & O'Neill, S. A. (2010). Students' motivation to study music as compared to other school subjects: A comparison of eight countries. *Research Studies in Music Education, 32*(2), 101–137. https://doi.org/10.1177/1321103X10384202

Meggitt, C. (2011). *Children and young people's workforce*. Hodder Education.

Mezirow, J. (Ed.). (2011). *Transformative learning in practice: Insights from community, workplace, and higher education*. Jossey-Bass.

Myers, I. B. (1962). *The Myers-Briggs type indicator: Manual*. Consulting Psychologists Press. https://doi.org/10.1037/14404-000

Nadal, K. L., & Rivera, D. P. (2008). Ethnic minority. In F. T. L. Leong (Ed.), *Encyclopaedia of counselling online*. London: Sage. http://sk.sagepub.com/reference/counseling.

Owens, M. T., & Tanner, K. D. (2017). Teaching as brain changing: Exploring connections between neuroscience and innovative teaching. *CBE – Life Sciences Education, 16*(2). https://doi.org/10.1187/cbe.17-01-0005

Payne, R. (2015). Using rewards and sanctions in the classroom: Pupils' perceptions of their own responses to current behaviour management strategies. *Educational Review, 67*(4), 483–504. https://doi.org/10.1080/00131911.2015.1008407

Pritchard, A. (2018). *Ways of learning* (4th ed.). Routledge.

Proctor, E. (2001). Practice notes: Remember, remember. *Music Teacher, 80*(8), 31.

Reid, J. M. (1987). The learning style preferences of ESL students. *TESOL Quarterly, 21*, 87–111. http://dx.doi.org/10.2307/3586356

Renwick, J. M., & Reeve, J. (2012). Supporting motivation in music education. In G. E. McPherson & G. F. Welch (Eds.), *The Oxford handbook of music education*, Volume 1 (pp. 142–162). Oxford University Press. https://doi.org/10.1093/oxfordhb/9780199730810.013.0009_update_001

Schunk, D., Meece, J. L., & Pintrich, J. R. (2014). *Motivation in education: Theory, research and applications* (4th ed.). Prentice Hall.

Shavinina, L. V. (2009). A unique type of representation is the essence of giftedness: Towards a cognitive-developmental theory. In L. V. Shavinina (Ed.), *International handbook of giftedness* (pp. 231–257). Springer.

Simonton, D. K. (2017). The genetic side of giftedness: A nature-nurture definition and a fourfold talent typology. In J. A. Plucker, A. N. Rinn, & M. C. Makel (Eds.), *From giftedness to gifted education: Reflecting theory in practice* (pp. 335–352). Prufrock Press.

Sternberg, R. J. (1998). Styles of thinking and learning. *Canadian Journal of School Psychology* 1998, *13*(2), 15–40. https://doi.org/10.1177/082957359801300204

Trinity College London (TCL) (2013). *TCL level 4 certificate for music educators: Specifications*. TCL.

Trinity College London (TCL) (2019). *TCL level 4 certificate for music educators, areas of study*. TCL.

UNESCO (2006). *Road map for arts education.* UNESCO. www.unesco.org/new/fileadmin/MULTIMEDIA/HQ/CLT/CLT/pdf/Arts_Edu_RoadMap_en.pdf.

UNESCO (2009). *Policy guidelines on inclusion in education.* UNESCO. https://unesdoc.unesco.org/ark:/48223/pf0000177849?posInSet=1&queryId=65c98 10b-4110-4108-a59d-8f9eda710551.

UNESCO (2010). *Fact sheet: A summary of the rights under the convention on the rights of the child.* www.unicef.org/spanish/crc/images/Rights_overview.pdf

Warm, A., Murray, C., & Fox, J. (2003). Why do people self-harm? *Psychology, Health & Medicine, 8*(1), 72–79. https://doi.org/10.1080/1354850021000059278

Waters, S., McPherson, G. E., & Schubert, E. (2014). Facilitators and impediments for elective music and sport in adolescent males. *SAGE Open, 4*(2), 1–13. https://doi.org/10.1177/2158244014529779

Watts, E. H., Kimberly, M., & Blair, D. V. (2016). Assistive technology to support students in accessing the music curriculum. In D. V. Blair & K. McCord (Eds.), *Exceptional music pedagogy for children with exceptionalities* (pp. 85–104). Oxford University Press.

5   Planning for Inclusive Teaching and Learning

To Guide Your Reading

• How can we plan for successful musical learning that meets individual learning needs and aspirations of all children and young people?

• How can Universal Design Learning become a possible 'praxis' for your teaching in order to promote inclusive learning?

Lesson planning:

• How should we plan and devise learning outcomes and learning objectives?

• What learning activities can be used to promote a sense of ownership, creativity, enjoyment and engagement?

• How can we identify and address potential risks or hazards that might affect children and young people's well-being?

Introduction

The systematic planning of teaching and learning is one of the essential key skills teachers and educators need to have or develop. It is a crucial activity to prepare for the inclusion of all children in the teaching and learning process. Specifically, it is during the lesson planning stage that teachers conceptualise ways for allowing all learners to have access to the means necessary for developing the required knowledge, skills and know-how and, hence, how they will have the chance to progress and succeed. It is also at this stage that teachers conceptualise levels of support as well as scaffolding and the means required to support learning. This chapter begins by arguing that Universal Design Learning can provide a basis that teachers can use to guide their teaching ('*praxis*'), and advocates for its combined use alongside Learning Power Theory (introduced in Chapter 1, as '*ethos*'). Following this, ten steps are sequentially presented and discussed with the goals of supporting music teachers in the development and creation of inclusive lesson plans. Various teaching methodologies are presented in step four of the ten mentioned steps.

Universal Design Learning

It is at the planning stage that teachers will reflect on the 'ethos' and 'praxis' guiding their teaching. While 'ethos' refers to principles, namely ideas and theories that guide teaching, 'praxis' refers to *how* those principles, ideas and theories are applied practically in day-to-day teaching. In Chapter 1, I argued that Learning Power Theory (LPT) can provide an 'ethos' for teaching. Here, I argue that Universal Design Learning (UDL) can provide the 'praxis' and seek to demonstrate how this can be achieved. LPT and UDL are both holistic, embedded in the latest learning theories, and have been successfully tested. Therefore, I advocate for their combined use.

UDL has been developed by researchers at the Center for Applied Special Technology[1] (CAST). It is a highly prominent concept within Special Education, and has been researched in the context of expanding learning opportunities for learners with disabilities. However, it is also applicable to various other learning contexts and not dissimilar to good teaching principles outlined in non-CAST publications. UDL proposes that the individual needs of a learner with a disability (or with other specific circumstances/life situations) can and should be considered as a catalyst for designing changes to be made to the teaching of all learners in that class, including typical learners. This does *not* mean that individual adaptations will not be made, but that the learning environment devised will be such that the processes of planning, designing, teaching and assessing are inclusive of all types of learners (McCord et al., 2014). UDL is based on three main teaching principles:

- **Providing multiple means of representation**: concepts should be represented using different learning modes (i.e., visual, aural, kinaesthetic/tactile), thereby providing learners with various ways for acquiring knowledge and information.

- **Providing multiple means of action and expression** through which learners can showcase what they know.

- **Providing multiple means of engagement**, to promote learning and motivation.

As Jellison (2016) notes, by using UDL in music teaching, inclusive learning environments are developed. This means that:

- Music becomes accessible to all types of learners.

- While expectations are high for all learners, learning differences are considered on a continuum and diversity is valued.

- Standards, goals and the quality of the music learning experiences are not compromised.

- By using flexible strategies, learning is promoted and so also is the potential to develop learning through different modes and means (depending on the specific circumstances).

Through the inclusion of a variety of different learning activities and teaching methodologies in every lesson, teachers can provide multiple: means of representation of concepts; means of action through which learners can express themselves; and means for engaging in the learning process. While this helps to cater for differences in various learning styles, it also proves itself to be invaluable in terms of challenging learners to use different approaches and thereby enables them to gain a variety of different learning insights as a result. Proactive teachers with active, inclusive approaches to teaching and learning can better motivate a wide range of personalities and styles of learning. In this way, their classroom promotes the development of independent, flexible and creative learners.

Creating Inclusive Lesson Plans

Planning requires being able to imagine what is going to happen in the classroom and produce teaching and learning decisions accordingly. This is necessary at both the macro and micro levels. The macro level considers the bigger picture and figures out: how a lesson fits into the course overall; how a lesson fits into its subject curriculum; how it connects with the broader curriculum of other subjects and with learners' wider life aspirations; and promotes self-proficiency and a musical identity. The micro level considers questions such as: how will a ten minute warmup work best in the context of the rest of the lesson? How can a lesson address specific learning needs?

Specifically, lesson planning is the process of outlining learning activities for a learner and/or group of learners. It does so in coherent and logical ways with the goal of helping learners to understand, learn and put into practice the content being taught. Each lesson should be designed with wider, common goals in mind: to promote learners' motivation for learning; to strengthen their musical knowledge and skills; and to promote increasing levels of musical participation and learning independence. The initial lesson planning stages involve considering 'what' is needed to be covered in the lesson, and vis-à-vis the overall course of lessons, the 'why' and 'how' of it all. The 'what' and the 'why?' work together symbiotically as it is only possible to decide 'what' to teach when it is known 'why' it should be taught. The choice of 'how' will in many cases directly affect learners' motivation levels for learning and thus their understanding and mastery of the new concepts being taught.

An inclusive lesson plan integrates the following key components:

- Setting out clear learning outcomes and learning objectives, with considerations on the inclusion of all learners.

- Breaking down the learning objectives into progressive steps in order to facilitate learning. Choosing the best sequence to go from the basics to progressively increasing levels of complexity and difficulty.

- Conceptualising different learning activities which provide various sensory approaches to learning. This can be done via multiple means of representation of concepts (e.g., visual, aural, kinaesthetic/tactile); promoting multiple means of action and expression for learners to showcase what they know; and multiple means of engagement, to promote learning and motivation (as per UDL principles).

- Understanding what elements of the lesson can be tailored to meet the needs of specific learners.

- Planning strategies for checking learners' understanding of the materials being taught.

- Considering what resources you and your learners will need to deliver the lesson.

- Considering how to create a safe learning environment which is conducive to learning and which meets the various needs of all learners.

- Building in flexibility in planning and delivery of teaching and learning. This is necessary so you can adapt, change or even abort a certain lesson plan if the approach is not working for some reason. This should be gauged by how learners respond and react to the lesson.

Planning also helps teachers to become more confident in their own teaching. When there is a clear understanding of what learners are required to achieve, teaching performance becomes more sharply focused upon the main teaching and learning outcomes. This enables the lesson time to be used more effectively (Gazard, 2010).

Obviously, the wide diversity of music teaching and learning contexts we encounter therefore requires various different, and specifically directed, approaches to lesson planning. Teaching in one-to-one settings is clearly different from teaching in small or larger group settings. Furthermore, each learner is unique, and the group dynamics and contexts of learning are also unique. Since these can be (and often are) highly varied, this implies a pressing need for each lesson to be *specifically tailored* for a specific learner or groups of learners, at a specific point in time, and in a specific context. Nevertheless, there are some common principles applicable to all lesson planning. These will now be presented in general terms, in the form of ten steps for lesson planning. By following the ten steps outlined later, you will ensure you cover the essential aspects of lesson planning. This will ensure that your lessons are tailored to *your* learners and *your* teaching context.

Step 1: Know Your Learner/s and the Educational Context

Even when deploying lesson plans taken from a course book template, and even when using given guidance on how to teach specific concepts to specific year groups, decisions still need to be made about 'what' is really important to cover. Answers to this will be found by devising answers to the following questions:

- Who are the learners? What are their ages, musical backgrounds, musical preferences, previous learning experiences, learning needs, specific circumstances and/or conditions?

- What are your own aims as a teacher for their development (considering the course overall and appropriate recommended progression pathways)?

- In which context is learning going to occur? If schools, is there an institutionalised music education curriculum to follow? Or is it a community activity, a group or one-to-one teaching?

The information gathered at this juncture is vital for success in the planning and delivery of teaching and learning. Obviously, knowing learners is a cumulative process, and every day we teach, we discover more about them and ourselves. As you gain more experience as a music educator, the insights you accrue about your learners should inform your planning at all times.

Step 2: Outline Learning Outcomes and Learning Objectives

Learning outcomes describe and/or list measurable and essential knowledge, skills and competencies that learners can demonstrate they have achieved by the end of a lesson or a course. The word 'outcome' is pertinent given it denotes that there needs to be an 'end-product' that can be assessed against predefined criteria. For this reason, learning outcomes need to be clear, specific and measurable so that they can be assessed properly. Clear and measurable learning outcomes will not only provide information about *what* the learner has achieved but also report on the success (or otherwise) of teaching and appropriateness of the assessment processes in place. Although learning outcomes are certainly helpful from the point of view of assessment, their main purpose should be to provide direction towards specific and tailored learning trajectories. These must be achievable and realistic, and they must allow each learner to further develop their musical potential. Where possible, learners should have a say in regard to developing and agreeing upon their learning journey and trajectory. This will help to create and develop independent learners who take ownership for their learning.

While learning outcomes can be considered as statements concerning the overall goals of teaching, learning objectives describe the individual stages which learners must progress to on the way to reach the intended learning outcomes. To clarify differences between learning outcomes and learning objectives, see Table 5.1. Consider how the learning objectives work in the given case, acting as progressive steps towards the achievement of the given learning outcome.

When devising learning outcomes and learning objectives, it is helpful to consider what learners ought to learn and be able to do at the end of the lesson. Answering the following questions will help you in the process:

- What is the topic of the lesson?

- What are the learners' learning needs? Accordingly, what do they need to learn?

- What should learners be able to understand and do at the end of lesson?

When it comes to the actual writing of learning outcomes and learning objectives, the SMART acronym credited to both Peter Drucker (1955) and George Doran (1981) is a very helpful tool. It stands for goals/outcomes/objectives which are:

Specific **M**easurable **A**chievable **R**ealistic **T**imely

Hence, in order to ensure that your lessons are successful, it is important to ensure that the desired outcomes are SMART, both for learners but also yourself as their teacher.

SPECIFIC

Objectives describe the desired result in detailed, focused and clearly defined ways. To be specific, an objective should have a description of a specific behaviour, achievement or outcome. When writing down learning objectives, use verbs which are action-orientated to define and describe the actions which need to be undertaken by learners to fulfil the objectives. Figure 5.1 provides a list of some action verbs that you might want to consider when devising

Table 5.1 Example of a proposed learning outcome and aligned learning objectives for a Music Theory lesson

Learning outcome:	'By the end of the lesson, learners will demonstrate knowledge on the construction of major scales'.
Learning objectives:	'By the end of lesson:
	1. Learners will identify the location of tones and semitones in major scales.
	2. Learners will describe the practical application of accidentals in relation to major scales construction.
	3. Learners will understand and apply the circle of fifths to describe key signatures of given major scales'.

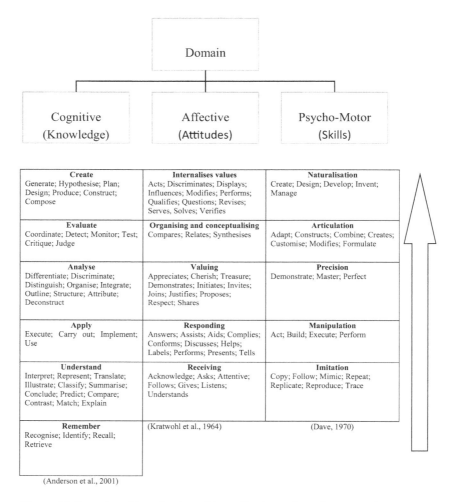

The following table appears within the figure:

Cognitive (Knowledge) (Anderson et al., 2001)	Affective (Attitudes) (Kratwohl et al., 1964)	Psycho-Motor (Skills) (Dave, 1970)
Create Generate; Hypothesise; Plan; Design; Produce; Construct; Compose	**Internalises values** Acts; Discriminates; Displays; Influences; Modifies; Performs; Qualifies; Questions; Revises; Serves, Solves; Verifies	**Naturalisation** Create; Design; Develop; Invent; Manage
Evaluate Coordinate; Detect; Monitor; Test; Critique; Judge	**Organising and conceptualising** Compares; Relates; Synthesises	**Articulation** Adapt; Constructs; Combine; Creates; Customise; Modifies; Formulate
Analyse Differentiate; Discriminate; Distinguish; Organise; Integrate; Outline; Structure; Attribute; Deconstruct	**Valuing** Appreciates; Cherish; Treasure; Demonstrates; Initiates; Invites; Joins; Justifies; Proposes; Respect; Shares	**Precision** Demonstrate; Master; Perfect
Apply Execute; Carry out; Implement; Use	**Responding** Answers; Assists; Aids; Complies; Conforms; Discusses; Helps; Labels; Performs; Presents; Tells	**Manipulation** Act; Build; Execute; Perform
Understand Interpret; Represent; Translate; Illustrate; Classify; Summarise; Conclude; Predict; Compare; Contrast; Match; Explain	**Receiving** Acknowledge; Asks; Attentive; Follows; Gives; Listens; Understands	**Imitation** Copy; Follow; Mimic; Repeat; Replicate; Reproduce; Trace
Remember Recognise; Identify; Recall; Retrieve		

Figure 5.1 Domains of learning (cognitive, affective and psycho-motor) based on the work of Bloom et al. (1956) and some of his followers

learning objectives, and which traverse the three main interconnected domains of learning. They are:

- **Cognitive**: mental skills (knowledge);

- **Affective**: growth in feelings or emotional areas (attitude or self);

- **Psychomotor**: manual or physical skills (skills).

These domains of learning were established by Bloom et al. (1956) and later adapted and further developed by several authors, including Anderson et al.

(2001); Krathwohl et al. (1964) and Dave (1970). Their categorisation separates each of the three domains into subdivisions, starting from the simplest processes or behaviours and working towards the most complex. There are other systems or hierarchies that have been devised, such as the Structure of Observed Learning Outcome (SOLO, see Biggs & Collis, 1982). However, Bloom's taxonomy, apart from being easily understood, is also widely used today. The categories can be thought of as incremental stages or degrees of difficulties. For this reason, the first ones must normally be mastered before the next one can be achieved. The verb list shown in Figure 5.1 is not exhaustive but has been reproduced here to assist you in the writing of learning objectives.

MEASURABLE

In order to ensure that learning objectives are measurable, a system is required to be in place to confirm that the expected knowledge retention and/or expected action or behaviour has occurred. The system needs to be such that it enables the systematic collection of evidence of achievement (more on this in Chapter 7). The questions that follow can assist in devising such system:

- How will I know that learning has occurred?

- What elements will tell me that learning has occurred?

- How can this be measured?

- For the standard required, what should I define as a benchmark for measurement?

ACHIEVABLE

Although learning objectives can be testing, they should never be thought of as being unachievable by learners. Setting objectives that are unachievable will quickly result in lowering learners' motivation, which will in turn culminate in lower levels of engagement and enthusiasm for learning. By contrast, setting objectives at too low a level can be just as discouraging for learners who have already attained the standard now required. Consider the following questions when evaluating whether objectives are achievable:

- Will learners, with a reasonable amount of effort, work and application, be able to achieve what the objective requires from them?

- Is it possible to devise a system or process to measure the required objective?

- Are you aware that other learners with similar characteristics have been able to do it?

- Are the necessary resources available when required?

- Are there limitations preventing the achievement of the objectives? If so, how can they be overcome?

In order to be realistic, objectives need to consider what is *possible* considering the learner or group of learners in a given context. They must also contain elements related to the environment where learning is to occur. In setting realistic expectations, it is essential to have as deep as possible knowledge about the learner or group of learners, particularly in terms of:

- Their subject-specific knowledge;

- Level of proficiency;

- Skills and needs in development;

- The resources available to support learning (e.g., the availability of musical instruments during the lesson, or of computers and music production software in the lesson and/or at home), as well as possible sources of funding.

You should also consider the following questions to ensure the learning objectives you have set are realistic:

- Is it realistically possible to achieve this objective?

- Do learners have the necessary proficiency level and skills to do the required task or tasks *well*? Managing to merely scrape through will, in the end, demotivate learners.

- Are the resources required to accomplish this objective available?

- If more resources and materials are needed, who is going to fund it and how?

TIMELY

Learning objectives should always be time-bound. A deadline will keep learners focused on learning and help to make the objective measurable. Ask yourself if the learning objective can indeed be achieved in the suggested timeframe? What other competing demands might learners be exposed to? After you have outlined the learning objectives for the lesson, rank them in order of importance. This will help you to manage your teaching time more effectively, helping you decide what aspects need to be given more time in your lessons.

Also, if perhaps you are pressed for time, you might then use the time available to focus on the most important learning objectives.

As teachers working towards developing inclusivity and enabling participation, we know that a 'one-size-fits-all' approach is unachievable, unrealistic and inappropriate from a timing perspective. It might be that a learner's previous lack of access to music education opportunities has resulted in the learner not having the necessary knowledge and development to work at the standard required. Or, there could be a specific condition preventing the development of specific musical performance skills. Therefore, differentiating learning objectives in ways where learners' different talents and needs are valued will help to foster motivation. Learners who are able to participate reasonably well do, in fact, enjoy that participation and feel they are achieving set expectations.

Step 3: Develop the Lesson Introduction

Once the learning outcomes and learning objectives are devised, it is time to start designing the type of musical activities you will use in order to help learners understand, experience and apply what they are about to learn.

If you are teaching a group of learners, it will be a diverse body of learners with different academic and personal experiences, different musical backgrounds and musical preferences. They may or may not be familiar with the topic you are introducing. Hence, you might want to begin the lesson with a warm-up that they are *already* familiar with, and which leads up to the learning of new material, while at the same time giving you a sense of where the learners are in terms of their musical skills/aptitude (e.g., pulse regularity, pitch discrimination, etc.). In all cases, it is vital to develop an interesting introduction which contextualises the topic: this will stimulate motivation for engagement in the learning to follow. Ways to induce this can include asking leading questions; sharing a musical story; discussion of a historical event; presentation of a controversial idea; and showing a short video/audio clip.

Step 4: Plan Specific Learning Activities and Teaching Methodologies

When planning learning activities, try to consider a variety of ways for learners to engage experientially with the learning material. This can include gestures and movements; clapping rhythms; singing; real-life performance situations; audio and visual material; and various other ways. This will help keep learners engaged and appeal to a variety of different learning styles. There are a variety of different learning methodologies which you might want to consider, such as play; differentiation; talk and discussion; collaborative learning; high order thinking and problem solving; guided discovery, or inductive approach; integration; and peer tutoring.

Through **play**, learners can grasp useful insights that will result in more efficient learning and increased motivation for engaging in learning. Play stimulates creativity and imagination: these are crucial for development at all levels. There are many different forms of play (Zosh et al. (2017). These include:

- **Imaginative play**: Learners can pretend that they are someone else or somewhere else.

- **Manipulative/constructive play**: using natural and man-made musical instruments, toys and other equipment, learners physically engage in learning. Fine and gross motor skills are important.

- **Creative play**: involves creating something that was not available prior to the activity starting.

- **Language, Rhythm and Pitch games/Musical memory games**: these games draw on memory and the capacity to use, understand or manipulate rhythm, pitch, language and other musical elements.

- **Cooperative play/Competitive play**: here different types of collaboration can be established in an interactive process aimed towards commonly agreed and shared objectives, and at times with a competitive element of wining or loosing.

- **Free flow play/structured play**: when teachers structure the activity and plan for specific learning outcomes, the control lies with the teacher. However, if the teacher observes the learner, and provides opportunities for the learner to choose tasks and outcomes, the control is with the learner.

Differentiation refers to adapting teaching to suit learners of different abilities and diverse learning characteristics including different learning styles (Standerfer, 2011). Teachers need to recognise the different needs of learners and plan accordingly to meet those needs. This results in removing some of the possible learning barriers and granting enhanced access to learning. Differentiation strategies include differentiation by adapting teaching style; pace of teaching and learning; use of different learning resources; varying the type of support provided with more support given to the learners who need the most; learning objectives; setting different tasks for different learners; by grouping learners strategically; and effective use of content. Using differentiation effectively requires being empathetic with learners and sensitive to their individual traits, as well as ensuring all learners feel equally valued and supported.

Through **talk and discussion** carried out in the classroom, much can be discussed with learners with the aim of exploring their views, emotions and reactions through reflection and verbal translation of their experiences.

Collaborative learning, whereby learners work collaboratively with each other (or others) in the learning process, allows for the interchange of ideas and viewpoints helping to enhance understanding (Baker & Harvey, 2014).

Cooperating with others will potentially impact positively upon learners' development at personal and social levels and thus help to foster appreciation for working cooperatively.

Higher order thinking and problem solving skills are developed through analysing, summarising, making inferences, concluding, discovering and being creative (Lewis & Smith, 1993). Learning activities to develop these skills can include visualisation; role play; exercises involving sequencing and logic; problem solving; tasks involving changing circumstances; and social interaction. The environment should be such that making an unexpected judgement is as equally valued as finding a solution, and where learners can freely express their viewpoints.

Guided discovery, or inductive approach, is an inquiry-based method where guided discovery problems may be presented prior to the introduction of relevant content (Reynolds, 2016) and where learners are asked to uncover the rules for themselves.

Peer tutoring requires that learners work in pairs as tutee and tutor, where both benefit from the experience (Darrow et al., 2005). Pairing can be of learners with similar ability levels or mixed level abilities, and also with learners experiencing difficulties in the role of tutors.

An important element at this stage is estimating how much time is required for each activity, and accounting for this with the possible need of devoting extended time to further explanations and discussion. This is frequently required for cementing learning when new, more advanced concepts are introduced. On the other hand, you can move quickly into another activity in cases where learners have already mastered the concepts or skills required.

The lesson plan and lesson delivery need to work together symbiotically. Specifically, teachers need to be ready *to adapt the plan in accordance to the immediate learning needs of learners* while ensuring that the lesson provides a positive learning experience. As a music teacher, you must be able to improvise from time to time, much like a Jazz pianist. To do this, lessons must be designed to enhance learners' motivation, sense of self-efficacy as well as learning retention and which highlight the transferability of concepts. For these reasons, when creating a lesson plan, it is advisable to plan a variety of content appropriate activities for specific circumstances. These could include:

- For when learners are struggling to grasp certain concepts;

- For when learners have mastered the content;

- For when a group has mixed reactions to the learning material. For instance, when a group of learners has mastered the content, but either a few or a larger number of learners have not.

Regarding this last case, and if the teaching and learning setting is in a group environment, consider: how could more advanced learners in the class help to promote learning as a peer learning activity? Strategies along this line can be quite helpful: indeed, as a teacher for the past 25 years, I have witnessed how many of the brightest students enjoy adopting an explanatory role. To guide you at this level, consider the following questions:

• What will you do to present and explain the topic in interesting ways?

• What demonstrations or analogies can help learners understand the topic?

• What will learners need to do to help them understand the topic better?

• How will you know that learners are following and understanding the material?

Step 5: Plan to Check for Understanding

This step requires considering the ways in which you can check whether learners are following, effectively grasping and able to apply the learning being undertaken. Consider:

• What specific questions can you ask the learners in order to check for understanding?

• What can you ask learners to do in order for knowledge/skill demonstration to occur and check whether each of the objectives has been achieved?

Anticipating learners' difficulties and questions is an important element in terms of lesson management but also in considering strategies to support students in accomplishing the set learning objectives.

Step 6: Develop a Lesson Conclusion

At the end of the lesson, it is important to summarise the main learning points of the lesson and obtain feedback from learners on their learning experience. This will help with planning subsequent lessons. Summarising the main learning points can be done in a number of different ways. You can recapitulate the main points yourself or ask learners to help you summarise the main points.

In order to obtain insights regarding how learners' learning experiences are progressing, you can ask them questions such as:

• What did you think of today's lesson?

• What was difficult?

• What was easy?

• What did you like the most?

• What would you like to learn and do in the next lesson?

The end of the lesson is also the correct time for pointing towards any work that they should/could complete before next lesson (in instrumental music lessons, this will usually be advice for practice) and by briefly previewing the next lesson. This will help learners stitch concepts together and promote their curiosity.

Step 7: Create a Timeline

When considering time management, it is important to keep in mind that a list with many learning objectives is not realistic. It is best to narrow it down to the two or three main key concepts, ideas or skills you want learners to learn and develop. Teachers often need to adjust the plan to the learners' learning pace during each lesson. A pragmatic timeline, side by side with alternative activities, will assist you in becoming flexible and adaptable. It is good practice to estimate the time needed for each activity and write it down next to each activity. You should also plan for some extra time at the end of the lesson to clarify questions. Also, make sure to have ready an extra activity in case there is time left, and be adaptable by focusing on what is more relevant for learners.

Step 8: Consider the Resources Available to You and Your Learners

Make a list of all the resources needed for the lesson and ensure that the needed resources are available to you on the day, considering any steps you might need to take to ensure this is the case. Main resources required include:

- Location and type of room (appropriateness of location and room, accessibility);
- The environment of the lesson and how it should be prepared (temperature, safety considerations, room setting);
- Equipment required;
- Support required from others;
- Time management, including the amount of time you need to prepare the room and whether there will be time to do so (e.g., there could be a different lesson in that room just before yours). How much time do you need to prepare the room? Will you require someone to assist you in carrying musical instruments or other materials in a timely fashion? If so, who?

Step 9: Consider Potential Risks and Hazards

A significant factor to always keep in mind is that you are fully responsible for creating, developing and maintaining a safe and appropriate learning environment for the learners. As part of your lesson planning, give due time and consideration to examining what could go wrong and what actions you will take in such scenarios. In the following list there are some questions you might want to consider regarding this issue:

- Will I use electronic devices in my lesson, and if so, are there any issues that could arise? (e.g., how will I ensure that electronic devices and wires are safely placed and accidents are prevented?)

- If using school-based wind instruments, how will I ensure the instruments are appropriately clean and safe for use by learners?

- If children will be using headphones, how will I ensure these will not be a source for the proliferation of ear infections? And how will I ensure healthy sound levels are maintained in order not to cause any hearing difficulty or damage?

- Could the planned activities have the potential for disruptive behaviour to occur? (e.g., use of musical instruments)? What type of behaviour is likely to occur? What can I do to prevent such situations from happening and what will I do if such situations occur?

For teachers teaching at schools or public institutions, policies are likely to be in place for Health and Safety; First Aid; Child Protection; Internet Safety; Handling of Electrical Equipment; Manual Handling; Fire Safety; Data Protection; and others as appropriate. It is also likely that risk assessments on the venue have been carried out. Nevertheless, it is still your responsibility to get acquainted with **ALL** the policies and steps that should be taken in case of any eventuality. It is also strongly advised that you seek information on the policies and ensure that the institution has taken all necessary steps to provide a safe learning environment for yourself and your learners. If any matter has not been considered, you should raise it with your line manager. When it comes to ensuring a safe environment, we all have a collective responsibility, and any hazard or potential hazard found should be immediately reported to your line manager and appropriate action taken.

If you are teaching in your own studio, you need to:

- Carry out a risk assessment on your own teaching space and surrounding area. Ensure you revise it periodically (either annually or bi-annually) and consult with the appropriate authority on Health and Safety.

- Have in place policies and required training on Health and Safety; First Aid and associated protocol; Fire Policy; Child Protection; and Data Protection. Ensure revision of these policies and undergo training updates as required. These policies need to be written following the pertinent legal requirements of the given context and updated as required.

- Have in place the required insurances as per legal requirements.

Some professional bodies in the UK, such as the Musicians Union, European Piano Teachers Association (EPTA) and Incorporated Society of Musicians (ISM), offer an array of benefits for members, including some of the previously listed insurances as well as legal advice and support. It is strongly advised that you become a member of a professional body who can advise you on all these matters as per your specific circumstances and current legal requirements.

This given list is not exhaustive, as there is a myriad of context-specific situations that need to be considered. Therefore, carefully matching the environment where the lessons will occur, the group of learners and the types of activities planned is essential for building a detailed risk assessment. This is a crucial and vital step in your planning.

Step 10: Plan for Reflection on Your Lesson Plan and Lesson Delivery

Include time in your plan for reflection on what worked well and why, and what requires improvement. This will help you to develop a strategy for working on any points that need improvement. Plans may not always work as well as previously anticipated for a variety of different reasons. As teachers and educators, each lesson we plan and deliver provides a great learning opportunity, and such learning can only take place by reflecting both on the planning and the delivery of the lesson. The more we do it, the more genuine and fruitful learning takes place.

Obtaining feedback from others on our teaching is another important way to gain deeper insights on our planning and teaching performance. Use the following feedback sources to improve your teaching:

- **Learners' feedback**: consider how learners have reacted to the lesson in terms of physical behaviour but also in relation to their expressed emotions and verbalised content. Learners' feedback can be obtained either formally (administration of short anonymous questionnaires, where learners rate your teaching performance, depending on learners' ages) or informally by chatting to them.

- **Parents' feedback**: parents can provide relevant insights on your learner's attitudes towards learning the topic you teach and their attitudes towards music and music making in general. They can also provide you with a range of other information which can be useful to you as a teacher.

- **Peer observation**: ask teacher colleagues to sit in on your lessons to observe your teaching and provide you with their views on what and how you can improve further.

- **Video recording of your teaching**: this will provide you with a heightened awareness on issues such as how you use your vocal intonation and gestures to express yourself among other elements that perhaps you were unaware of. If video recording your teaching, be aware that written permission needs to be requested and given by the learners' parents or guardians in cases where they are minors, and also at the institutional level if you teach in a school or institution.

Through continuous reflection on your planning and delivery of teaching, you can develop yourself as a reflective practitioner (more on this in Chapter 10).

To wrap up this chapter, Table 5.2 contains a summary of the lesson plan steps outlined in the previous sections, side by side with some relevant aspects to consider in each step.

Table 5.2 Summary of lesson planning steps and some aspects to consider

Lesson planning steps	Some aspects to consider
Step 1: Know your learner/s and the educational context	• Who are the learners? • What aims do you have as a teacher for learners' overall development? • In what context is learning going to occur?
Step 2: Outline learning outcomes and learning objectives	• Create learning outcomes and learning objectives which are: specific, measurable, achievable, realistic and timely.
Step 3: Develop the lesson introduction	• Choose a warm-up that students are familiar with. • Create an interesting lesson introduction which helps contextualise the topic/s and motivate learners.
Step 4: Plan specific learning activities and teaching methodologies	• What will you do to present and demonstrate the topic interesting ways? • What demonstrations and examples can help learners understand better? • What will learners need to do to help them understand the topic better?
Step 5: Plan to check for understanding	• What questions can you ask learners to check for understanding? • What can learners do to demonstrate knowledge or skill development? • Going back to your list of learning objectives, what can you have learners do to check whether each objective has been achieved?
Step 6: Develop a lesson conclusion	• Summarise the main learning points of the lesson. • Obtain feedback from learners on their learning experience. • Point towards any work learners should/could complete before the next lesson. • Briefly preview the next lesson and how this lesson relates to what comes next.

(Continued)

Table 5.2 (Continued)

Lesson planning steps	Some aspects to consider
Step 7: Create a timeline	• Create a timeline, by estimating the time needed for each activity. • Have alternative activities which can be done if there is time. • Plan for some extra time at the end to answer questions and sum up main points.
Step 8: Consider the resources available to you and your learners	• Consider the location and type of room needed, while considering accessibility to prepare the room before the lesson. • What environment is needed (room temperature, safety considerations, room setting)? • What equipment is required (musical instruments, other)? • What support may be required from others? • What time is required, including room preparation time?
Step 9: Consider potential risks and hazards	• Carry out a risk assessment. • Are the required policies in place (e.g., Child Protection, Fire Safety, Data Protection, etc.)? • Have you undertaken up-do-date required training (Child Protection, First Aid, etc.)? • Are the required insurances in place as per legal requirements?
Step 10: Plan for reflection on your lesson and lesson delivery	• Plan for ways to obtain feedback on your teaching from a variety of different sources (i.e., learner's feedback, parents' feedback, peer observations, video recording of your teaching once relevant permissions and written consent is obtained). • Develop yourself as a reflective practitioner (more on this in Chapter 10).

Reflective Questions

<table>
<tr><th colspan="5">1. In preparation for creating your lesson plans, reflect on what elements you need to consider at the planning and environment preparation stage to enable inclusive teaching and learning</th></tr>
<tr><td rowspan="6"><ul><li>Consider what structure would be useful to use for your lesson plan template, considering the 10 steps of lesson planning presented in this chapter.</li><li>Consider introducing an introductory note at the start of the plan giving details about the student or students you will be teaching. While you may know your students well, your mentor and course assessors need details in order to understand how this plan is appropriate for your learner/s.</li><li>Explain how you plan to develop students' agency and ability to undertake ownership and decision making in relation to their learning.</li><li>Reflect on how, exactly, you will promote and help develop creativity.</li><li>Ensure you create appropriate learning outcomes and learning objectives.</li><li>Explain how you will check for understanding and that learning has occurred.</li><li>Include opportunities to gather children and young people's feedback on their enjoyment and the quality of their learning experiences.</li></ul></td><td colspan="4">Aligned with CME, Level 4 Unit (U) or Area of Study (AOS) and Assessment Criteria number of ABRSM (2014) and TCL (2013, 2019)</td></tr>
<tr><td colspan="2">ABRSM</td><td colspan="2">TCL (2013)</td></tr>
<tr><td rowspan="4">U2:</td><td rowspan="4">All learning outcomes for this unit</td><td>U2:</td><td>All learning outcomes for this unit</td></tr>
<tr><td colspan="2">TCL (2019)</td></tr>
<tr><td>AOS3:</td><td>All learning outcomes for this unit</td></tr>
<tr><td></td><td></td></tr>
</table>

2. What learning activities and teaching methodologies will be useful to apply in your context to promote independent learning, decision making, agency and creativity?				
• The content on lesson planning in step 4 of this chapter might provide you some ideas. • Outline specifically what you plan to do to develop each of the mentioned components.	**ABRSM**		**TCL (2013)**	
	U2:	2.3.2	U2:	1.2
			TCL (2019)	
			AOS3:	1.1.7 1.1.8

3. How will you identify and address potential risks or hazards that might affect children and young people's well-being and provide a safe learning environment?				
• Consider the content on lesson planning in step 9. • Carry out a risk assessment to your teaching context and use it as an appendix to your lesson plans. Take action to ensure safety for each risk or hazard identified.	**ABRSM**		**TCL (2013)**	
	U2:	2.2.2 2.3.2	U2:	2.2 2.3
			TCL (2019)	
			AOS3:	2.1.8 2.1.9

4. What will do to ensure you effectively plan inclusive teaching and learning?				
• Consider the principles of UDL and define them (or other inclusive methodologies you may be aware of). • Explain how you will practically apply UDL principles in your teaching. • Outline the components of an inclusive lesson plan and ensure these are embedded throughout your lesson planning.	**ABRSM**		**TCL (2013)**	
	U2:	2.2.1 2.3.1	U5:	2.1 2.2 2.3 2.4 3.1 3.2
			TCL (2019)	
			AOS3:	1.1.4 1.1.5 1.1.6 1.1.7 2.1.3

Note

1. The Center for Applied Special Technology (CAST) is a non-profit research and development organisation founded in 1984, in the US. It develops 'innovative educational products' and has its own publishing house, CAST Professional Publishing. See: http://castpublishing.org/

Further Reading

Darrow, A. A., Gibbs, P., & Wedel, S. (2005). Use of classwide peer tutoring in the general music classroom. *Update: Applications of Research in Music Education, 24*(1), 15–26. https://doi.org/10.1177/87551233050240010103

Jellison, J. A. (2016). Inclusive music classrooms: A universal approach. In G. E. McPherson (Ed.), *The child as musician* (2nd ed., pp. 361–372). Oxford University Press.

McCord, K., Gruben, A., & Rathgeber, J. (2014). *Accessing music: Enhancing student learning in the general music classroom using UDL*. Alfred.

Standerfer, S. L. (2011). Differentiation in the music classroom. *Music Educators Journal, 97*(4), 43–48. https://doi.org/10.1177/0027432111404078

Zosh, J., Hopkins, E., Jensen, H., Liu, C., Neale, D., Hirsh-Pasek, K., Solis, S., & Whitebread, D. (2017). *Learning through play: A review of the evidence*. Lego Foundation. www.legofoundation.com/media/1063/learning-through-play_web.pdf

References

Anderson, L. W., Krathwohl, D. R., Airasian, P. W., Cruikshank, K. A., Mayer, R. E., Pintrich, P. R., Raths, J., & Wittrock, M. C. (2001). In W. Anderson & D. R. Krathwohl (Eds.), *A taxonomy for learning, teaching, and assessing: A revision of Bloom's Taxonomy of Educational Objectives*. Longman.

Associated Board of the Royal Schools of Music (ABRSM) (2014). *Level 4 certificate for music educators: Assessment framework*. ABRSM.

Baker, W., & Harvey, G. (2014). The collaborative learning behaviours of middle primary school students in a classroom music creation activity. *Australian Journal of Music Education*, (1), 3–14.

Biggs, J. B., & Collis, K. (1982). *Evaluating the quality of learning: The SOLO taxonomy*. Academic Press.

Bloom, B. S., Engelhart, M. D., Furst, E. J., Hill, W. H., & Krathwohl, D. R. (1956). *Taxonomy of educational objectives handbook 1: Cognitive domain*. Longman Group Ltd.

Darrow, A. A., Gibbs, P., & Wedel, S. (2005). Use of classwide peer tutoring in the general music classroom. *Update: Applications of Research in Music Education, 24*(1), 15–26. https://doi.org/10.1177/87551233050240010103

Dave, R. H. (1970). Psychomotor levels. In R. J. Armstrong (Ed.), *Developing and writing educational objectives* (pp. 33–34). Educational Innovators Press.

Doran, G. T. (1981). There's a S.M.A.R.T. way to write management's goals and objectives. *Management Review, 70*(11), 35–36.

Drucker, P. (1955). *The practice of management*. Heinemann.

Gazard, P. (2010). *You can teach primary music*. Rhinegold Education.

Jellison, J. A. (2016). Inclusive music classrooms: A universal approach. In G. E. McPherson (Ed.), *The child as musician* (2nd ed., pp. 361–372). Oxford University Press. https://doi.org/10.1093/acprof:oso/9780198744443.003.0019

Krathwohl, D. R., Bloom, B. S., & Masia, B. B. (1964). *Taxonomy of educational objectives: The classification of educational goals. Handbook II: The affective domain.* David McKay.

Lewis, A., & Smith, D. (1993). Defining higher order thinking. *Theory into Practice, 32*(3), 131–137. https://doi.org/10.1080/00405849309543588

McCord, K., Gruben, A., & Rathgeber, J. (2014). *Accessing music: Enhancing student learning in the general music classroom using UDL.* Alfred.

Reynolds, R. B. (2016). Relationships among tasks, collaborative inquiry processes, inquiry resolutions, and knowledge outcomes in adolescents during guided discovery-based game design in school. *Journal of Information Science, 42*(1), 35–58. https://doi.org/10.1177/0165551515614537

Standerfer, S. L. (2011). Differentiation in the music classroom. *Music Educators Journal, 97*(4), 43–48. https://doi.org/10.1177/0027432111404078

Trinity College London (TCL) (2013). *TCL level 4 certificate for music educators: Specifications.* TCL.

Trinity College London (TCL) (2019). *TCL level 4 certificate for music educators, areas of study.* TCL.

Zosh, J., Hopkins, E., Jensen, H., Liu, C., Neale, D., Hirsh-Pasek, K., Solis, S., & Whitebread, D. (2017). *Learning through play: A review of the evidence.* Lego Foundation. www.legofoundation.com/media/1063/learning-through-play_web.pdf

6　Leading Music Learning

To Guide Your Reading

How to use appropriate strategies, resources and pedagogical approaches that will:

- Support children and young people to engage in musical learning which develops their personal and musical competencies?
- Motivate musical creativity and the skills and confidence required to communicate musically, confidently, fluently and expressively?
- Promote the inclusion of all participants in musical learning activities?
- Promote physical, emotional and intellectual well-being?

Introduction

Music teaching is a multifaceted area of work. As such, a teacher can find themselves working in a variety of different music teaching contexts. To succeed it is crucial that teachers obtain knowledge of the specificities of each context where they work. This chapter provides useful overviews of the main, overarching music teaching contexts. These are the early years sector; primary and secondary schools; instrumental and vocal music teaching settings; and community music facilitation. This is done with an awareness that these music teaching and learning contexts are not mutually exclusive nor are they the only ones. Furthermore, recognition of the need for optimising connections between contexts via thoughtful teaching interventions is made. For each context, a brief review is made of relevant concepts and current issues, followed by guidance points aimed at assisting teachers conceptualising their working practices for each setting.

Being a teacher, educator or facilitator requires interacting with learners and sensing their feelings and attitudes towards learning. We must also be able to grasp understandings on how learning is progressing while simultaneously adapting teaching and teaching planning as needed in order to provide positive learning experiences. The process of interaction involves interacting not only with learners but also intercommunication between/with parents, the school administration (if teaching in institutional settings) and other fellow teachers, and understanding learners' socio-cultural environments. Successful teachers take all of the factors into consideration while keeping up-to-date with recent developments in music education. They are flexible and adaptable in trying new approaches while also being able to justify particular methods and decisions. They constantly reflect upon their teaching experiences and take them as their own lessons, grasping an enhanced concept of teaching self-awareness and using it as a pillar for their own development.

Early Years

Music, alone or combined with other art forms, and when used as a safe space for exploration, imaginative play and self-expression offers an excellent platform where creativity can be fostered, nurtured and developed. Music in early years also has the potential to enhance other areas of development, such as the physical, emotional and psychological well-being of learners and the promotion of collaborative skills, namely motor skills, physical co-ordination while also boosting children's ability to develop relationships with peers and others, including parents and carers.

Interactive music learning experiences can involve parents, babies and children, carers and music teachers/educators/facilitators, in small groups or one-to-one settings. In each of these scenarios it is embedded in the child's family, community and cultural musical day-to-day experiences. It can take place at home, in nurseries, schools, playgrounds, arts centres, museums, libraries, concert halls, theatres, hospitals and private classes in rented premises or homes (Young, 2018). It can include a combination of different musical activities such as singing; structured and unstructured play with and without musical instruments; music and movement classes; instrumental music classes; foundation music skills programmes; and programmes led by community musicians or peripatetic music teachers. In many cases the musical activities are combined with other art forms such as drama, dancing, drawing, etc.

Discussions among music educators and researchers on what effective early music provision should look like reveal a major point of contention. On the one side, there are those that advocate for an early years music provision specifically focused on achieving particular learning outcomes and argue for intensive music training to commence from a young age on the grounds that it can lead to improved ability in the discrimination of pitch and better fluency in technical skills development (e.g., Suzuki, 1983). This argument has led to the development of many pedagogical approaches (e.g., Dalcroze,[1] Kodály, 1965; Orff,[2] Suzuki[3] and many others) that teachers sometimes use in isolation but at other times in combination. On the other side of the argument are those that recommend that music provision in early years should be freer and fluid, stating that there is no evidence that intensive music training necessarily leads to musical attainment and engagement later on (e.g., Trehub, 2006).

Regardless of the position you adopt (a midpoint between the two is perfectly acceptable) your main mission as a music teacher, educator or facilitator when working with early years, and in accordance with recent insights from developmental psychology, should revolve around:

- Encouraging children's self-expression through music and in all possible ways;

- Promoting, nurturing and developing creativity, through the use of music as a safe space for exploration, imaginative play and self-expression;

- Making sure these take place in a safe and enjoyable environment designed to promote and sustain the joy of music making, and which is so evident in early years (Trehub, 2006), as well as fostering a sense of self-proficiency, self-confidence and self-esteem (McPherson et al., 2012).

Additionally, in any setting you work (and irrespective of the pedagogical approach(es) you use), you can implement (fully or partially) what Young (2018) advocates as good practice. She states that early years music education activities and initiatives should provide opportunities for self-initiated play on musical instruments rather than exclusively focusing upon acquisition of skills in preparation for further formal music education. After a systematic observation of 95 children in three different nurseries, engaging in self-initiated play, she emphasises that spontaneous engagement in music making has a role in terms of embedding self-expression, creativity and embodiment in meaningful ways when compared with more guided and structured learning geared towards achievement of certain learning outcomes.

Giving opportunities to young children to take ownership in expressing themselves through music (using the means and ways they choose rather than fully dictating ways of engagement to them) is crucial for the development of creativity according to recent research. This doesn't mean that there shouldn't or couldn't be some structure to the music sessions you develop, deliver and/or facilitate. In fact, both structured and unstructured musical activities enhance the lives of early years' children. The following guidance points can assist you in conceptualising your working practices in early years music settings:

- Establish dialogue-based interactions and musical interactions with your learners rather than fully teacher-led ones.

- Ensure that each child's contributions and ideas are welcomed, valued, accepted and used as departure points for new learning/experiences of learning.

- Provide opportunities for imaginative play and exploration, using a variety of activities and the resources you have available. These activities may include: singing; making sounds with one's own body; using home-made and conventional instruments in addition to listening to music; and recording and composing music (Creech & Ellison, 2010).

- Establish two-way partnerships with families and carers (Creech & Ellison, 2010), where the family and children's musical background is acknowledged and shared with music teachers/educators and also with other children and families in cases of group work.

- Recognise the variety of musical experiences and musical diversity that children bring to early years settings and support the continuity of the music made in the home environment in order to enhance children's self-concept and to promote experiential learnings on the value of diversity in society (Young, 2018).

- Devise multimodal approaches which include the use of creative music making with exploration of sound and music, in conjunction with movement, other art forms and possible situations where creative play can be nurtured (Young, 2018).

- Develop and establish partnerships with other professionals for the sake of creating and delivering innovative music learning experiences which will benefit children's learning and development. These can be with other music educators or with colleagues in other fields and disciplines, as well with those in power who can make various initiatives happen (e.g., funders, councils, local authorities, politicians) (more on this in Chapter 9).

- For more, check out Nicola Burke's (2018) *Musical Development Matters in Early Years*, published by The British Association for Early Childhood Education. Here, the main themes of hearing and listening, vocalising and singing, moving and dancing, exploring and playing are each considered from birth to five years old side by side with insights on what music educators can do to promote learning and development. A link to this resource is available in the CW Resource 2. The suggested age/stage of development statements should not be taken as necessary steps that each child needs to go through and are used by the author simply to pinpoint different stages in typical development.

- Engage in professional development activities and adopt a continuous professional development attitude through networking with other music teachers and other professionals and being up-to-date with the latest developments in your area of work.

Knowing the importance of the use of music in early years, at both developmental and personal levels, helps to conceptualise what you do as a music teacher at a broader level. So, if someone asks you the question 'Do you teach music?' you may as well reply with 'Yes!'. But you can also answer with: 'I teach music and much more!'. This is indeed the case because music is not done solely for the sake of music. Music is much more than music. See beyond the music, see the child and how music can help support the child's growth and development as an individual, and as a member of society.

When we realise this wider purpose, we worry less when a child is perhaps singing slightly or fully out of tune, or is unable to yet feel the regularity of pulse, when clapping a given rhythm. Instead, we realise the spark of happiness in the child's eyes for being part of something with their mates, for instance singing together in a group and learning how to take turns. Or maybe it's learning collaborative skills and how it feels to sing together? Maybe it's improvising a different and perhaps unregular and unexpected rhythm saying his/her name? You will then help by supporting the child to achieve a better pitch by demonstrating the intended pitch and seeing if the child attempts to match it, without being judgemental. Or you might mimic a regular pattern to see how the child reacts.

In parallel with some musical modelling, you will also give space for spontaneous musical self-expression and encourage the child's efforts, while striving for the child's development of enjoyment and fun in music making activities through positive reinforcement. You will promote the joy of music making and strive towards building strong foundations for children to develop their potential and have the best possible start in life. You will do so by focusing on creativity development and on strengthening partnerships with children, parents, the wider family and a range of other professionals aimed at raising and sustaining a consistent quality of early years' experiences for children and their families.

Primary School

Taught either by generalist[4] or specialist music teachers,[5] the experience of music making in primary school contexts varies considerably from one school to another, from country to country, and from culture to culture. This depends upon perceptions regarding the value, use and functions of music in a given situation, making it difficult to provide a generalised view of education and likewise of music learning and teaching. Notwithstanding the variability in terms of the type and quality of music offerings available, the benefits of music education provision in primary schooling for those who can receive it are immense and are directly connected to the quality of provision available.

In the UK, the Office for Standards in Education, commonly known as Ofsted (2009, whose role it is to inspect schools independently and impartially around the UK) published a 2009 report that revealed that in three-quarters of schools inspected, music's impact on learners' personal development was rated as good or outstanding. All of the teachers interviewed agreed on music's potential to enhance learners' confidence, concentration and social skills and that for these reasons, music should feature as an essential part of a balanced and broad primary school curriculum. Contributing to the findings reported earlier was the Wider Opportunities Scheme, created under the Government's

Music Manifesto in England and Wales (DfES, 2006), now led by voluntary apolitical partnerships independent from the government. This scheme offers to children, who wish to do so, an opportunity to learn to play a musical instrument at primary school. Children welcomed the chance of practically engaging in music making with peers and friends. However, less than half of the schools inspected by Ofsted in the 2009 report were participating in the scheme. This raises questions about the other half, particularly with regard to equal access to opportunities and ideas of democracy in education which assert that music should be 'for all'.

Three years later, Ofsted's 2012 report revealed that some Wider Opportunities programmes lasted for only a term or less, and in some cases the length of the initial opportunity was so short that it was of little benefit, either to learners' long-term musical progress or to the overall music curriculum (Ofsted report, 2012). Shockingly, this latest Ofsted report (2012) rated only a third of the schools inspected as offering outstanding (five out of 90 total schools inspected) or good music provision (28 out of 90) (a link to this report is available in CW Resource 3). While the benefits of quality music education provision in primary schooling are widely recognised, there appears to be a mismatch between such recognition and priority given to its implementation in UK primary schools, even where funding may be available (Creech & Ellison, 2010). This is evidenced, for example, by the limited amount of time dedicated to music learning in comparison to time devoted to the learning of other subjects and by the place given to music within the curriculum. In the UK, for instance, it is estimated that only 4% of time is devoted to music within the wider Primary Curriculum, as estimated by the Qualifications and Curriculum Authority (2005).

Furthermore, in many other parts of the world the primary school music curriculum, rather than having a place of its own as a subject with its own merits in the curriculum, is instead embedded within a wider rubric, generally referred to as 'Understanding the Arts' or 'the Arts'. This is typically comprised of a variety of artistic subjects such as Drama, Design, Dance and Music. In this way, Music becomes a not entirely compulsory subject in the curriculum, and despite being mentioned in the 'written curriculum', in many cases it is not a part of the learning experiences of children in their day-to-day learning. Teachers have the freedom to shape the delivery of the Arts rubric of the curriculum, deciding where the emphasis lies and any cross-curricular connections they might establish. Where teachers feel less confident about music or have more resources and preferences towards other art forms, they might offer music less frequently, or even not consider music at all. Therefore, children miss out on the wide-ranging benefits of music making.

Regardless of your role as either a generalist, specialist, head teacher at a primary school or the person in charge of delivery of music provision services to primary schools, it is important that you consider what you are currently already doing *and* what you could possibly do to further enhance the current music provision on offer to learners. If you are a generalist teacher, you have in-depth knowledge of other curricular areas and spend a considerable amount of time with the learners. Therefore, you are in a privileged position to know what learners' learning needs are and hence the best way to establish cross-curricular connections between music and other subjects.

As a generalist teacher, you may not have been trained specifically to 'teach' music. It is therefore hardly surprising that you may feel less confident to deliver material you don't feel fully proficient in. In addition, it is a great pressure to be asked to deliver in all areas of the curriculum. I truly appreciate that you are considering going outside of your comfort zone to provide high quality learning experiences which your learners deserve. As you will probably realise, every time we step out of our comfort zone, we learn much about ourselves and develop to a higher level of awareness and ability. After a period of time, it will likely start to feel less daunting and you will grow in confidence.

You may perhaps not play a musical instrument, nor particularly enjoy singing or feel proficient at reading music. The fact is that you actually don't necessarily need these skills in order to be able to facilitate high-quality musical learning experiences in your classroom. Whereas if you are a specialist teacher, you might be inclined to place a high emphasis on the quality of the sound or tone production, you may also emphasise music notation sometimes too much and teach music that accords with your own musical background. In truth, there is a lot that could be gained by having generalist and specialist music teachers working more closely together: many points could be exchanged which would take music provision to higher level.

In what follows are some pointers for those teaching in primary school contexts, some of which are more applicable to generalist teachers and others more so for both generalist and specialist teachers. Regardless of you being a generalist of specialist teacher, it is important to understand not only the challenges that you may be facing but also how you can help your colleagues (generalist or specialist teachers) overcome difficulties they may also be facing. In fact, by working together, we can certainly improve the quality of education we provide to our learners, and improve our teaching substantially. Consider the following:

- If you are a generalist teacher, **recognise your own "innate ability to be musical and teach music as a positive force"** (Burnard & Murphy, 2017, p. xix). I have a few questions for you: have you attempted to sing a song before? Have you felt inclined to clap the pulse of music you enjoy listening perhaps while driving? Do enjoy moving to music If you answered at least one of these questions in the affirmative, you are musical! You have been exposed to the experience of 'communicative musicality' and 'musical enculturation' processes, and by extension assuming normal neurological functioning and development, we can all be considered to be musical to some extent (Welch, 2005). Being musical doesn't necessarily equate to knowing how to play a musical instrument or being an excellent singer. What it means is that you are equipped to engage in a range of music making activities. Alongside your learners, you will gain from the benefits of music making, while ensuring you are providing them with a solid and well-rounded educational provision, where music is an essential and important ingredient for their personal development.

- **Know and understand what the music curriculum you are asked to deliver is all about**. Obviously, institutional guidelines for the delivery of music (if existent) will be different from one context to another, and it is important that you find out exactly what you are being asked to deliver and what your learners are expected to know, learn and be able to do and their respective key stage. For the most part, in the Western world the institutionalised music curriculum for both primary and secondary schools is comprised of three main strands: listening and responding; performing; and composing. Planned musical activities within each strand revolve around developing an awareness of and sensitivity to the interrelated elements of music: pulse, duration, tempo, pitch, dynamics, structure, timbre, texture and style. There will be (in most contexts) specific guidelines for specific learning stages aimed at ensuring learning progression

- **Change your mindset from 'teaching music' towards 'facilitating music'**. The word 'teaching' is many times conjoined with the assumption that there is content that necessarily needs to be of an expository/explanatory nature. In the case of music, you might feel that you necessarily need to perform (sing or play musical instruments) in a quite proficient manner, or teach learners how to read music notation. However, what your learners actually require is that you 'facilitate' musical experiences in their classroom. Using your own creativity, there are many ways you can do so effectively, utilising your own musical strengths and reflecting on the right type of activities for your students (Odena, 2012). Facilitating music is about enabling music to happen. This means that time spent in activities that are not intrinsically musical is time **not** well spent and will not help your learners to develop musicianship (e.g., activities such as filling in forms on music related definitions, drawing musical instruments or instances where you are giving learners a lot of explanations and definitions to learn).

In order to 'facilitate music' you need to provide music making experiences in relation to listening and responding, performing and composing, and where the learners actually 'make music' and develop a critical awareness about sound. Moreover, they should be able to use sound creatively to express themselves. For instance, for listening and responding, recorded musical material can be presented and learners then asked to identify patterns and reflect upon the musical elements used. You may focus on a few elements only and briefly provide a definition of what they mean prior to starting the listening experience. For responding, a certain rhythmical pattern can be clapped, and each learner can be asked to provide an answer to the pattern given, taking turns. With regard to performing, for singing based activities, recorded songs can be helpful and used for learning the melody, lyrics and singing along. When exploring how to produce sound using given musical instruments learners should be made to experience different approaches and reflect on the different sounds produced, highlighting which ones they prefer and why. Alternative music notation, created by the learners in your class (where certain meanings are agreed upon for certain symbols) may be used, and it serves as another interesting strategy to develop creativity and develop critical awareness about sound.

In terms of encouraging learners to compose music, there are a wide variety of apps which learners will in most cases be happy to explore. Additionally, there are a variety of websites and apps designed to reinforce music theory-based concepts (for a list see CW, Resource 4). You will need to put aside some time to learn how to use the apps and software you plan to use (most are quite intuitive and user friendly these days) and ensure that technology is used to promote deeper musical understandings rather than simply for learning how to use certain software.

- **Use the musical sound as the driving factor for facilitating learners' musical understanding.** Your learners' musical understanding needs to be essentially derived from the experience of listening, responding and music making itself. You need to be prepared not only for guiding learning through sound but also accurately listening to and interpreting your learners' musical responses. Furthermore, through demonstration and modelling, help them to refine the quality of their music making in a positive learning environment, where a sense of self-proficiency in music making is equally developed. This is not to say that talking and writing about music are not important or helpful. But talking and writing about music should be considered as *supporting* rather than *driving* learners' musical understanding (Ofsted, 2012).

- **Make your main purpose to be to develop creativity, self-expression, self-proficiency and self-esteem.** In order to successfully develop creativity, you will need to instil an environment where children can experiment with sound and express themselves through music freely, and where there is no such thing as a 'wrong idea'. Nurture an environment of self-expression through music. By doing so, you are welcoming your learners' contributions and promoting their creativity in a safe space but also allowing yourself to display your vulnerability, and your learners will admire you for that.

You might want to first introduce them to some relevant concepts and ask them to compose or improvise while using a certain musical pattern, or when appropriate in conjunction with the learning outcomes, provide more free style tasks. Use musical improvisation to nurture collaboration, participation and develop listening and aural skills. Your learners' sense of self-proficiency is intimately linked with the feedback they receive from you whenever they complete what you have asked them to do. **I cannot stress enough** how important it is that you **provide words of appreciation** for the efforts your learners are making and that you promote an enjoyable learning environment where the tasks requested from learners are accessible, realistic, appropriate for their level of understanding and interesting, but also meaningful to them.

- **Find the 'right' balance between structured versus less structured learning activities.** Concerning the development of creativity, it is important to find a balance between structured versus learning activities which are somehow freer and less constrained, where learners are invited to 'think outside the box', create and/or improvise. However, new levels of knowledge and understanding also have the potential to promote creativity at higher levels. This is where the balance between set learning outcomes and unexpected or more fluid learning outcomes in parts of some sessions (or even full sessions) needs to be carefully considered. A learning outcome might be to come up with something completely new or fully original, not constrained to any rules. Or, learners can be asked to elaborate on pre-existing concepts, notions, or patterns. By offering both structured and unstructured learning activities (still nevertheless properly planned) those learners who like freedom to create will benefit from having such an opportunity; equally, those who feel more or less challenged will start learning how they can navigate in a less structured environment, and vice-versa.

- **Realise, welcome and use your learners' musical backgrounds in the classroom.** Learners' musical backgrounds may differ from yours, and if this is the case, do not impose your musical background on learners. Instead, offer an inclusive musical repertoire and varied opportunities for music making where the backgrounds of your learners are welcomed and represented. In addition, take your learners musical interests and knowledge as a departure point for planning learning in the classroom.

- **Don't feel threatened by the wealth of musical knowledge and previous musical experiences learners bring to your classroom**. Instead, be humble and ready to learn from and with your learners, using their knowledge as departure points for learning. If you don't feel comfortable singing in front of your class, find out who among the learners would like to lead a singing based activity and support the learner in the 'facilitation' of the activity.

- If you are a generalist teacher, **schedule time for music for your class** on your timetable (weekly and daily). Prioritise music as being as important as other school subjects, based upon an awareness of the wide-ranging benefits that music will have in the life and development of your learners and don't let other priorities or commitments to get in the way.

- **Develop in your school a culture focused on high quality participatory music making rather than solely presentational or performance-based music making**. Such inner cultural change might take time to achieve as the idea of performative music in the form of end of term shows is still quite engrained in primary and secondary schools. In many cases, the intense preparation to build these shows by teachers and learners alike can make the whole experience highly stressful, particularly when the focus is solely placed on a polished musical performance, instead of what really matters: the quality of the learning experience of music making.

  This is not to say that presentational and performance-based music making should *not* be part of the musical learning experience. However, preparation for any presentational and performance-based activity should be enjoyable for learners and teachers alike and contributions therein equally valued. Consideration needs to be given as to whether presentational music making is the best way to develop musical appreciation, enjoyment and musical understanding, from the perspective of your learners rather than from the school/institution's own agendas or priorities. The best interests of learners should be at the heart of all decision making in this regard.

- **Be a learner in your classroom, while also being teacher.** Don't be afraid of trying out new things in order to acquire new insights. Being creative about teaching, such as devising strategies and activities for the particular learners you have in your classroom, is a very important skill that needs to be developed by doing. Learn from learners but also from other teachers, musicians, managers, learners' parents and so on. Engage in independent learning by searching out people, books, articles, web content and the latest insights from research which can help you in the facilitation of music teaching.

- **Seek support from colleagues** (generalist and specialist teachers) and within the hierarchical structure in your school (e.g., the head of subject, direct line manager and even the school principal). It is amazing what we can learn through informal discussions with colleagues on strategies they have used and the wealth of knowledge some of our experienced colleagues have amassed. It is even more amazing to know that in most cases they are actually quite happy to share such knowledge and help us develop further as teachers. While informal discussions tend to be good, the process can even be formalised by creating a discussion group which can meet regularly to discuss music teaching, as well as other teaching matters.

- **Identify your own music teaching needs for development and continuous professional development opportunities (via both guided and independent learning).** All teachers, regardless of how many years they have been teaching and of how well qualified they are, should remain engaged in finding out what else they can improve in their teaching to support their learners more efficiently. If you are not confident about music teaching, what *exactly* are you not confident about? What could help you overcome the problems you have identified? Or perhaps you are very confident, but unsure why some learners are not progressing as expected? Is there a course with content matching the problem identified? Or is there information in books or reliable internet sources where you can learn more about it? If guided learning is costly, independent learning through reading reliable articles and books can be as helpful as guided learning in many instances. At this point, I cannot recommend two websites highly enough that contain a wide variety of music related courses: Udemy.com and Skillshare.com

- **Be an advocate for high quality music provision for all in your school and beyond.** Why should some children receive high-quality music education while others do not? Perhaps music is not taken as seriously as it should be in your school? Or are there inequalities of access to musical learning and participation? There are many reasons why providing music might be difficult, ranging from economic reasons to not realising the important place music can have in learners' personal development. While there could be a number of barriers to music access, it is extremely important that you identify the barriers and consider what is in **your** power to remove such barriers (or at least temporarily overcome them). This might include developing persuasive skills for communicating the importance of music to others (e.g., head of school, politicians, etc.) or developing creative solutions for music making experiences. I acknowledge that in some parts of the world the resources might be scarce or completely nonexistent. But I am certain that when you decide to take action, and engage in thinking about what can be done, you will come up with something that is possible to be done. It might not solve all the problems, but it will most certainly make a difference in the life of a child.

- **Congratulate yourself every time you see joy on your learners' faces** as the time for music lesson arrives and as they happily undertake the music learning activities you have planned.

Needless to say, the selection of learning content needs to be based on children's learning needs and their previous musical experiences, in conjunction with their own musical aims, interests, preferences and socio-cultural environment. It might be that in certain circumstances the best course of action might be to adopt the content suggestions given for a previous level, instead of those recommended for the children's particular age group. It is also important that an appropriate sequence of content is maintained and that appropriate musical literacy concepts are not only presented as 'theory' (often perceived as being very dull, much like grammar in language lessons) but also side-by-side with its practical application and sound translations of musical rhythms and melodies.

Secondary School

Music in secondary schools is usually tied to a set curriculum, which may be imposed either at national or regional levels, or implicitly within the 'standards' for the subject. Usually, it is a part of the compulsory curriculum until around the age of 14; however, music then often becomes an elective subject for learners between the ages of 14 to 18, is taught by specialist teachers and is structured according to specialist courses and examinations. Common challenges in engaging learners in the music secondary school environment include a reported low level of learner enjoyment. Learners tend to lack motivation for engaging more actively in the lessons as the repertoire does not seem relevant or appealing for adolescents. When music is an optional route there is low update by learners and there are issues of inclusion of social groups based around race, culture and gender despite evidence of young people's strong musical engagement with music outside school (Philpott & Wright, 2012).

Many of the challenges can be linked with the quality of teaching. The Ofsted 2012 report highlights a number of teaching related problems in secondary school music provision in England, including use of inappropriate starter activities which were either not musical, not engaging or not relevant to the main learning focus that followed. There were frequently lengthy spoken introductions with a focus on completing tasks rather than making music, with little explanation or modelling by the teacher with regard to the use of the language of musical sound. Cross-curricular activities often did not focus appropriately on musical attainment, and frequently resulted in insufficient musical learning, as music was used to serve the learning interests in other fields thereby resulting in distinctly **un**-musical learning. Music technology focused on many occasions on *mastering aspects of the technology* rather than on *seeking musical responses and deeper musical understandings* through technology (to read the full report please go to CW, Resource 3).

Given these and other challenges, it may be useful to consider the pointers in the following if you work in a secondary school environment:

- **Give due attention to the transition between primary and secondary school** as advocated, for example, by the Musical Bridges initiative funded by the Paul Hamlyn Foundation. Some learners may come from primary schools where the music provision was either non-existent or poor. Teachers should understand where learners are at and depart from there, going back as required to the basic elements of music when necessary (i.e., pitch, rhythm, dynamics, texture, timbre and structure).

- **Provide learners with the basic knowledge they need to understand and express themselves musically, but ensure you and your learners move from 'single components' to a more holistic understanding of how everything connects.** Focus on the interrelations between different aspects of the curriculum rather than isolated components. Ensure learners can understand, for example, how a certain music style evolved to become distinguished as its own, and what led to such changes? Consider, for instance, how music performance can support the development of listening skills? How can learners' compositions provide a basis for further development in terms of their aural and performance skills? How can learning about chord progressions facilitate internalisation of sound? Through singing, perhaps? When assessing learners, consider their progress holistically, taking into account where they were at the start, where they currently are, and how you can ensure you will take them to where they should be. It might be that you still need to go back to basics. But surely, it is better to do this rather than causing them to feel they are unable to follow.

• **Ensure your planning considers learners' musical learning progression over the period of time you will be together**. This requires consideration of the need for improving the quality, depth and breadth of learners' musical responses while also being continuously aware of what learners have achieved musically in previous lessons. In doing so, it is essential that you are clear about how each of your lessons intends to build upon previous musical learning in progressive and structured ways. Consider the quality of your learners' musical responses in terms of accuracy, sensitivity, feeling and expression and devise ways in which you can support their development towards higher levels of sophistication.

• **Make your priority to be to teach through music and music making. Your role is not to teach *about* music but to teach *through* music.** Realising this as an essential and integral aspect of your work means that you need to be able to do and demonstrate to learners exactly what they are expected to do musically. To achieve this you must engage, together with your learners, in life music making in the classroom. Moreover, you need to be able to listen carefully and interpret your learners' musical responses, and through demonstration and modelling, help them to refine the quality of their responses in ways where their effort and perseverance are recognised and where they are made aware of the progress they have achieved.

When having to tackle content of a more theoretical nature, think outside of the box and devise musical activities where the content can be musically enacted and experienced at a musical level rather than providing non-musical learning experiences which are 'about music', but not intrinsically musical. For example, if working on explaining/revising key signatures, explain the theory but relate this to how it sounds in practical learning experiences that help learners realise connections and differences aurally. If working with a certain musical app or software, ensure the purpose of its use is to enhance musical understandings and quality of musical responses through technology rather than simply learning how to use technology. This point applies also to assessment: devise musical ways for assessment to take place, particularly when undertaking baseline assessments. So rather than using questionnaires and written tests 'about' music, focus instead on assessing integral aspects of music making (listening, performing and composing).

• **Nurture creativity, self-expression, self-proficiency and self-esteem, considering the balance between freedom of expression versus structured learning.** Some learners will enjoy full freedom while others will crave structure. Start by introducing learners to some relevant concepts, tied to the learning outcomes/curriculum and ask them to compose or improvise while using a certain musical pattern. Parallel to this, free composition tasks can be given, where basically there are no rules, or where each learner or group makes the rules for themselves. Composition can also be more intimately connected to musical improvisation to nurture collaboration, participation and develop listening and aural skills. Consider how can composition and improvisatory activities be used to promote self-expression and enjoyment of music making? If a learner has a rationale on why they wish to bring an unexpected element into his/her composition, it should not be criticised on the grounds of your own musical taste, or that in your view it is not necessary. Freedom of expression should always be encouraged in musical composition while ensuring that agreed rules/expectations and application of given concepts are understood.

The way you as a teacher welcome your learners' musical creative work is decisive in relation to how able and proficient they see themselves as composers/musicians, the enjoyment they derive from the activity and on how much time outside of the classroom they will engage in the creative process of music making. Use your learners' creative work as a window to understand more about their uniqueness, and also for strengthening the relationship you have with them. Doing this effectively, crucially requires that you reflect on how your own musical background may influence your perception of what musical creativity is, and the expectations you have from your students (Odena & Welch, 2007).

• **Consider what is preventing learners from engagement with music at either GCSE, A level, and other musical provision available and devise strategies to tackle specific problems.** Learners are your best source of information. Through an anonymous questionnaire I am certain you would obtain relevant information which would then help you plan for further engagement. The anonymous aspect will ensure a greater level of honesty from learners. Also have conversations with learners who are not engaging by asking them what their reasons are? You may find that some learners' answers can be about not feeling confident or knowledgeable enough to do or pursue music. Unfortunately, such assumptions are derived from poor quality music education experiences, including low quality teaching. Therefore, reflecting on the quality of our teaching from the point of view of how we can (in our specific teaching contexts) pro-mote learners' enjoyment, knowledge, skills and sense-of-self-proficiency in music is crucial in terms of engaging learners with music. The goal should not be to promote engagement solely for the time where learners are in school but rather musical engagement as a lifelong pursuit.

• **Take the initiative to devise meaningful music making experiences for learners.** Consider equality of access, but realise that meaningful music making experiences will be different for different learners, or groups of learners. Learners will have different musical preferences and identify with different music styles; therefore, the repertoire needs to be varied and provide opportunities for exploration of preferred styles. For instance, it is a well-known fact that girls disproportionally engage more with singing activities (such as choirs) than boys, and that boys tend to engage more in music technology-based activities than girls.

Concerning choral singing, the Ofsted 2012 report revealed that in Eng-land boys were not particularly interested in the musical style promoted by choirs nor the way that the activities were structured. In other con-texts, there might be other reasons, or a different picture altogether, and it is your job as a teacher to understand these reasons and put in place activities where the musical style promoted agrees with boys and girl's identity self-concept and preferences. Boys only choirs have resulted in increased numbers of boys engaging and participating. Additionally, in choirs where the director/conductor was a male, an increased number of boys have been observed to join (Hall, 2005). Concerning music tech-nology, the stereotyped notion that boys are better at STEM subjects can make girls less confident in interacting with technology. To address this, perhaps only girls' music technology groups could be created. However, it remains to be seen whether this would produce the engagement and mind-shift required. Only by trial and error will it become possible to know what works and what doesn't.

• **Support learners enacting their own agency and provide them with opportunities for assuming leadership roles.** Provide opportunities for learners to experience conducting small ensembles or to engage more closely as artistic directors. Support them in creating specific groups which match their own musical styles and ambitions. This can be done both as part of classroom work and as extra-curricular provision. Help learners develop the expertise to organise their own musical experiences. This will help to foster sustained community music making, through people making music together as a hobby, for instance. This requires that schools consider their role in developing and fostering musical leadership skills in a variety of roles such as rehearsing, arranging and conducting (Jones & Langston, 2012). Apart from utilising and further developing their musical skills, this also encourages the development of non-musical skills needed for organising music making, be it event management, publicity, public relations writing programmes, logistics, marketing, etc.

- **Connect learners to musical opportunities that already exist in the community** (e.g., choirs, bands, orchestras). Direct your learners to easily accessible groups, where they will utilise the musical skills and knowledge they are developing at school.

- **Create musical opportunities within the community**. School music teachers have what it takes to create or participate in community-based music initiatives. This requires that teachers consider establishing deeper music-based community links and see where the school can cooperate/ collaborate to provide community based musical experiences/offerings, where teachers and learners alike, and as members of the community, actively participate.

- **Aim for improving the quality of singing.** Singing is the most natural way of musical expression for human kind. As a participatory activity it has wide ranging personal and social benefits. Participatory singing activities provide relevant opportunities for improving the quality of singing, which should not be missed. Therefore, teachers should listen carefully to the sound produced, advise on correct breathing techniques, promote a healthy approach to singing including voice warm-ups and aim at developing each learner's musical and singing potential to higher levels through demonstration and modelling.

- **Consider using a variety of different teaching methodologies,** including those where informal music learning is used in formal learning such as with Musical Futures. An increasing number of schools are currently using the Musical Futures model for their teaching and curriculum approach for learners aged between 11 and 14 years old. Musical Futures is an approach where learners' musical interests are taken as the basis for their learning, promoting learner agency, encouraging learning through the use of methods used by popular musicians such as playing by ear and promoting learners' musical interests in popular styles. This is then complemented through wider developments in terms of their social and personal skills, enhancing their ability to participate in community choirs or orchestras. This model has had a considerable and beneficial role in engaging young people in music education, with repercussions on their musical development. When using informal learning methodologies, ensure you define exactly the role you have in terms of supporting your learners' learning and ensure you use principles of good teaching practice as this model has been shown to work effectively only when these elements were considered and implemented (Ofsted, 2012).

- **Make a deliberate effort to connect with the wider community of teachers and music teachers to share knowledge and experiences**

and contribute to advances in music education. Professional isolation remains a problem for teachers working in the secondary school environment, with cases of schools where the music department is staffed by only one music teacher who have no one else with musical expertise with whom to share and discuss good practice. Despite there being several online music teaching forums, only a minority of teachers actively engage in professional dialogue with colleagues either online or in the development of partnerships with other colleagues. In addition, not all engage in professional membership of relevant bodies (e.g., the Musicians' Union in the UK), or in regular area, regional or national meetings (Ofsted, 2012). Reasons put forward by teachers for not engaging more widely include pressures of planning, preparing, assessing and delivering public musical performances in their own schools. However, by being connected to other teachers you will come across ideas that may help solve some of the challenges you may be facing, while at the same contributing to the wider community of teachers.

Many of the problems between adolescents and music education, particularly concerning engagement and enjoyment, are directly related to the fact that young people feel that their rights of inclusion, enhancement and participation are not being met in the music classroom (Philpott & Wright, 2012). This directly relates to your choices of repertoire, approach(es) to teaching, teaching methods, level of agency you transfer to your learners and your willingness and ability to take the initiative to make a positive difference with regard to these aspects wherever you are.

Vocal and Instrumental Music

Instrumental and vocal music teachers teach people of all ages and various levels of proficiency in a variety of contexts, music styles and genres, either in an employed or self-employed capacity. Many instrumental and vocal music teachers have portfolio careers, which combine music performance, teaching, composing and community music and teaching in a variety of different contexts. These can include nurseries; primary and secondary schools; music institutions, such as academies and conservatoires; community based institutions and businesses; young offender institutions; collaborations across arts and non-arts sectors; care homes, working with the elderly; and at their own music tuition business, at times home-based or rented spaces or at learners homes.

Rapid changes in society, propelled by intense change at various levels (i.e., cultural, musical and technological), are causing the landscape of instrumental and vocal music teaching and learning to evolve at a faster pace than ever before. Whereas in the recent past instrumental and vocal teaching was undertaken mostly in face-to-face contexts (either in one-to-one teaching, in most cases, or group settings), we are starting to observe variants which include virtual online teaching (in real time), web-based interactive teaching and video recorded sessions or courses that learners can access at a time of their choosing. To keep their provision well-suited, appealing and more widely accessible for learners in the twenty-first century, teachers are being required more than ever to step out of their comfort zones and include technology as an aid to support teaching and learning.

Although more research is needed to ascertain the effectiveness of teaching and learning in interactive one-to-one instrumental/vocal virtual environments, video conferencing web-based platforms such as Skype, WhatsApp, FaceTime, Zoom, Microsoft Teams and others have been used with some success. Dammers (2009) considered nine trumpet lessons provided via real-time, online and one-to-one formats, focusing on the feedback and progress made by learners. Despite reported difficulties such as occasional video delays (latency) and limited visual perspectives to do with the software capabilities, this study showed that one-to-one online teaching can be considered a viable alternative to the more traditional face-to-face teaching or as a complement to blended learning.[6]

A larger scale study involving instrumental music teaching in a variety of different instruments across North Yorkshire, UK, using Skype in combination with a Roland VR-3EX, an AV mixer offering three camera angles revealed that learners were motivated to learn, concentrated well and made good progress in online one-to-one lessons (King et al., 2019). This same study also showed that teachers teaching behaviours during online lessons was much the same as the teaching behaviours they enacted in face-to-face, one-to-one teaching (more on teaching behaviours ahead). Although teachers felt that they spent more time talking in online teaching settings, the data analysis didn't show consistent differences at this level. The main difference between teaching in each of these two settings had to do with accompanying, which teachers found difficult to do when teaching online and, therefore, was used much less in online settings. Teachers participating in this study found teaching in online settings more challenging in comparison to their face-to-face one-to-one teaching. Nevertheless, they stated they would be keen to do it again. This study showed among other findings, how instrumental music teaching and learning can, through online teaching, help to overcome access barriers in areas where teachers would need to travel for long distances between schools, and where there are transportation problems.

Group teaching has advantages of maximisation of the use of resources, time and monetary payments making possible for learners' tuition fees to be shared or reduced. In this way, group teaching can become more accessible for learners, while simultaneously promoting peer learning and a sense of community through social musical activities such as ensemble playing (Hallam, 2006). Disadvantages include difficulties when teaching learners of different ages and levels of proficiency in the same group, despite the learning advantages that this can offer. A 'middle ground' and compromise may be needed, meaning that learners who are more proficient may lose interest if the learning feels repetitive or seems too easy. Those who are struggling may feel unable to cope with the learning demands, and this will impact upon their sense of musical self-proficiency, possibly resulting in a loss of interest.

Group teaching can occur in face-to-face settings where all learners meet in the same room, or virtually with a teacher, in the form of a webinar, for example, where there can be varying degrees of interaction between teacher and learners and between learners accessing the same virtual learning room. The degree of interactivity will of course relate to the functionalities of platforms used and teacher chosen methodologies. Yet, it remains unclear how effective online group teaching might be when compared with face-to-face group teaching, with the caveat that at first consideration can be assumed that virtual scenarios (group or one-to-one), while offering access options, also potentially promote the development of 'lone' musicians (King et al., 2019).

Video recorded teaching is also becoming a very popular approach where teachers create lesson videos and learning resources such as downloadable music, backing tracks, contextual information and other advice. In some cases, teachers have conceptualised, developed or helped to develop more or less interactive apps and websites that can support learning of music theory, sight reading, aural skills and other integral elements related to instrumental and vocal music learning. There is evidence that these resources can promote learning and even promote a greater level of independence in learning as documented in various sources (e.g., Savage, 2012). Therefore, technology developments of various types (web and non-web based) seem to offer interesting opportunities for enhanced learning experiences with potentially equal or enhanced levels of effectiveness when compared with teaching that doesn't use technology. However, more research is needed to ascertain best practice and approaches.

Approaches to Instrumental and Vocal Teaching

The 'master-apprentice' model of individual lessons, characterised by transmission of knowledge using a didactic approach,[7] has dominated instrumental learning across generations and cultures (Campbell, 2006) and has a number of limitations. It tends to be focused on listening and responding in the moment to particular music being played by a learner while focusing on specific instrumental/vocal points of technique. This immediate and reactive approach focuses on the short-term rather than on long-term learning, ignoring in many instances the development of aspects such as: learning motivation; progressive learning goals; creativity and evaluation of development (Creech & Gaunt, 2012). Hallam (1998, adapted from Pratt & Johnson, 1998) proposed alternative approaches, which can be used simultaneously, and which she suggests move away from a teacher-centred towards a more learner-centred approach. They are:

- Engineering: delivering content.

- Apprenticeship: modelling ways of being.

- Developmental: cultivating the intellect.

- Nurturing: facilitating personal agency.

- Social reform: seeking a better society.

In addition to these, mentoring models have been proposed over the past decade or so, and closely align with ideas of facilitation. Mentoring has been defined in a variety of ways, depending on the contexts where it is used, but it differs from coaching, advising and counselling. As applied to the instrumental/vocal teaching and learning context, Creech and Gaunt, 2012 define it as:

- Essentially focused upon considering each learner as unique in a given context(s) and recognising the interdependence between personal and professional development, with a view to supporting learners' integration as a fully functioning individual within their society.

- Mentors help mentees make informed decisions by themselves, and promote, foster and encourage mentees independence.

- Mentors assist mentees in developing self-confidence through creation of a relationship of trust and commitment where it is safe to explore a variety of performance related options and avenues.

- Communicative interactions between mentor and mentee are fluid, embedded in layers of dialogue which move flexibly from social exchanges, to modelling of musical skills, collaborative exploration of artistry, insights into career direction/s and career planning, and therefore help to foster development of personal and professional identities.

- Mentors are credible professionals in certain areas of expertise and have the ability to be self-aware, self-reflective and let go of their ego. Hence, they are open, flexible and non-judgemental, and have both empathetic and listening skills. They also have the ability to communicate well using a variety of communicational strategies in order to ask appropriate and relevant questions to help the learner think in different and perhaps new ways, and thereby opening up new opportunities for self-expression.

Although the earlier principles are important for theorising different approaches teachers can take with regard to their teaching, effectively enacting preferred approaches requires more than understanding the basic principles or defining elements of the approach. It also requires a recognition of how we teach, and what we might need to change in order to enact the approach faithfully and in ways that our learners can benefit from.

Various observational studies in instrumental music teaching and learning have shown that teacher talk is dominant, with learners making little contribution to the dialogue even at advanced stages of learning (Rostvall & West, 2003). Teacher talk tends to be about technical aspects of playing/singing and questions asked in many cases tend to be interpreted as rhetorical and aimed at reinforcing instructions given or at seeking agreement rather than promoting critical thinking and independence from learners (Creech & Gaunt, 2012). Teacher modelling – advocated by Hallam (2006) as a way of ensuring that learners are prepared for their practice by having a strong aural representation of the music they are learning – is used somewhat less, with more time allocated to learners playing through sections or whole pieces. One-to-one teaching on the whole (as observed in the studies mentioned earlier) was mostly teacher-directed, with learners having limited opportunities and space to develop creativity, independence and critical thinking.

Creech (2009) studied how interpersonal interaction between teachers, learners and parents impacted upon learning outcomes in violin teaching and learning in one-to-one contexts (learners aged 8–18 years old). Learner attainment was measured both by examination grades but also by learners' measures of self-efficacy, enjoyment, motivation, satisfaction and self-esteem. While the 263 UK based violin teachers in the study used a variety of teaching methodologies and had different levels of teaching experience (ranging from 1 to 30 years), the most effective teaching and learning was found in what the researcher classed as 'harmonious trios'. These were defined as a parent-teacher-child partnership characterised by mutual respect and reciprocal communication among the three participants. This study also revealed that mutual respect and child-centred, rather than teacher-centred goals, provided positive learning outcomes. Psychological remoteness between teacher and learners had a detrimental effect on learning (more on this study in Chapter 9).

Moreover, where learners have had a say with regard to establishing and influencing learning objectives, a positive effect was seen in regard to musical attainment, thereby evidencing the importance of giving learners an active voice and establishing partnerships with learners in opposition to adopting teacher-centred approaches. Interestingly, constructive and proactive partnerships established between teachers and learners also resulted in higher levels of teacher teaching satisfaction. These teachers demonstrated an ability and willingness to enact teaching and learning guidance which they perceived as most appropriate while also being responsive to the learning needs of their learners as individuals. They recognised that each learner was an individual with a certain identity, story and personal circumstances. Learners were reported to be most comfortable in situations where they idealised their teachers (Gaunt, 2010). This demonstrates the importance of teachers investing in the continuous development of their performing knowledge and skills, as well as regularly and actively engaging in performance.

While the previous content is essentially focused upon one-to-one teaching, it is possible to widen the concept of mentoring to group teaching and include partnerships developed between various music teachers, musicians, teachers of other subjects and other professionals within the cultural and community environment. An alternative model functioning along these lines has been initiated in Australia. This model attempts to enhance children's experiences of music by combining their cultural contexts of school, home and community within a 'mentoring programme' (Temmerman, 2005). This collaborative venture offers school learners the opportunity to work with composers and performers, and to learn about employment within the music industry, through partnerships with an array of professionals who work with the children in group and one-to-one settings. Teachers also benefit from initiatives such as this and through the augmentation of existing school programmes and sharing expertise.

Other approaches to instrumental and vocal teaching relate to informal learning, achieved for example through socialisation or enculturation, as exemplified by the gharanas (households) of India where families have their own distinct musical styles based on familial traditions (Farrell, 2001). Green (2001) also describes how professional and non-professional rock musicians learn by using strategies whereby they 'pick up' skills through watching other musicians and teaching themselves, while also usually being supported by their families and peers. This has led to approaches such as the one advocated by 'Musical Futures'. Similar informal learning approaches have been (and are) widely used across the world in participation ensembles: many of these existed long before Musical Futures was conceptualised. Operating within distinct, self-enclosed cultures, ensembles can transmit musical traditions and offer a broad spectrum of skills development, from socialisation to identity formation.

Scaffolding and Teachers' Teaching Behaviours

Teaching a learner to play a musical instrument requires teaching each learner in an individual way. Through scaffolding, a teacher selects and introduces specific tasks just beyond the learner's current capabilities (see Adachi, 1994; Barrett, 2005; Kennell, 2002; Young, 2005). The ways in which teachers scaffold learning are intimately related with the teaching behaviours they enact. Teacher behaviours can be defined as specific and delimited behaviours with specific pedagogical intentions and functions manifested by teachers verbal content and/or gestures they enact (Simones, Rodger et al., 2015). Both verbal and gestural elements are equally important (Simones, Schroeder et al., 2015) and work in integrated ways as gesturing is an integral component of language when synchronous and co-expressive with speech (McNeill, 2005) and beyond.

In Table 6.1 you can see the Teacher Behaviour and Gesture (TBG) framework I have developed through observation of video recordings of instrumental music teaching and through a review of literature in the subject. The TBG framework provides a categorisation and definition of instrumental music teachers teaching behaviours and gestures used while teaching. You can use it to analyse video recordings of your teaching in order to examine more closely your verbal utterances, teaching behaviours and gestures. In so doing, you will obtain more insights on how you scaffold your learners learning by focusing on areas where improvement is needed.

Figure 6.1 shows excerpts of how this framework has been used to analyse video recordings in the context of piano teaching. You can either do written

Table 6.1 Categorisations used in the Teacher Behaviour and Gesture Framework (TBG)

Categorisation 1: Teacher behaviour categorisation

Adopted and adapted from Carlin, 1997; Zhukov, 2004)	Giving information	Providing general and/or specific conceptual information
	Giving advice	Giving a specific opinion or recommendation aimed at guiding the student towards the achievement of certain specific aims, without demonstration or modelling
	Asking questions	Enquiring
	Giving feedback	Evaluation of a student's applied and/or conceptual knowledge made known to the student
	Demonstrating	Showing how to perform a particular action, without actively engaging the student in the action and where the student mostly listens and observes
	Modelling	Actively engaging the student in performing actions alongside teachers' explanations
	Giving practice suggestions	Provision of suggestions of ways to practice a particular element or passage, or discussing a practising schedule
Simones, Schroeder et al., 2015	Listening/ observing	Internally processing the material presented and performed by students for diagnosing students' needs in musical development and establishing appropriate teaching plan to the student.

Categorisation 2: Teachers gesture categorisation

Spontaneous co-verbal gestures (McNeill, 1992, 2005)	Deictic	Pointing.
	Iconic	Express images of actual objects or actions.
	Metaphoric	Express images of the abstract
	Co-verbal beats	Vertical/perpendicular movements of hand, arms and/or head with the purpose of highlighting information that is external to the gesture in itself, occurring at the meta-level of discourse.

(Continued)

Spontaneous co-musical gestures (Simones, Schroeder et al., 2015; Simones, 2019)	Musical beats	Up and down movements of hand, arms and/or head that only denote the tempo or speed, at which the music should be played without providing expressive musical information.
	Conducting style	Up and down movements of hand and arms that assume generally a more circular shape providing temporal and expressive information about the music.
	Playing musical instruments or singing	Instances where teachers intentionally and actively engage with music making in the form of instrumental and/or vocal music making.

Categorisation 2: Teachers gesture categorisation

| | Mimics with instrument manipulation | Instances where teachers appear to mimic a certain mental image of a gesture that they consider appropriate to perform a particular musical sound-producing action, delivered while expecting the student to imitate the gesture shown. Mimics can be subdivided into two sub-categories (only for instrumental music teaching): a) Mimics with instrument manipulation b) Mimics without instrument manipulation |
| | Touch | Instances where teachers have made intentional physical contact with the student in the course of instrumental music teaching. |

Source: Reprinted from Simones (2019), under a Creative Commons CC-BY licence; adapted from Simones, Rodger et al. (2015)

(Time in Minutes/ Seconds)	3:04	4.24	4.31	4.33	4.45	4.50
Speech Transcript	Look, you are here now	that sounded much better than last week	there were only a few mistakes	what is this note here	yes, it's a G sharp, but you played G natural actually	listen, this is how it should sound when you play G sharp
Teaching behaviour	Giving information	Giving feedback	Giving feedback	Asking questions	Giving Feedback	Demonstrating
Teacher gestures	Diectic	Co-verbal beat	Co-verbal beats	Diectic	Co-verbal beats	Playing the piano

Figure 6.1 Annotation template example A

Source: Reprinted from Simones (2019), under Creative Commons CC-BY licence

records of your video observations using a timeline of events or use software tools for video analysis. Several of these tools are freely available from the internet, including Elan software (developed by the Institute of Psycholinguistics, Nijmegen (Netherlands) and Anvil software. Both Elan and Anvil software are specifically designed for manual annotation and transcription of audio or video recorded material using a tier-based model for inserting data.

In particular, it is worth analysing not only the proportion of time you spend enacting particular teaching behaviours but also the level of scaffolding quality you demonstrate when enacting such behaviours. For instance, teacher talk time considered on its own doesn't say much about the *relevance* and *importance* of said talking (i.e., sometimes a lot of teacher talk may be necessary, other times not). If the talk was aimed at promoting learner agency, creativity and learning independence, and there was a reciprocal communicative interaction between yourself as a teacher and the learner (either through musical or verbal questions and responses), we can reasonably assert that this is a good use of teacher talk time. However, the lesson should not be entirely focused on talk: rather, the lesson should be conceptualised as a period of musical communication, established in various ways.

Effective lessons include high amounts of demonstrating and modelling teaching behaviours and giving feedback to these. Demonstrating teaching behaviour is about **showing** the learner *how* to perform a particular action while providing an aural template of the sound (type and quality) required and without actively engaging the learner in the action. Modelling is more intense as it involves *actively engaging* the learner in the performance of a certain action in conjunction with the teacher's verbal or gestural explanations of what is required.

Demonstrating and modelling are absolutely essential in instrumental and vocal teaching and learning and yet, studies show that these teaching behaviours are in many cases lacking in lessons (e.g., Hewitt, 2002). Reasons for this absence may relate to teachers feeling intimidated or fear of making mistakes in front of learners. If this is the reason, I suggest practising the pieces you are teaching to learners: learn them to the best of your ability, play sections which can be helpful to learners, play at a much slower tempo if this helps the learner realising particular nuances and don't be afraid to show to learners that you are human – and that we all make mistakes. Learners are not going to think less highly of you because you made a mistake or because suddenly you appear to be struggling on a certain section. On the contrary, show your learners that you are not afraid of making mistakes. By doing so, you are providing a great example of how to face and accept mistakes. To do this effectively, you must keep a chilled and relaxed attitude and use mistakes as opportunities to learn something new.

In many instances, fear of performance is developed through the relationship learners established with teachers and how teachers have reacted when learners have made mistakes, using utterances such as: 'stop right now!', 'what is this?', 'that is wrong'. In many instances these utterances are accompanied

Table 6.2 Pillars of effective instrumental music teaching and constituent elements

Pillars of effective teaching	Constituent elements
A framework	• Posture: refers to all things physical, including interaction with our instrument and everything concerned with technique. • Pulse: deals with all things rhythmical. • Phonology: concerns the way we control sound and all things aural. • Personality: is all about the character of the music. Whatever we play, must be suffused with musical intentions.
An environment	• Lessons should be fun and pleasurable: of course, there is always serious and hard work going on, but a lesson should never become stifling, boring or unpleasant. • We need to be creative: thinking creatively, using our imagination at all times, developing ever-more intriguing ways to teach and learn, and if we're creative our learners will develop the confidence to be creative too. • Practising must be desirable: we need to enable learners to go and develop their playing on their own, and to do so because they **want** to. • Self-evaluation: what am I doing? How am I doing it? Am I doing it well? We need to teach learners how to self-evaluate. • A love of performing: which needs no explanation.
A method	Simultaneous learning: • Teach proactively rather than reactively: Creating a flow of continuous appropriate and achievable musical activities thereby leading to real understanding and ultimately producing independent and positive-thinking learners. • Everything connects: teachers know how the various parts of music connect and interact and make these connections clear and comprehensible to learners. • Teach from the ingredients: identify the relevant ingredients (in a piece for example, we would identify the key, rhythmic patterns, markings, character, etc.) and then base the lesson around exploring a number of these ingredients, mixing and matching them.

Source: Adapted from Harris (2012, pp. 11–13)

by facial expressions and behaviours which have conveyed strong disapproval, disappointment, frustration and sadness. This approach promotes stage fright, whereby learners focus intensely on the mistake and as such, are unable to focus on what is to be played next. Teachers using such approaches are preventing learners from developing the ability to deal with mistakes. They are living in an unrealistic (and quite frankly cruel) world where the mantra is that 'practice will make perfect': however, when it doesn't it almost feels like it's the end of the world. Instead, don't interrupt learners because of a mistake.

When the learner has finished playing, focus upon what was good and then refer to what requires improvement, providing strategies for correction of a wrong note or whatever else may need to be improved. Welcome mistakes; be thankful for them and teach your learners to be thankful for them also. Give them a new mantra: 'the definition of learning is making mistakes and learning from them'.

Giving feedback as a regular part of your teaching behaviour has strong repercussions in relation to the quality of learning and teaching you provide. You will want to provide proactive, specific and constructive feedback, starting with something the learner did well, then focusing upon what can be done better and how. Ensure the feedback is specific. For instance, 'well done' is not specific enough. To help learners, using an instance where they did something right, they need to be made aware *exactly* of what was done well and how it can be applicable to other instances in their playing. For example:

> Well done for performing the crescendo in this phrase [*one may physically indicate the exact portion on sheet music*]. This ensured the emotion in this section of the piece increased in intensity and therefore led well into the fortissimo which is about to come in the next phrase. What worked really well was the way you used the weight of your hands and arms progressively and the way you heard it before playing it in your head. The same can be done in the third section of the piece.

Moving from the micro to the macro aspects of teaching, apart from the need for considering teaching behaviours, verbal content and gestures, Harris (2012) proposes the need for considerations on what he calls the "three pillars of effective instrumental music teaching". These are: a **framework**, an **environment** and a **method** (see Table 6.2).

Harris (2012) recommends the following structure for instrumental music lessons:

- Warm-ups: physical and mental aimed at removing tension, both in mind and body, moving on to some pulse games and then some sequential aural-based musicianship activities. It is important to keep the warm-ups connected to practised work and for new material to be introduced **later** in the lesson.

- Development Section: taking ingredients used in the warm-up to explore the music pieces further, experimenting, developing specific skills and musicianship and imparting appropriate knowledge and values, sometimes with and sometimes without notation.

- Recapitulation: aimed at ensuring that learners understood what has been taught through gentle questioning and applying what was worked to different contexts, however, not by using explicit testing. Also ensuring that learners know what they are to do in their subsequent practice sessions.

As for all other music teaching contexts, a clear lesson plan will prove itself to be very helpful for providing a general outline of what learning outcomes and objectives you should be working towards. It will also help you to devise a coherent and appropriate structure for the lesson, while taking into account your overarching aims vis-à-vis enhancing learners' motivation, providing a coherent learning trajectory and evaluating how learning and teaching are progressing in terms of outcomes and effectiveness. The pointers that follow can assist you in developing your instrumental and vocal teaching further:

- **Consider ways in which you can widen access of instrumental and vocal music to children in your community and beyond**. This will require being versatile and being able to teach in a variety of teaching settings, for instance one-to-one; group teaching; in face-to-face versus virtual environments; preparing video recorded resources; and establishing partnerships with other teachers and other professionals for providing a rounder approach to learners' personal and your professional development.

- **Make your priorities to be to develop creativity and self-expression**. Do not limit your teaching solely to technique or a certain music style, or the use of Western classic music notation or other types of notation. Instead, be open-minded and focus on what music really is about – an experience. Ensure you appropriately guide learners through the experience and that there are aims and sequentially logical trajectories towards development. Ensure the experience is at all times meaningful to the learner (be it in the lesson, during practice or performance). Encourage creativity through, for example, asking learners for alternative ways of musical interpretation, creation of a composition and engaging in improvisatory musical exchanges during lessons.

- **Ensure your teaching is musical at all times**. There is no point in teaching notation without relating sound to symbol or without promoting aural development and active listening skills. Learning to play an instrument or to sing, needs to be considered in the wider context of developing musicianship, promoting a musician's identity, enjoyment and independence.

- **Consider offering a learner-centred approach, closely aligned with mentoring**. In doing so, you might consider including some elements of learner-led learning or inclusion in your 'formal' teaching of 'informal learning elements'.

- If you work in one-to-one settings, **consider developing opportunities for learners to work collaboratively with other learners**. This could include some small group sessions, duet or ensemble playing/rehearsals, or other activities perhaps undertaken in partnership with other teachers and professionals in the community.

• **Be flexible in regard to experimenting with technology and apps in your teaching, but before doing so, consider its usefulness**. Consider how can it potentially promote learning? How will learners react to the experience? (Particularly, be aware that there is no 'size-fits-all' in regard to the use of technology either).

• **Provide strategies and weekly plans for practice**, ensuring that learners have clearly understood the strategies proposed and assess during the following lesson if it has worked or not. If not, consider adapting and changing as you see it would most benefit the learner. Practice plans need to be individualised as what may suit a learner might not necessarily suit another, even if they are of the same age, learning level and learning stage.

• **For learners that don't engage with practice, use the lesson as an opportunity for practice**. Emphasise any gains obtained (small or large) and that the work undertaken during the lesson resulted in progress while predicting and informing the learner of what he or she could achieve with daily practice in a certain amount of time (e.g., three months, six months, etc.).

• Also in relation to the previous point, **consider what might be preventing the learner from engaging more actively with practice** (e.g., being busy with too many activities, lack of motivation, feeling unable to progress as the task might be too hard to overcome, not having the technical background fully developed to overcome the challenge, loss of motivation, not feeling particularly connected with the given repertoire, personal life challenges such as parental separation). Once you are able to identify possible reasons you might then be able to act on aspects that are under your control (e.g., choice of repertoire, varying the level of difficulty of the tasks by introducing something more feasible).

• **Consider analysing your teaching behaviours**, and in particular check if the amount of talking you do is mostly focused on technical aspects, or does it include elements aimed at promoting learners' independent thinking, development of creativity and allowing learners' self-expression (through musical behaviours and verbal utterances)? Does the talking you do provide opportunities for developing learner agency? Does it provide opportunity and space for allowing learners to state what they want to achieve their musical interests (and by when), and does it make them comfortable to express how they think their learning is progressing in terms of learning but also in terms of the type of experience they get from you as a teacher?

• Still in regard to teaching behaviours, **consider the amount of the lesson you dedicate to demonstrating and modelling**. Learners need to be provided with an aural template of what they are aiming towards in terms of how it should sound (pitch, rhythms, but also intonation, phrasing, articulation, etc.). How often do you break the musical material into small chunks and work in short sections where learners are commonly stumbling? Play those small chunks to learners while providing an aural template but also explain why perhaps you are not stumbling and what they can actually do physically or mentally to overcome the same problem over and over.

- **Consider the type and quality of feedback you provide to your learners**. In many cases, it is through the feedback you provide that learners will develop perceptions of themselves as either being (or not being) a musician; being good at it or not good; being something they can do; or something which is not really for them. You will want to provide proactive and constructive feedback at all times.

- **Consider ways to establish and work in partnership with other teachers and professionals**. There is so much that can be done by joining forces together in usual but also unusual partnerships. Be creative and think outside of the box when thinking what else can be done and how.

Community Music

Community music is a wide-ranging area of music practice which has witnessed relevant developments over the past 20 years or so. New levels of understandings on the benefits of community-based music making for all ages and people in various settings have had a profound influence on the currently expanded remit of activity of community music. This ranges from the diverse face-to-face interactions within the same physical space in a variety of settings, to virtual communities and various new forms of interactions and musical participation (Elliott, 2012).

As a term, 'community music' is difficult to define since it assumes continuously evolving different meanings in different cultural and geographical contexts. On the one hand, 'community' can only be defined in relation to the characteristics of a specific community (e.g., shared values, benefits, types and nature of participation and others). On the other hand, even if some sort of agreed definition is established, communities are always evolving and changing, new dynamics are established overtime, resulting in new conceptualisations. It is in this continuously dynamic and fluid environment that community musicians work – a shared space in which the community and community musicians collaborate, in various roles, capacities and dynamics in order to achieve shared goals (more or less delimited) while working with people of all ages and backgrounds.

Equally difficult to define is the term 'community musician'. Broadly speaking, it can be said that community musicians promote, develop and deliver "music-making interactions outside of formal music institutions" and establish "partnerships between the formal, nonformal, and the informal music education settings" (Higgins, 2012, p. 3). Coming from a diversity of musical disciplines, genres and traditions, community musicians create and facilitate opportunities for participation through music, using a variety of musical activities, which can include workshops, creative music making projects, performances and demonstrations, in a wide range of settings. These can include: early years settings; hospitals; supermarkets; community centres; prisons; hospices; day care centres; factories (Creech, 2010); arts centres; schools; recording studios; places of worship; sporting grounds and so on (Higgins & Bartleet, 2012).

Community musicians work across a wide spectrum of diverse and multifaceted roles. These roles include workshop leader; community music worker; project manager; music animateur; music educator; music facilitator; cultural development worker; musician in residence; music outreach worker; freelance workshop provider; project leaders; and a variety of other jobs and various other titles. They are also seen working collaboratively with a range of other professionals and musicians, such as visual artists; actors; teachers; composers; and health professionals, to name but a few. Frequently, community musicians are invited into schools to promote and develop music making opportunities, and as a result the cultural life of the school and its curriculum are enriched. These partnerships with schools provide experiences of: ensemble performing; approaches to composition; repertoire access; and styles of music beyond curricular offerings. In this way, community music links community and schools in more effective and realistic ways. It also provides the school with a variety of resources as well as culturally specific and cross-cultural music approaches that school teachers might adopt for curricular purposes (Higgins & Bartleet, 2012).

The following elements are key differentiators of community music in relation to other music teaching contexts:

- The term 'facilitation' is commonly used instead of 'teaching'. Facilitation in this context is defined as an intentional intervention, aimed at facilitating group music making experiences, without a prescribed or set curricula provided by a skilled music leader or leaders.

- Community musicians facilitate people making music through a variety of music making activities, musical styles and diverse social-musical relationships and are strongly committed to lifelong musical learning.

- Community musicians' objectives can be wide-ranging and include a particular focus on personal growth, therapeutic elements, community development, social or celebratory, and others, each with repercussions on other areas such as skill acquisition, social skills and community development (Creech, 2010).

- At the heart of the work of community musicians are fundamental ideals of access and equality in which musical participation is a right that all human beings should be able to exercise, including immigrants, low income families, those with physical and mental conditions and indeed, all groups in society. Therefore, the main purpose of what community musicians do intrinsically relates to creating accessible music making experiences that promote musical participation and equality of opportunity in diverse learning environments.

*   Similarly, as with other contexts of music teaching and learning, musical participation involves performance, invention, improvisation, listening and responding.

*   In relation to their own professional development, community musicians tend to use the term 'training' instead of 'education' (which is more commonly used in the routes to teaching described in the previous sections).

*   Although situated within the general community, community musicians won't be delivering formal music lessons as part of music as unit of study at schools, colleges and other statutory organisations. However, they may work in partnership with these institutions to deliver after school music programmes and classes that might be one-off or sustained across a period of time.

Widespread resistance from community musicians in relation to professionalisation of the field resulted in no regulatory pedagogical requirements being required to work as a community musician. This resistance stems from one of the main premises in community music – that of access – and that in the event of regulatory requirements imposition, access, engagement and musical participation may be prevented (Higgins, 2012). Nonetheless, this has not prevented high quality training from being developed and delivered in a variety of settings: at both the community level but also at Higher Education institutions, in the UK and many other parts of the world.[8]

Although community music encompasses a diverse range of different types of activities and approaches, for the purposes of this book I will only focus on activities which can be said to have an educational and/or facilitation element with children and young people. The insights provided are applicable to formal, non-formal and informal contexts, both within and beyond school-based environments.

Principles and Approaches

Broadly speaking, community musicians' objectives can be classified as educational, community development, personal growth, social, therapeutic or celebratory (Creech, 2010) and are shaped by a variety of different factors which Veblen and Waldron (2012) categorised into:

*   The kinds of music and active music making;
*   The participants;

- The intentions and aspirations of those involved;

- The teaching/learning practices;

- Interplay between informal and formal social/educational/cultural contexts.

There will be contexts where a didactic approach may be needed, such as when leading large ensembles (e.g., large orchestra, choir or band). When working with large ensembles, although the objectives may still be highly inclusive and aimed at promoting community participation, the ethos of the group may be such that (although not always) it prioritises high-quality musical performance and in this way is highly focused on the 'end product' as it were rather than on children and young people's experiences of engagement and participation. Community musicians working in contexts of this nature, tend to enact a 'director' role, whereby the work is highly structured, guided and supervised by the leader/director and aimed at developing music performance skills. They will, however, also assume that such development will contribute to participants' personal growth.

In the context described earlier, it is not unusual for a child or young person interested in joining a choir to be required to sing individually for the choir director before being allowed to join the group, or to be asked to do a short performance of a piece before the go-ahead is given to join a local orchestra or band. In such instances, community music principles such as inclusion and hospitality (discussed in the next sections) may at times be at odds with conditions for participation. It is important that community musicians working in these types of contexts consider what opportunities they are providing for children and young people to express themselves musically and creatively, and what opportunities children and young people are being given to develop agency but also shape the work being developed.

Where the objectives allow for a prioritisation of participants' experiences and contributions, facilitation is a highly suitable approach as it creates opportunities for establishing a partnership with and between children and young people for the development of shared objectives and shared achievements (Higgins, 2012). Through facilitation dialogue is encouraged among children and/or young people with differing perspectives, thereby promoting exploration of a range of diverse assumptions and options. As an approach, facilitation encourages individual responsibility for contribution at all levels including individually and towards the group, musically and in terms of organisation and logistics needed for the group. Facilitation aligns effectively with the latest principles on inclusion, participation, hospitality and ethics of care (more on this later). These have been the subject of a good amount of work by contemporary authors and specialists in community music. Links for interesting and innovative initiatives on Community Music with children and young people can be found in CW Resource 5 which I encourage you to access in order to acquaint yourself with the latest and innovative developments in community music-based work with children and young people across the globe.

In community settings people learn through the interactions and relations they establish with each other, and music is based in the context of the particular community setting. The social aspect is an important component, and although music is an important aspect in the social activity in and of itself, the intended benefits achieved through the use of music and social interactions (such as healing, networking, self-expression and celebration of cultural heritage) are equally important. In some situations, they can actually be even more important than the music itself (Veblen & Waldron, 2012). Indeed, participation in music making with others has been shown to boost intracommunity[9] and intercommunity[10] networking, create friendship making opportunities and contribute to mental and social stimulation, with significant benefits in terms of health at all levels (Jones & Langston, 2012).

Musical participation, therefore, is regarded as a conjoint activity where those engaged in it (of all ages and backgrounds) do so for the 'goods' (values, benefits) it provides (Elliott, 2012). Therefore, community musicians need to have deep understandings on community interaction and dynamics and of ways facilitating the generation of 'goods' through participation, and thus be able to promote the personal growth of participants. It is important to be aware that the 'community' spoken of in community music is not about achieving consensus. Instead, it is about establishing an inclusive environment and a participatory ethos where everyone is welcome. Community musicians stimulate active participation and provide a platform where children, young people and adults can express themselves. This reflects the notion that community is a 'place' where ideas are communicated, expressed and negotiated, but where there might also be some struggle and unity (Higgins, 2012).

Concerning the 'good' that can be achieved through music participation, researchers working with an at-risk youth group in a project entitled "Positive Youth Development" (Catalano et al., 2004) discovered a number of benefits achieved through musical participation, including increased: positive bonding with others; resilience; self-determination and self-efficacy.

Inclusion, Hospitality and Ethics of Care

The work of community musicians is embedded in the concept of hospitality, defined as an unconditional welcome without reservations towards potential musical participants (2012). This implies a need to be flexible and adaptable and to have the ability to mediate and negotiate should a conflict or unforeseen circumstances arise (e.g., where less or more participants are attending than initially expected, disagreement or altercation between participants etc.). In considering community interactions and dynamics, the addition of new members keeps a sense of fluidity as the group continuously re-invents itself. Community musicians therefore need time to understand how a specific community group defines itself, and for a newly created group, time will be needed to allow such definitions to take shape.

Cohen et al. (2012) state that three aspects of Noddings (1984) relational ethics theory can be brought to bear on community music. They are:

- The emphasis on the need for understanding the other person's reality, no matter how difficult it may be. In a group setting, acquiring such understanding for each participant may be challenging. However, it is possible to achieve varying degrees of success with regard to such understandings with different participants and at different points in time.

- That the process of understanding the other person's reality is such that the behaviour of the community musician/facilitator/teacher is determined by the needs of the participant. Ideally, community musicians foster an environment where each learner cares for the broader musical goals of the group and in the process realises others' needs in the process of music making. Additionally, community musicians and teachers in general have a duty to understand the learners' needs, including musical backgrounds and preferences, cognitive and affective abilities, and where they are on the at-risk continuum, if the group is considered as an at-risk group.

- That the process is embedded in caring, from aesthetical, natural and ethical perspectives. *Aesthetical* care is the care for ideas or things, which should always be based on caring for the people performing and/or bringing about the ideas or things, more than caring for the ideas or things in and of themselves. *Natural* caring is about what is felt as being naturally appropriate in our dealings with others in relation to their needs and circumstances. For example, in a case where a child who might be crying, a natural inclination would be to reassure the child and support him/her in or order to make them feel safe. Ethical caring is about promoting social bonds and skills that allow for socialisation to take place in effective ways.

These principles provide a solid framework for enacting a much needed ethics of care, not only in community music environments, but indeed in all other contexts of music teaching and learning.

Facilitation and Workshops

Regardless of the fact that ideas surrounding community music have many different orientations, facilitation and workshops have been emphasised by community musicians as key mechanisms through which they enact their work. As an approach, facilitation as used in community music is a process which uses music as means for developing participation, nurturing participants' ability to work collaboratively, and builds their confidence through conversation, negotiation and play. Workshops, in the educational literature, are often associated with creativity development and group work. They constitute a space for experimentation adopted by community musicians due to their settings being conducive to the creation of democratic spaces favourable for creative music making, as viewed from the perspective of being generative spaces for new ideas from each participant and also as a group (Higgins, 2012). A facilitator can be described as a self-reflective individual, focused upon the process of facilitating/assisting groups of people to achieve their goals together by using their human skills, knowledge and experiences (Hogan, 2002). As Higgins (2012) states, community music facilitators need to be able to find a comfortable balance between:

• Being prepared and able to lead.

• Being prepared and able to hold back, thus enabling the group or individuals to discover the journey of musical invention for themselves.

Being a facilitator requires the flexibility to move in and out of roles as per the needs of the group or situation, and having trust in the creative ability of others, while also recognising and welcoming the contribution of participants. Facilitators give control to the group and need to be ready to experience unpredictable outcomes. This way music becomes a personal invention for the participants, owned by and meaningful to them, and with the potential to generate an experience that can shape, create and have an impact upon identity formation (Higgins, 2012, p. 148). Such work, necessarily needs to take place in a safe space where children and young people feel welcomed, respected and accepted as they are.

As in other contexts of music education, planning (be it for a new community music project/initiative, or for a facilitation session) needs to be informed by knowledge of the children and young people participating. Who are they? What age ranges are there? What are their backgrounds? What kinds of music and active music making do they identify with? What are their ranges of musical abilities and preferred ways for musical expression? What are their motivations, intentions and aspirations in joining the group? What is the context in which the work is to be developed (i.e., purposes, aims, teaching and learning practices where it is embedded) and what will be the interplay between formal, informational, cultural and educational contexts? Facilitators should aim for challenges which are sufficiently demanding to stimulate all concerned, but should also ensure that they don't set the bar too high with regard to what children and young people cannot realistically do or hope to achieve.

The interaction between facilitator and each child or young people, be it on a one-to-one basis or in a group environment, is of paramount importance in promoting and enabling functional and successful learning. Such interaction needs to be cemented in the notions of hospitality and ethics of care, side-by-side with trust, respect and responsibility. Higgins (2012) defines trust and respect as intertwined and inseparable ideas that work when participants, or facilitators, are able to rely upon the actions and decisions of one another. In order to be developed successfully, it requires that the relationship be based on respect and listening and where a positive feeling of esteem is developed among all involved.

Peer teaching, peer learning and peer mentoring where more advanced or experienced members of the group work with smaller groups or in dyads to support the learning of group members, is another helpful key strategy that should be promoted as much as possible. By doing so, children and young people have opportunities to learn to work together while developing team work, leadership and negotiation skills which are transposable to all walks of life and also learn to value diversity in society.

Specific contexts of community music require specific attributes from facilitators. For instance, when working with early years, it is imperative to know developmental expectations for the children ages and how to devise opportunities for musical experimentation for this particular age group. This is vital since the type of experimentation offered for this particular age group will be quite different to that offered to, say, a group of 15 year olds. In addition, perhaps the group of children may be from an at-risk group, in which case knowing the specifics will allow for the design of an appropriate type of intervention. It is also essential to plan for continuously reviewing and evaluating the intervention to ascertain if children and young people are benefiting from it, or if a change of approach is needed. Since community musicians work in a variety of different contexts, and particularly in the case of work with children and young people, please read the specific parts of this book where there are relevant aspects to the contexts where you work *apart from* this specific section on community music. These varying contexts can include learners from early years; children in formal education; children with learning disabilities; migrants; at-risk children; and more general 'youth'.

It is also relevant that you become acquainted with professional associations and professional bodies for community music in your own national and international context, as well as national and local guidelines with regard to providing community music in the contexts where you operate. In the absence of specific guidelines, consider how the aspects mentioned earlier may relate to your context, and which specific elements may need to be added and considered at a deeper level.

The role of community musicians is dually creative. On the one hand, there is the element of facilitating participants self-expressing and nurturing their creativity. On the other hand, there is the need to continuously consider what else you can offer to the community in general, or to certain groups in the community, and which could bring them 'goods' achieved through music and be meaningful to them. This requires awareness of society as a whole and an ability to think outside of the box. In this way, you can create new innovative avenues where music can help, heal, support, develop and promote a wide variety of persons and good causes. Obviously, you must also consider the 'how?' part of how this would be achieved in your specific context. Doing so requires being an active member of society, in conjunction with development of effective leadership and facilitation skills. In what follows are a few pointers that you may wish to consider in your community music work:

- If working in a context where a didactic approach is needed, **allow children and young people to have a say on the repertoire selected**, and consider developing activities which instigate musical creativity and self-expression. Promote active rather than passive participation. The following questions may help with conceptualising an approach that includes a mixture of didactic versus facilitative approaches being used at planned times of the session. These can be used to promote creativity and agency. Ask yourself: what opportunities can I create for children and young people to honestly let me know about their experience as members of this community? What opportunities can I give them to shape the repertoire we use, and the approach I take? What opportunities for peer learning can be created (maybe working in smaller groups)? How can I act on children's and young people's feedback and provide (partially or totally) what they feel they need and what they would like to have?

- As a community facilitator working with early years, children and young people it is important to **have a working knowledge of other dimensions of the musical life of participants**. For example, if working with a group of young children, to know what musical experiences they are offered at school, what is in the music curriculum they are exposed to, and how this connects, complements or differs from the provision you facilitate?

- It is important to **realise, recognise and make the most of the fact that the roles of music educators and community musicians are intertwined.** "Music educators serve community music functions and community music facilitators serve music education functions" (Jones & Langston, 2012, p. 120). From this perspective, seek to engage in partnerships with music teachers and educators working in both formal and informal music education settings while aiming to provide a variety of rich musical experiences to children, both in terms of community and civic involvement. The lessons from this can then be carried over into their adulthood, and you will thereby be promoting a lifelong interest in musical engagement and participation.

- **Create longer-term projects and use participant's feedback to improve the project delivery and outcomes at various stages of implementation.** Creech (2010) points out that one of the problems with many community music projects relates to the fact that many projects are offered on a short-term basis, which makes it difficult to evaluate and document their impact. Obviously, this frequently relates to an absence of funding. However, when conceptualising a project, carefully consider the amount of time required for the intervention to achieve its main objectives and the various levels of benefits that can be achieved at different stages of the project, so that funders can **clearly see** a strategy running through the project in terms of its fruitful continuation. With regard to funding proposals, a key element for success is being able to document the type and nature of impact of the project for those involved, in conjunction with a clear alignment of the project's activities with funders' specific priorities. Therefore, collecting feedback from participants at different points in the project, and in a number of different ways (both qualitative and quantitative), is instrumental both for documenting the project's impact but also for achieving ongoing funding.

Reflective Questions

1. After reading the section of the chapter specifically focused on your teaching context, are there any new elements that might be beneficial to include in your lesson plan and delivery, with a view of supporting learners developing personal and musical competencies? If so, outline them.				
• You might find it useful to make two separate lists. One of the elements you found in the specific section of the Chapter that you already use, and the second on new elements you wish to include. • Reflect on the new elements you wish to include (if any) and consider how you will practically start doing so.	Aligned with CME, Level 4 Unit (U) or Area of Study (AOS) and Assessment Criteria number of ABRSM (2014) and TCL (2013, 2019)			
	ABRSM		TCL (2013)	
	U2:	2.3	U2:	All the learning outcomes included in learning outcome 3
			TCL (2019)	
			AOS3:	All the learning outcomes included in learning outcome 2
2. After reading the contents of this chapter, outline strategies you might use to promote independent learning, agency, independent learning, and creativity.				
• Consider not only sections on your specific work contexts, but also what is suggested for other contexts and whether some approaches may be transferable.				
	ABRSM		TCL (2013)	
	U2:	2.3	U2:	All the learning outcomes included in learning outcome 3
			TCL (2019)	
			AOS3:	All the learning outcomes included in learning outcome 2

3. When reading the content on other music teaching contexts that you have not taught in previously or recently, did you find any elements that would perhaps be beneficial to try out and bring into your current teaching context(s)?	
• Think as widely as possible and consider the pros and cons of each element. • If the pros outweigh the cons how and when do you plan to implement these new elements? • How will you evaluate the introduction and effectiveness of these new elements? • How will you share your innovative approaches with your community of practice?	

Notes

1. Dalcroze (born 1865–1950) emphasised the body as the primary source of knowing in a world still heavily influenced by a long philosophical tradition of consciousness as the source of knowledge (e.g., Descartes). Tone and rhythm, the essential ingredients of the Dalcrozian teaching and learning method (entitled 'Eurhythmics'), are to be learned through bodily movement in 'whole gesture songs' – intended to train the body to simultaneously internalise and respond to music (Jaques-Dalcroze, 1921). For more, see: Jaques-Dalcroze, Emile. *Rhythm, Music & Education*. London & Whitstable: The Riverside Press Ltd., 1967. (First published 1921) and Crosby, A. (2008). Dalcroze's Eurthymic techniques for choral rehearsal: moving to "O Magnum Mysterium." *Choral Journal*, *48*(11), 30–41.
2. Orff (Born 1895–1982): Carl Orff's Schulwerk pedagogy consists of fundamental guiding principles for teachers with no systematic stepwise procedure to be followed. The basic pillars of the approach are to teach music and movement 'by doing', through which the percussive rhythm is considered as a basic and natural form of human expression. The driving idea behind Orff's work was to provide opportunities for children to experience art, music and movement in the Güntherschule in Munich, an educational centre for music, gymnastics, dance and rhythmic movement. The approach incorporates familiar, easily grasped tunes and a rather improvisational approach. Orff's work was deeply influenced by Dalcroze's method. For more, see Orff, C., & Keetman, G.(1950) Musik für Kinder I. Mainz: Schott.
3. Suzuki: The Suzuki method is an internationally known music curriculum and teaching philosophy dating from the mid-twentieth century, created by Japanese violinist and pedagogue Shinichi Suzuki (1898–1998). The method aims to create an environment for learning music which parallels the linguistic environment of

acquiring a native language. The central belief of Suzuki, based on his language acquisition theories, is that all people can (and will) learn from their environment. The essential components of his method spring from the desire to create the 'right environment' for learning music (he believed that this positive environment would also help to foster excellent character in every student).

4. In many parts of the world (including the UK), primary school teachers are expected to teach all subjects of the primary school curriculum, including music, and for this reason, they are referred to as generalist teachers.

5. Specialist music teachers are those who are trained to teach music specifically.

6. Blended learning involves a combination of methods which include face-to-face teaching and online lessons.

7. Didactic approach refers to a manner of instruction in which information is transmitted directly from the teacher to the student. It can be said to be a teacher-led and teacher-centered approach, as the teacher fully selects the learning materials and controls how learning, learners' responses, classroom interactions and assessment takes place.

8. The UK has been a prolific environment for training for community musicians, particularly from 1994 onwards with training delivered by: 1) local providers such as Youth Music, Sound it Out, Music Leader, Community Music Wales and others; 2) Conservatoires such as Royal College of Music, Birmingham Conservatory, Leeds College of Music, which have also expanded their offering to include programmes in community music at postgraduate level; 3) universities such as the University of Edinburgh and University of York have also followed suit. Outside the UK, there are various training opportunities for community musicians, including the Irish World Academy of Music and Dance; the Universities of Washington, New York and Boston, in the US; in Brazil, run by several non-governmental organisations; at the University of Witwatersrand in Johannesburg; and in Japan, the Creating Music Culture Foundations organisation delivers a variety of lifelong learning programmes deeply connected to facilitation of community music (Higgins, 2012).

9. Intracommunity: within a single community.

10. Intercommunity: between communities.

Further Reading

Burnard, P., & Murphy, R. (Eds.) (2017). *Teaching music creatively* (Learning to teach in the primary school series). Routledge.

Cohen, M. L., Silber, L. H., Sangiorgio, A., & Iadeluca, V. (2012). At-risk youth: Music-making as a means to promote positive relationships. In G. E. McPherson & G. F. Welch (Eds.), *The Oxford handbook of music education* (Vol. 2, pp. 184–202). Oxford University Press.

Creech, A., & Gaunt, H. (2012). The changing face of individual instrumental tuition: Value, purpose and potential. In G. E. McPherson & G. F. Welch (Eds.), *The Oxford handbook of music education* (pp. 694–711). Oxford University Press.

Gazard, P. (2010). *You can teach primary music*. Rhinegold Education.

Harris, P. (2012). *The virtuoso teacher: The inspirational guide for instrumental and singing teachers*. Faber Music.

Higgins, L. (2012). *Community music in theory and in practice*. Oxford University Press.

King, A., Prior, H., & Waddington-Jones, C. (2019). Exploring teachers' and pupils' behaviour in online and face-to-face instrumental lessons. *Music Education Research, 21*(2), 197–209. https://doi.org/10.1080/14613808.2019.1585791

Miendlarzewska, E. A., & Trost, W. J. (2014). How musical training affects cognitive development: Rhythm, reward and other modulating variables. *Frontiers in Neuroscience, 7.* https://doi.org/10.3389/fnins.2013.00279

Odena, O. (2010). Practitioners' views on cross-community music education projects in Northern Ireland: Alienation, socio-economic factors and educational potential. *British Educational Research Journal, 36*(1), 83–105. https://doi.org/10.1080/01411920902878909

Odena, O. (2012). Creativity in the secondary music classroom. In G. E. McPherson & G. F. Welch (Eds.), *The Oxford handbook of music education* (pp. 512–528). Oxford University Press.

Odena, O., & Welch, G. F. (2007). The influence of teachers' backgrounds on their perceptions of musical creativity: A qualitative study with secondary school music teachers. *Research Studies in Music Education, 28*(1), 71–81. https://doi.org/10.1177/1321103X070280010206

Odena, O., & Welch, G. F. (2009). A generative model of teachers' thinking on musical creativity. *Psychology of Music, 37*(4), 416–442. https://doi.org/10.1177/0305735608100374

Office for Standards in Education (Ofsted) (2012). *Music in schools: Wider still, and wider, Quality and inequality in music education 2008–2011.* Ofsted.

Phelan, H. (2012). Sonic hospitality: Migration, community, and music. In G. E. McPherson & G. F. Welch (Eds.), *The Oxford handbook of music education* (Vol. 2, pp. 168–184). Oxford University Press.

Philpott, C., & Wright, R. (2012). Teaching, learning, and curriculum content. In G. E. McPherson & G. F. Welch (Eds.), *The Oxford handbook of music education* (Vol. 1, pp. 440–459). Oxford University Press.

Simones, L. L. (2019). Understanding the meaningfulness of vocal and instrumental music teachers' hand gestures through the teacher behavior and gesture framework. *Frontiers in Education, 4.* https://doi.org/10.3389/feduc.2019.00141

Simones, L. L., Rodger, M., & Schroeder, F. (2015). Communicating musical knowledge through gesture: Piano teachers' gestural behaviours across different levels of student proficiency. *Psychology of Music, 43*(5). https://doi.org/10.1177/0305735614535830

Veblen, K. K., & Waldron, J. L. (2012). Fast forward: Emerging trends in community music. In G. E. McPherson & G. F. Welch (Eds.), *The Oxford handbook of music education* (Vol. 2, pp. 202–220). Oxford University Press.

Young, S. (2018). *Critical new perspectives in early childhood music: Young children engaging and learning through music.* Routledge.

References

Adachi, M. (1994). The role of the adult in the child's early musical socialization: A Vygotskian perspective. *The Quarterly, 5*(3), 26–35.

Associated Board of the Royal Schools of Music (ABRSM) (2014). *Level 4 certificate for music educators: Assessment framework.* ABRSM.

Barrett, M. (2005). Musical communication and children's communities of musical practice. In D. Miell, R. MacDonald, & D. J. Hargreaves (Eds.), *Musical communication* (pp. 261–280). Oxford University Press.

Burke, N. (2018). *Musical development in the early years* (part of the legacy of the Tri-Music Together project). The British Association for Early Childhood Education. https://network.youthmusic.org.uk/musical-development-matters

Burnard, P., & Murphy, R. (2017). Introduction. In P. A. Burnard & R. Murphy (Eds.), *Teaching music creatively* (pp. XVIII–XXI). Routledge.

Campbell, P. (2006). Global practices. In G. E. McPherson (Ed.), *The child as musician: A handbook of musical development* (pp. 415–437). Oxford University Press.

Carlin, K. (1997). *Piano pedagogue perception of teaching effectiveness in the preadolescent elementary level applied piano lesson as a function of teacher behavior* [Unpublished doctoral dissertation, Indiana University, Bloomington].

Catalano, R. F., Berglund, M. L., Ryan, J. A. M., Lonczak, H. S., & Hawkins, J. D. (2004). Positive youth development in the United States: Research findings on evaluations of positive youth development programs. *The ANNALS of the American Academy of Political and Social Science, 591*(1), 98–124. https://doi.org/10.1177/0002716203260102

Cohen, M. L., Silber, L. H., Sangiorgio, A., & Iadeluca, V. (2012). At-risk youth: Music-making as a means to promote positive relationships. In G. E. McPherson & G. F. Welch (Eds.), *The Oxford handbook of music education* (Vol. 2, pp. 184–202). Oxford University Press. https://doi.org/10.1093/oxfordhb/9780199928019.013.0013

Creech, A. (2009). Teacher-parent-pupil trios: A typology of interpersonal interaction in the context of learning a musical instrument. *Musicae Scientiae, XIII*(2), 163–182.

Creech, A. (2010). The role of music leaders and community musicians. In S. Hallam & A. Creech (Eds.), *Music education in the 21st century in the United Kingdom: Achievements, analysis and aspirations* (pp. 314–328). Institute of Education, University of London.

Creech, A., & Ellison, J. (2010). Music in the early years. In Susan Hallam & A. Creech (Eds.), *Music education in the 21st century in the United Kingdom: Achievements, analysis and aspirations* (pp. 194–210). Institute of Education, University of London, Bedford Way Papers.

Creech, A., & Gaunt, H. (2012). The changing face of individual instrumental tuition: Value, purpose and potential. In G. E. McPherson & G. F. Welch (Eds.), *The Oxford handbook of music education* (pp. 694–711). Oxford University Press.

Dammers, R. J. (2009). Utilizing internet-based video conferencing for instrumental music lessons. *Update: Applications of Research in Music Education, 28*(1), 17–24. https://doi.org/10.1177/8755123309344159

Department for Education and Skills (DfES) (2006). *Music manifesto report No. 2: Making every child's music matter.* DfES.

Elliott, D. J. (2012). Commentary: Music in the community. In G. E. McPherson & G. F. Welch (Eds.), *The Oxford handbook of music education* (pp. 99–103). Oxford University Press.

Farrell, G. (2001). India. In D. J. Hargreaves & A. C. North (Eds.), *Musical development and learning: The international perspective* (pp. 56–72). Continuum.

Gaunt, H. (2010). One-to-one tuition in a conservatoire: The perceptions of instrumental and vocal students. *Psychology of Music, 38*(2), 178–208. https://doi.org/10.1177/0305735609339467

Green, L. (2001). *How popular musicians learn.* Ashgate.

Hall, C. (2005). Gender and boys' singing in early childhood. *British Journal of Music Education, 22*(1), 5–20. https://doi.org/10.1017/S0265051704005960

Hallam, S. (1998). *Instrumental teaching.* Heinemann.

Hallam, S. (2006). *Music psychology in education.* Institute of Education.

Harris, P. (2012). *The virtuoso teacher: The inspirational guide for instrumental and singing teachers.* Faber Music.

Hewitt, M. P. (2002). Self-evaluation tendencies of junior high instrumentalists. *Journal of Research in Music Education, 50*(3), 215. https://doi.org/10.2307/3345799

Higgins, L., & Bartleet, B.-L. (2012). The community music facilitator and school music education. In G. E. McPherson & G. F. Welch (Eds.), *The Oxford handbook of music education* (pp. 494–511). Oxford University Press. https://doi.org/10.1093/oxfordhb/9780199730810.013.0030

Hogan, C. (2002). *Understanding facilitation: Theory and principles.* Kogan Page.

Jaques-Dalcroze, E. (1921). Rhythm, music and education. *Journal of Education, 94*(12), 319–319. https://doi.org/10.1177/002205742109401204

Jones, P. M., & Langston, T. W. (2012). Community music and social capital. In G. E. McPherson & G. F. Welch (Eds.), *The Oxford handbook of music education* (Vol. 2, pp. 119–137). Oxford University Press. https://doi.org/10.1093/oxfordhb/9780199928019.013.0009

Kennell, R. (2002). Systematic research in studio instruction in music. In R. Colwell & C. Richardson (Eds.), *The new handbook of research on music teaching and learning* (pp. 243–256). Oxford University Press.

King, A., Prior, H., & Waddington-Jones, C. (2019). Exploring teachers' and pupils' behaviour in online and face-to-face instrumental lessons. *Music Education Research, 21*(2), 197–209. https://doi.org/10.1080/14613808.2019.1585791

Kodály, Z. (1965). *Let us sing correctly.* Boosey & Hawkes.

McNeill, D. (1992). *Hand and mind.* The University of Chicago Press.

McNeill, D. (2005). *Gesture and thought.* The University of Chicago Press.

McPherson, G. E., Davidson, J. W., & Faulkner, R. (2012). *Music in our lives: Rethinking musical ability, development and identity.* Oxford University Press.

Noddings, N. (1984). *Caring: A feminine approach to ethics and moral education.* University of California Press.

Odena, O. (2012). Creativity in the secondary music classroom. In G. E. McPherson & G. F. Welch (Eds.), *The Oxford handbook of music education* (pp. 512–528). Oxford University Press.

Odena, O., & Welch, G. F. (2007). The influence of teachers' backgrounds on their perceptions of musical creativity: A qualitative study with secondary school music teachers. *Research Studies in Music Education, 28*(1), 71–81. https://doi.org/10.1177/1321103X070280010206

Office for Standards in Education (Ofsted) (2009). *Making more of music: An evaluation of music in schools 2005–2009* (No.080235). Ofsted.

Office for Standards in Education (Ofsted) (2012). *Music in schools: Wider still, and wider, Quality and inequality in music education 2008–2011.* Ofsted.

Orff, C., & Keetman, G. (1950). *Musik für Kinder I.* Schott.

Philpott, C., & Wright, R. (2012). Teaching, learning, and curriculum content. In G. E. McPherson & G. F. Welch (Eds.), *The Oxford handbook of music education* (Vol. 1, pp. 440–459). Oxford University Press. https://doi.org/10.1093/oxfordhb/9780199730810.013.0027_update_001

Pratt, D., & Johnson, J. (1998). The apprenticeship perspective: Modelling ways of being. In D. Pratt (Ed.), *Five perspectives on teaching in adult and higher education.* Krieger Publishing Company.

Qualification and Curriculum Authority (QCA) (2005). *Music: 2004–2005 annual report on curriculum and assessment.* QCA.

Rostvall, A. L., & West, T. (2003). Analysis of interaction and learning in instrumental teaching. *Music Education Research, 5*(3), 213–226.

Savage, J. (2012). Tom's story: Developing music education with technology. *Journal of Music, Technology and Education*, *4*(2), 217–226. https://doi.org/10.1386/jmte.4.2-3.217_1

Simones, L. L. (2019). A framework for studying teachers' hand gestures in instrumental and vocal music contexts. *Musicae Scientiae*, *23*(2), 231–249. https://doi.org/10.1177/1029864917743089

Simones, L. L., Rodger, M., & Schroeder, F. (2015). Communicating musical knowledge through gesture: Piano teachers' gestural behaviours across different levels of student proficiency. *Psychology of Music*, *43*(5), 723–735. https://doi.org/10.1177/0305735614535830

Simones, L. L., Schroeder, F., & Rodger, M. (2015). Categorizations of physical gesture in piano teaching: A preliminary enquiry. *Psychology of Music*, *43*(1), 103–121. https://doi.org/10.1177/0305735613498918

Suzuki, Shin'ichi (1983). *Nurtured by love: The classic approach to talent education* (W. Suzuki, Trans.). Suzuki Method International, Summy-Birchard Inc.

Trinity College London (TCL) (2013). *TCL level 4 certificate for music educators: Specifications*. TCL.

Trinity College London (TCL) (2019). *TCL level 4 certificate for music educators, areas of study*. TCL.

Temmerman, N. (2005). Children's participation in music: Connecting the cultural contexts – an Australian perspective. *British Journal of Music Education*, *22*(2), 113–123. https://doi.org/10.1017/S0265051705006091

Trehub, S. E. (2006). Infants as musical connoisseurs. In G. E. McPherson (Ed.), *The child as musician* (pp. 33–50). Oxford University Press. https://doi.org/10.1093/acprof:oso/9780198530329.003.0002

Veblen, K. K., & Waldron, J. L. (2012). Fast forward: Emerging trends in community music. In G. E. McPherson & G. F. Welch (Eds.), *The Oxford handbook of music education* (Vol. 2, pp. 202–220). Oxford University Press. https://doi.org/10.1093/oxfordhb/9780199928019.013.0014

Welch, G. F. (2005). We are musical. *International Journal of Music Education*, *23*(2), 117–120. https://doi.org/10.1177/0255761405052404

Young, S. (2005). Musical communication between adults and young children. In D. Miell, R. McDonald, & D. Hargreaves (Eds.), *Musical communication* (pp. 281–299). Oxford University Press.

Young, S. (2018). *Critical new perspectives in early childhood music: Young children engaging and learning through music*. Routledge.

Zhukov, K. (2004). *Teaching styles and student behaviour in instrumental music lessons in Australian Conservatoriums* [Unpublished doctoral dissertation, University of New South Wales, Sydney, Australia].

7 Assessing Music Learning

To Guide Your Reading

- How can we assess musical attainment in order to evaluate the effectiveness of teaching strategies and support further musical learning?

- What assessment methods and tools can be used to support and evidence young people's musical progress and attainment in relation to learning objectives and personal goals?

- How can we support and encourage young people in evaluating their own music making and that of their peers?

- What is the best way to gather assessment information and feedback from children and young people to evaluate our own planning and teaching and to inform future planning and teaching?

Introduction

In general, assessment is geared towards understanding the ability of learners to learn. As such, it also provides important clues regarding the teacher who is teaching. Specifically, it attempts to systematically understand where learners are in their learning journeys at specific points in time, while also generating valuable information on where exactly learning development is required. For these reasons, assessment is intimately tied up with various sets of learning outcomes, namely with what the learner is expected to know and be able to do as a result of engaging in learning. With this in mind, this chapter provides an overview of the main purposes of assessment in music education, while considering what should be assessed. The terms *formative* and *summative* assessment are defined, and best practice regarding the design and conducting of these different types of assessment is also considered. The chapter concludes with an outline of some methods and tools that music teachers might want to consider for assessing and recording learners' understanding, participation level and skill development in music learning.

The Purposes of Assessment

Colwell and Hewitt (2014) highlight various ways in which assessment helps improving teaching and learning:

- It helps to ensure that learning content and tasks provided by teachers match the needs of learners, taking into account their growing level of understanding and expertise, as well as their overall learning progress.

- It helps to identify gaps or weaknesses in learning but also specific help that a child may require in music. In this way, it acquires a diagnostical function.

- Assessment can also be used to confirm a teacher's belief that a specific learner has exceptional musical ability which should therefore be carefully nurtured. Verification can be done by seeking a colleague's opinion, or by administering a specific test or standardised test(s) of musical aptitude.

- **Formative assessment**, defined as continuous reflection on day-to-day learning and teaching, provides the teacher with insights on what support learners require in order to optimise their learning. It is effective in terms of meeting short- and long-term learning goals and objectives.

- **Summative assessment**, used at predetermined intervals, for example as at the end of a learning unit. This type of assessment is particularly helpful for recording and reporting progress in systematic ways to parents and other fellow teachers or professionals. It provides insights into what learners have achieved thus far in their music education.

- Assessment can also assume a planning and evaluative role when the level of effectiveness of teaching and assessment methods are reviewed by the teacher, and this information results in decisions being made about how teaching and learning should proceed.

As a process, assessment requires that important actions be taken to ensure that it is designed to accurately reflect typical musical processes and learning activities used in the lessons. It must also carefully consider *what* should be assessed and *how*. Therefore, setting out the *type* of assessment methods used and establishing *how* the information obtained is going to be interpreted is crucial to ensuring that the process is fair, valid and reliable. Validity denotes the extent to which assessment accurately measures what it is intended to measure. Reliability is focused on the degree to which an assessment tool produces consistent results – if, for example, administered twice on subsequent occasions to the same learner, or if the learner's work is assessed by two different assessors. To complete this process of assessment, two further relevant steps must be included: consideration of how results will be communicated to children and parents; and planning for how results will be used proactively to promote further learning.

Decisions and approaches on the previous elements of assessment will depend on a variety of different factors, which include country specific regulations as well as institutionalised approaches to assessment. These can include, but are not limited to the type and nature of the teaching and learning context, particularly in relation to the degree of formality involved (formal, informal, non-formal); cultural perceptions regarding the place of music within educational systems; the value and functions of music in everyday life; and a wide variety of music learning experiences in various traditions of music teaching and learning across the world, each requiring specific assessment practices. On top of this, assessment terminology and related practices can also assume different meanings and interpretations in different parts of the world.

What Should be Assessed?

In music education, it is difficult to state exactly what should be assessed as each context has its own specificities. Therefore, assessment also needs to focus on different aspects as learners progress from one level to the next. However, generally speaking, in all music education settings the development of understanding of the interrelated musical elements (i.e., pulse, duration, tempo, pitch, dynamics, structure, timbre, texture and style) should form an integral aspect of assessment.

Let us consider some examples of aspects included in one way or another in music curricula all over the world, albeit with sometimes different terminologies. The terms used here (later in italics) are used, for instance, in the Northern Irish, Irish and Portuguese music curricula. When assessing *Listening and Responding to Music*, assessment should address the range of responses that learners make to music. These can include the use of words; vocal sounds; the use of small or large movements; and other means of emotional and self-musical expression. However, these also need to be considered alongside interpretation of musical elements, and openness, sensitivity and emotional reactions towards a variety of musical styles and genres from different historical periods, as well as to music from different cultures.

When assessing *Composing*, any assessment should consider how the learner demonstrates new musical ideas through improvisation, composition and by compiling and arranging sounds. This can be as an individual or via collaborative work with others. We should look for ways involving imagination, risk-taking and originality. The level of control of musical elements and musical material should also be taken into account: side-by-side comparative reflection up to the completed product of composition; the use of standardised and non-standard notation; and knowledge of electronic media to record ideas, as well as the learners' abilities to use these effectively in their evaluation of the compositional process.

Assessment of musical *Performance*, involving singing and/or playing instruments, should consider various aspects: accuracy; technique; interpretation; communication; and expression. At the early levels of learning, the following aspects should also be considered: commitment; sense of pulse; imitation of rhythms; and the singing or playing of melodies. As the learner's confidence begins to grow, dynamics and phrasing will inject meaning and expression into the child's singing and playing. In particular, when working with early years, we must also consider a child's emerging understanding of invented or standard musical notation. Assessment of instrumental music skills typically occurs within/through instrumental music lessons; rehearsals; concerts; festivals; music competitions; and by using music examination boards which provide accredited pathways for progression and professionalisation in instrumental music performance (e.g., ABRSM, TCL and LCM).

Instrumental and vocal music assessment still tends to be highly focused upon accurate pitch and rhythm production; production of good tone; the ability to produce varied set and appropriate use of dynamics; and the ability to change tone quality to suit the piece of music and agility. Even so, there is a need to consider musicianship as a broader concept, wherein creativity, improvisation and stronger development of aural skills should also be an integral part of the assessment process (McPherson, 2005). This is especially pertinent today since a noticeable decline in improvisational abilities and aural skills development has been witnessed over the past few decades in school-aged children. Such a decline can be attributed to the fact that teachers might not be focusing upon these elements as much as they should, simply because they are too rigidly focused upon what the learners are actually going to be assessed on in music performance exams to the detriment of a more nuanced development of overall musicianship.

In terms of assessing informal music learning and community music, considering that the main role of teachers in these contexts primarily revolves around helping learners to conceptualise their goals and supporting learners in achieving them (Fautley & Colwell, 2012), it would appear that the most appropriate form of assessment in these contexts is formative assessment.

Formative Assessment and Feedback

In music education, formative assessment constitutes an integral element of the day-to-day work undertaken in the classroom. This is true both with regard to the integral processes of music making as well as learning about music more broadly. This type of assessment involves working directly with learners to ensure that they know what they need to do in order to improve and solidify their learning. As such, it is geared towards accelerating learners' learning and its effectiveness intrinsically relates to the quality and timeliness of the feedback learners receive from teachers. Music teachers and educators formatively assess learners through continuous listening and observing of their learners' music making in various ways (e.g., the learners' performance skills, composing, listening, the types of questions learners ask, etc.) whereupon they provide immediate feedforward[1] constructive feedback (Goldsmith, 2012).

Formative assessment is a process that teachers incorporate into their teaching through the ongoing dialogue they establish with their learners (Fautley & Colwell, 2012). Therefore, formative assessment is intimately tied up with (necessarily useful and quality) feedback. For example, in a choir rehearsal, choir members will be given solutions as to how to improve their ability to effectively match pitch, or perform a certain complex rhythm effectively. At the same time, they will also be made aware of what was not working well and why. In instrumental music, after listening to learners' performances, teachers provide appraisal of elements that were improved, and guide learners towards the successful use of strategies aimed at realising the developments needed. When providing feedback to learners, be it in the context of formative or summative assessment, please ensure that your feedback is aimed at achieving the points in what follows. You should begin by focusing on reinforcing learners' achievements and improvements, specifically:

- Raising learners' consciousness of the strengths of their work.

- Boosting learners' confidence and self-concept regarding personal strengths and abilities.

- Providing guidance on areas for further development of skills and enhancement of their work.

- Enhancing learners' own judgement, their understanding of assessment criteria and ability to self-audit their own work.

Given the functions of feedback, it is not surprising that formative assessment tied to high quality feedback has been shown by research to have impactful and wide-ranging benefits among learners (Hattie, 2009). In this regard, it is important to emphasise the importance of detailed feedback. In terms of what *should* be assessed, considered or discussed, teachers need to not only consider the learning outcomes and expectations for the learners but also what aspects need to be addressed for learning to be more effective and meaningful. This is intertwined with what happens in real-time during the learning process at each stage of learning and for each learner individually. The *what* of what needs to be assessed is dependent upon how learning is progressing for each learner, and is primarily centred on learners' learning needs. Therefore, effective formative assessment:

- Is **dynamic**: done in real time, and in dialogue with learners, with teachers frequently using strategies such as demonstration and modelling to demonstrate what needs to/could be done to improve.

- Is **integral to the learning encounter**: it occurs within the teaching and learning process and therefore it is embedded within it.

- **Requires feedback from learners and teachers**: teachers act on feedback they receive from learners with regard to their learning. They also provide feedback through dialogue with learners (verbal, musical, gestural, etc.) aimed at promoting and cementing learning as well as developing motivation and self-confidence.

- Is **reactive**: as a result of how the learner is progressing, teachers need to be prepared to change their approach as and when this is necessary. This includes selecting a more appropriate repertoire that resonates better with the learner, or one which is more related with the learner's current skill level. They must also adopt other ways to explain a certain novel topic or new technique if their usual method does not work.

- **Provides learners with what they need in order to improve/develop further**: this requires that over time, teachers develop a strong understanding of what learners' specific learning needs are, both in terms of pre-set learning outcomes but also in the long term both in relation to their personal ambitions and interests for development. With this in mind, teachers should establish a vision for the learner at different points in time, delineating next steps and sharing their understandings with learners in relation to where they are and what they need to do in order to get to where they need/want to be. Formative assessment *as a process* should help learners develop the ability of self-assessment, and thereby being able to recognise what they need to work on. This helps learners to develop independence and strategies for learning.

(adapted from Fautley & Colwell, 2012)

Summative Assessment

Summative assessment is often a high stakes affair. Oftentimes, it may result in the learner being accepted onto a course or programme of studies, or allowed (or not) to progress further to the next level in their formal, structured studies e.g., from Grade 4 to Grade 5. Summative assessment is not necessarily a periodic, one-off event: it *can* consist of a single assessment which determines a learner's proficiency and achievement on its own; or it can consist of several smaller scale assessments which once combined, offer a broader picture of attainment over a period of time. In music education, summative assessment can take place via a variety of different formats, for instance auditions; recitals; instrumental music exams; musical contests and competitions; tests; a midterm exam; a final project (such as a composition); or an essay or paper etc. Information garnered from summative assessments can be used formatively by learners and teachers to guide their efforts and activities in subsequent lessons and courses.

Commonly, in summative assessment a numerical or categorical score is ascribed as the end result of the testing method chosen. It is important to associate qualitative descriptors to numbers or categories so that learners and teachers alike are granted assessment information that can be used to promote learning more effectively (e.g., the ABRSM 'merit' and 'distinction' passing differentials). Results of summative assessment provide important elements for reflection. For instance, for learners, they can ask themselves: what can I do to perform better next time? From a teaching point of view, a teacher can ask: why didn't my learner perform to the level he/she usually does during lessons?

In order for summative assessment to be meaningful, teachers and learners alike need to understand the logic underpinning grading systems. For example, what does a score of 75/100 obtained in a music test *actually mean*? Or what does a score of 99/150 in a piano exam signify? Or what does the term 'satisfactory' awarded for a composition project really mean? These questions naturally lead to the importance of defining assessment criteria: specifically, descriptive statements that provide learners and teachers with information about the qualities, characteristics and aspects of a given learning task. Well-defined assessment criteria allow teachers to assess learners' work in a more open, consistent and objective manner. When designing assessment criteria, it is important to keep the following considerations in mind:

- A criterion should normally be specific enough to provide evaluation on a single item, construct or skill. Namely, it helps if it is directly specific to *one* aspect.

- A criterion should be assessable, that is, it makes it possible to ascribe a hierarchy of attainment.

- A criterion should relate to information on a specific aspect of attainment.

- A group of criteria that work together to deconstruct the whole should, whenever considered together, provide an overall impression of the whole.

- Those elements deemed hard to assess, but nonetheless important, should not be omitted on the grounds of being difficult to assess. By the same reasoning, that which is easy to assess, should not be assessed simply because it is easy to assess at the expense of what is deemed as important.

(Fautley & Colwell, 2012)

For some examples of assessment criteria created in accordance to specific learning outcomes, and in various contexts of music teaching and learning, see the CW Resource 6. The examples given are not exhaustive and are only indicative. You can also consult the websites of the respective examining boards in your country. Many graded pieces also come with an accompanying "Teacher's Book" and these can be invaluable for ascertaining the precise metrics and reasonings by which exams are assessed. Since there are a multiplicity of context specific elements that you need to consider when designing assessment criteria, as well as many different ways for assessing content of similar nature, it is best to make sure you are up to speed with these *before* you commence with serious teaching directed towards helping your learners achieve their aims.

Interpretation of assessment data requires knowledge of the assessment criteria and standards required, and a full understanding of the assessment methods involved, procedures required and expectations placed upon learners. Again, here, the various 'Teacher's Guide' books available for both practical and theoretical exams offered by most major assessment bodies can be invaluable. In terms of communication to children and parents, it is important to be able to use summative assessment results in terms of the formative information they might provide. More precisely, they can be very useful in explicating how the formal assessment highlights strengths and perhaps weaknesses which may require improvements and thereby enable planning for how such results can and will be used proactively to promote further learning.

Methods and Tools

Assessment of music learning is more easily and realistically done when learners are actively engaged in music making. Assessment can be undertaken as they go along, progress and reflect upon their learning. For this reason, teacher observation is one of *the most* valuable assessment tools, be it in a one-to-one or group teaching context. Other recommended assessment methods and tools (as suggested, for example, by the Irish Music Curriculum (1999) and which are applicable upon contextualised adjustments to all music learning contexts) include tasks and tests designed by the teacher; samples of learners' work to be appraised and reflected upon; projects; portfolios; and records of learner achievement(s), as further detailed in the following section.

Teacher Observation

Through observation of learners' active engagement in music making activities, teachers can grasp relevant information on their work. This will prove itself to be crucial for monitoring progress. In order to make the most out of observation as an assessment tool, is it important to decide beforehand and be clear about the aspects of musical behaviour to be observed and what is expected that learners demonstrate, specifically in relation to the specified learning outcomes. Observation can be enhanced by the use of informal questions by the teacher as well as instigation of discussion and dialogue about specific elements of the work and intended knowledge, attitudes and skill development. Observations can be undertaken during learners' interactions in collaborative work, or in groups of two or three learners. This will facilitate focus on each child's engagement in musical activities. Observations (individual or in group) can be undertaken in an array of different situations, such as:

* Moving to music;

* Listening to music;

* Listening to the responses of others;

* Singing a song;

* Playing an instrument;

* Talking about and discussing the topic of the lesson;

* Selecting musical instruments;

* Reading a rhythmic or melodic pattern;

- During a performance rehearsal;
- Sharing of ideas for composition.

Teacher-Designed Tasks and Tests

Teacher-designed tasks and tests can range from performance tasks, to writing about a certain piece of music, or undertaking a rhythm dictation, singing or playing a tune from memory, etc. During performance assessment, it is possible to consider the product and process of performance. More precisely, it is possible to consider *how* a group composition resulted in a final product but also several other factors, for instance: the selection of instruments chosen; orchestration; other elements; and how learners worked collaboratively in the endeavour. In instrumental music contexts, performance assessments are undertaken in the formats of recitals, concerts and examinations.

Work Samples and Portfolios

A learner's work compiled and collected over time can provide relevant information on the breadth and depth of their learning in music. It can also illuminate their grasp of instrumental music with regard to aspects such as listening and responding, performing and composing. It might include drafts of compositions; a summary of pieces learned; a learner's self-assessment notes; and an audio or video recording of performance(s) and comments from teachers and peers. Teachers should consider the purposes that learners' work samples and portfolios will assume and use this information to decide on the type, nature and amount of work required. Namely it could be a compilation of all musically related work carried out by the learner or a collection aimed at showcasing their best work. Learners' reflections on their learning is a relevant tool for fostering reflection and higher-level thinking, which can be used to improve learning and teaching. Learning logs or learning journals are helpful tools at this level, providing as they do a record of learners' evolving attitudes towards their own musical development. The assessment of teacher-designed tasks, including portfolios, requires clarification as to the exact purposes of this type of assessment, and what teachers are expecting learners to demonstrate.

Projects

Projects can be assigned individually or to a group of learners. When assigning group work, the expectations for each individual group member of the groups (and also the assessment criteria) should be clearly determined. Also, the workload and responsibilities should be delegated as evenly as possible. Examples of group projects can include:

- Composing a song or a piece of music;
- Inventing a new form of music notation;

- Creating a dance sequence and/or choreography;

- Designing and building a musical instrument;

- Playing a tune in an ensemble;

- Playing a tune from memory;

- Selecting a certain number of pieces of music and giving a comparative critique.

Records of Learners' Achievements

These records are primarily based on a teacher's judgement of a learner's achievements and include indicators of achievement aligned to the learning outcomes. These can include: 'is able to recognise "legato" and "staccato"'; 'can differentiate between "major" and "minor" tonal patterns', etc. It includes assessment marks and/or qualitative teacher judgement(s) on tasks and work developed by the learner. It can also include any observations made by the teacher after the lesson or a group of lessons. This tool can provide a systematic and reliable way for assessing learners' learning towards the end of a course or the end of a school year.

Self- and Peer Assessment

Engaging learners in reflecting upon their own learning, their strengths and weaknesses and what they think they can do to improve is a key component in developing critically thinking and independent learners who will become more and more self-reliant with each step of their learning journey. This can be done in one-to-one meetings, or during lessons, through verbal discussions or, if appropriate, through a written form where learners are asked to self-assess themselves and their progress.

Questions guiding the construction of self-assessment tools should encourage reflecting upon 'what', 'why' and 'how'? Preferably, they should be open questions, where learners have the freedom to go deeper into what elements that they consider are important specifically to them. Peer assessment, where learners assess one another, can also be an interesting way through which experiential learning enables learners to understand the various learning outcomes more effectively and gain deeper understandings on the assessment process while simultaneously developing reflective and analytical skills.

To conclude, the assessment tools mentioned in this chapter provide a coherent and comprehensive structure for assessing and recording learners' understanding and their level of participation and skill development in music learning; and, moreover, they can be useful for discussions with parents and other teachers for framing future learning needs and support when required. It is strongly recommended that teachers keep a written record summary pertaining to each learner, kept on a file at the school, institution or as part of a private teacher learner file containing information on individual learner development in each area of work and any attainment demonstrated both at a formative and summative level alongside suggestions for further development.

While the previous discussion on assessment tools for music education has revealed a variety of methods and tools for assessment, it may be impractical to use all of these tools simultaneously. Therefore, teachers should give priority to tools and approaches which best reflect the work done in their class and which reflects different situations in learning undertaken in the classroom. Although teachers and assessors alike should be aware of what learners are required to demonstrate, teaching and learning should not *only* be about assessment. Nor there should be an overreliance on assessment when making judgements about learners. Rather, from a teaching and learning perspective, assessment should only matter insofar as it can help promote learning.

Reflective Questions

1. What methods can you use to assess your learners' musical attainment, in your teaching context/s? Why and how?				
• Consider the assessment methods proposed in this chapter and reflect on their appropriateness for use in your teaching context/s.	Aligned with CME, Level 4 Unit (U) or Area of Study (AOS) and Assessment Criteria number of ABRSM (2014) and TCL (2013, 2019)			
• How do you ensure that the methods chosen are reliable and valid?	ABRSM		TCL (2013)	
• Consider how assessment can be used for quality feedback to be provided to learners' and promote further learning.	U2:	2.4.3	U2:	4.1 4.3
			TCL (2019)	
			AOS3:	3.1.1 3.1.2 3.1.3 3.1.4 3.1.5 3.1.6

2. How has the assessment you have undertaken of your learners and other stakeholders contributed to changes, adaptations and/or improvements in your teaching?				
• Consider the learning challenges your learners face and how such challenges provide clues on changes you might undertake/undertook in your teaching to support their learning more effectively.				
	ABRSM		TCL (2013)	
	U2:	2.4.1 2.4.2	U2:	4.1 4.2
• How has reflecting on successes, challenges, failures and mistakes has helped you to make adaptations and improve your teaching?	U3:	3.1.4	U3:	1.3 1.4
			TCL (2019)	
			AOS3:	3.1.7
			AOS1:	1.1.4 1.1.5

3. How can you use assessment to identify and address misconceptions and difficulties children and young people may be experiencing in their learning?				
• Give specific examples of how you have used assessment to identify and address challenges and misconceptions your learners' might have experienced in their learning. • What, then, can be the importance of assessment beyond providing clues about a learner's ability to learn and attainment more generally?				
	ABRSM		TCL (2013)	
	U2:	2.4.1	U2:	4.1
			TCL (2019)	
			AOS3:	3.1.4

Note

1. Feedforward: the term 'feedforward' as used in relation to providing feedback to learners was originally introduced by Marshall Goldsmith (2012), with a view of shifting the focus of feedback from criticism to suggestions for future improvement.

Further Reading

Colwell, R. J., & Hewitt, P. (2014). *Teaching of instrumental music*. Pearson Education Limited.

Fautley, M., & Colwell, R. (2012). Assessment in the secondary music classroom. In G. E. McPherson & G. F. Welch (Eds.), *The Oxford handbook of music education* (Vol. 1, pp. 475–494). Oxford University Press.

References

Associated Board of the Royal Schools of Music (ABRSM) (2014). *Level 4 certificate for music educators: Assessment framework*. ABRSM.

Colwell, R. J., & Hewitt, P. (2014). *Teaching of instrumental music*. Pearson Education Limited.

Fautley, M., & Colwell, R. (2012). Assessment in the secondary music classroom. In G. E. McPherson & G. F. Welch (Eds.), *The Oxford handbook of music education* (pp. 475–494). Oxford University Press. https://doi.org/10.1093/oxfordhb/9780199730810.013.0029

Goldsmith, M. (2012). *Feedforward*. Round Table Companies. Retrieved from http://www.huffingtonpost.com/marshall-goldsmith/10-surefire-reasons-to-tr_b_571

Government of Ireland (1999). *Music curriculum, arts education*. The Stationary Office.

Hattie, J. (2009). *Visible learning: A synthesis of over 800 meta-analyses related to achievement*. Routledge.

McPherson, G. E. (2005). From child to musician: Skill development during the beginning stages of learning an instrument. Psychology *of Music, 33*(1), 5–35. https://doi.org/10.1177/0305735605048012

Trinity College London (TCL) (2013). *TCL level 4 certificate for music educators: Specifications*. TCL.

Trinity College London (TCL) (2019). *TCL level 4 certificate for music educators, areas of study*. TCL.

Section III

The Music Educator and Their Wider Professional Role

8 Safeguarding and Child Protection in Music Education

To Guide Your Reading

- What legislation is currently in place in the UK with regard to safeguarding children and young people? How does it apply to the context of music education?

- What are the roles of different individuals and agencies involved in safeguarding children and young people in their musical learning?

- How can we recognise different forms of abuse?

- What to do if you are concerned about a child or a young person?

- What to do if a child confides abuse to you?

- How do we promote safe practice in the use of ICT, the internet and social media?

- How can we avoid risks and possible consequences to self when working individually, in groups and/or as a class?

Introduction

Given that the CME course originated in the UK, this chapter considers a UK-based overview on current legislation and procedures for safeguarding children and is based on the government's advice on safeguarding (DfE-00129–2019; DfE-00130–2019). The chapter begins with a brief summary on policies and procedures, leading to considerations on the role of different individuals and agencies, including on how to recognise different forms of abuse and what to do if you are concerned about a child or young person's well-being. The chapter concludes with relevant content on: 1) guidelines for promoting safe practice in the use of ICT, the internet and social media; and 2) avoiding risks and consequences to self when working with children and young people. Please note that teachers working in the UK must ensure they abide by the latest governmental guidance, and teachers based in other geographical contexts should refer to their own country specific guidelines, policies and procedures.

The content on Safeguarding and Child Protection presented in this book does not replace accredited courses on Safeguarding. Therefore, it is essential that, in addition to reading the material in the next sections, you attend an accredited course and obtain a certificate in Safeguarding and Child Protection specific to the duties you undertake as part of your role and which are embedded within the legislation and procedures in place for the school and country where you work. Changing work contexts within or outside the same geographical area will always require that you familiarise yourself with the safeguarding and child protection policy of the new institution, as well as any pertinent legislation and procedures that you should follow to ensure you enact your role efficiently and within the law.

The UK Context: Legislation, Guidelines, Policies and Procedures

In 1989, the United Nations Convention on the rights of the child recognised that, for the full and harmonious development of his or her personality, the child should grow up in a family environment, in an atmosphere of happiness, love and understanding. It also emphasised and acknowledged children's rights to survival, to develop to their fullest potential, to be protected from harmful influences, abuse and exploitation and to participate fully in family, cultural and social life.

This convention is the most widely ratified human rights treaty in history. Countries that ratify the treaty pledge to protect children from violence, economic and sexual exploitation, and other forms of abuse and to advance the rights of children vis-à-vis education, health care, and a decent standard of living. Many countries have used the convention to strengthen their national legislation and consequentially adopted new policies to improve the lives of children. However, although many countries have instituted impressive legal protections for children, there is still much that needs to be done to ensure that the laws in place are not only fit for purpose but also effectively enforced.

Teachers and anyone working with children and young people (in whatever capacity and in any part of the world) owe them a duty of care. Duty of care is a moral, ethical or legal obligation to ensure the safety and well-being of others (DfE, 2019). To effectively act in accordance with the duty of care they hold, teachers need to not only be aware of and strictly follow their own country specific advice and regulations but also to continuously work in the best interests of the children in their care. This means being involved in advocating needed reviews of regulations and being involved in the development and implementation of fit-for-purpose policies, legislation and measures to ensure the safety and well-being of children, young people and other people involved in their care.

The UK takes a child-centred approach to safeguarding. It is aimed at keeping the child in focus when decisions are made about their lives and seeks to work in partnership with them and their families (links to the UK Government's specific documentation are available in CW Resource 7). Although the terms 'safeguarding' and 'child protection' are used interchangeably at times, they refer to different things. Safeguarding refers to the promotion of welfare and it encompasses:

> protecting children from maltreatment, preventing impairment of children's health or development, ensuring that children grow up in circumstances

consistent with the provision of safe and effective care, and taking action to enable all children to have the best outcomes.

(DfE-00129–2019, p. 4)

Child protection refers to the processes and procedures put in place to protect children at a significant risk of harm, or who have actually been harmed. Therefore, child protection is only a small portion of the wider work on safeguarding and promoting welfare albeit with a crucial and essential role within the wider framework on safeguarding.

The UK's four nations (England, Wales, Scotland and Northern Ireland) have their own child protection systems and laws to help protect children from abuse and neglect. Each nation has a framework of legislation, guidance and practice to identify children who are at risk of harm, and in this way takes action to protect those children and to prevent further abuse from occurring. This makes it difficult to discuss specific pieces of legislation and guidance for each of the four UK nations. The Children Act (1989) came to effect in the mentioned year in England and Wales, followed by the Children Order (Northern Ireland) and the Children Act (Scotland), both of which became law in 1995. These consisted of an amalgamation of previous child protection and family law and established relevant guidance for agencies with regard to the protection of children.

These duties and guidelines were further refined in a variety of subsequent documentation and legislation such as the Children Act 2004, the Statutory Guidance Keeping Children Safe in Education 2016 and 2019 (England and Wales); the Children and Social Work Act 2017 (England); the National Guidance for Child Protection 2014 (Scotland); and the Safeguarding Vulnerable Groups Order 2017 (Northern Ireland). Despite some differences across the four UK nations (mostly pertaining to terminology of roles, hierarchical structures and specific processes and procedures to follow), the legislation in place is based on the following key principles: 1) that the welfare of children and young people is of paramount importance; 2) that they are best looked after within their own families, unless compulsory intervention in family life is required.

The Roles of Different Individuals and Agencies

The roles, titles and duties given to individuals, group of individuals and agencies involved in safeguarding children and young people may differ slightly from country to country (this is true both within the UK and the wider context). However, it is assumed from the outset that anybody who works in an education setting has a duty of care to protect the welfare of children in attendance. This applies to all professionals working in education and beyond.

Within educational institutions, this duty of care extends to numerous persons in regular contact with children such as school governors; school principals; headteachers; teachers; designated safeguarding officers (DSOs); teaching assistants; dining staff; and anyone else who spends time with children. Hence, it is vital that these persons will have attended appropriate training such that they become well-placed to identify and recognise when there is a potential issue.

In the UK, Local boards for the safeguarding of children are strategic forums wherein local interagency strategic partnerships become responsible for the design, development, publication, distribution, dissemination, implementation and evaluation of child protection policy and practice. This is the case in the public, private and wider sectors in their local authority area(s). Their role is to provide individual and collective leadership but also direction for the management of child protection services within their local remit, and moreover to contribute to the provision of genuinely effective child protection.

School governors[1] and school principals/head teachers[2] have a responsibility to ensure that the school fully complies with safeguarding duties. This includes ensuring that there is in place a workable yet robust, fit-for-purpose and frequently updated and revised safeguarding and child protection policy. All within the workplace must be aware of, understand and follow this, not least including policies covering online safety. Given the centrality of internet culture to young people and children's lives, this latter point cannot be stressed strongly enough. This will include putting in place safer recruitment of staff through regular and frequent enhanced police checks for all staff who work with and have access to children and young people in educational environments. Ideally, the checks should be done on a yearly basis, or at a minimum every two years. These checks and/or disclosures contain information on all unspent and certain spent convictions of individuals, side-by-side with any other non-conviction information that the police or other government bodies think may be relevant, including checking against child barred lists.[3] It also comprises ensuring that all staff have undergone safeguarding training during their inductions and that this training is renewed regularly. Thorough security procedures and systems must be in place at the school. There must be physical security such as gates and railings as well as technology-based security to ensure that there is no unauthorised access to the school's computer systems. Monitoring of attendance and taking action if learners miss a lot of school time is also relevant.

The teacher in charge of safeguarding in schools, commonly referred to as a designated safeguarding officer (or DSO), must ensure that everyone follows the safeguarding policies. They are the person who will draw up and enforce the safeguarding policy, recognise issues, make referrals to social services where appropriate, work with families and be the first point-of-call for staff who have safeguarding concerns.

Teachers and educators all have a responsibility for the safe education and welfare of children and young people. Their work involves close observation of learners in the classroom, and this can frequently trigger concerns about health or welfare. Teachers should discuss any concerns with the DSO or equivalent in their institution/school.

Instrumental music teachers, tutors and community music practitioners working in schools and institutions need to familiarise themselves with and adhere to the Child Protection Policies of those establishments. If they are teaching in a private capacity (i.e., in their own home or studio), they should have their own written Safeguarding and Child Protection policy. It should be written and reviewed in accordance with latest legislation and recommended principles of good practice. They must also ensure that they fully understand their responsibilities and how to apply and work with safe practices effectively. They should attend regular training on safeguarding and child protection and check regularly that they are following and updating their policy. They should make sure that they know what they should do in a range of situations and take reasonable steps to ensure the safety and security of all the children and young people in their care.

A children's social worker has a variety of roles and duties, and in relation to child protection he/she will respond to new referrals from professionals and members of the public. They will investigate allegations of neglect, physical, sexual and emotional abuse so that a child or young people is protected from harm.

A child protection case conference is arranged where there is concern that a child or young people may be considered to be at risk of significant harm. It involves a range of relevant professionals, family members and the child (if appropriate) and will consider whether a multi-agency child protection plan and/or review of an existing child's plan is required to reduce the risk of significant harm to the child. A lead professional who is responsible for co-ordinating the work will be identified. The case conference will decide whether to place the child on the Child Protection Register, an administrative tool designed to alert practitioners that there is sufficient professional concern about a child to have warranted an inter-agency child protection plan being in place. A child and family are supported by a core group of those professionals who are involved in delivering the child protection plan. The core group are of critical importance in working directly with the child and family to reduce the risk of harm to that child.

Understanding and Recognising Different Forms of Abuse

Children and young people can be vulnerable to neglect, abuse or exploitation from within their family and people they come across in their day-to-day lives. According to the DfE (2019), threats and abuse can take different forms, including:

- Sexual abuse and or sexual exploitation;

- Physical;

- Emotional;

- Neglect;

- Online abuse;

- Influences of extremism leading to radicalisation;

- Trafficking and or exploitation by criminal gangs and organised crime groups.

Music teachers and other professionals working with children and young people need to understand what each of these forms of abuse can entail. They need to be able to recognise possible signs of abuse at both physical and behavioural levels.

SEXUAL ABUSE

Sexual abuse involves enticing or forcing a child to take part in sexual activities, which may or not involve physical contact and not necessarily involving high levels of violence. This can include:

- Watching sexual activities;

- Non-penetrative acts (kissing, touching, masturbation);

- Involving children in looking at or in the production of sexual images;

- Grooming a child with the intention of abuse (this can also occur via the internet).

Physical signs that abuse might be occurring can include discomfort while sitting and walking; stomach pains; genital soreness; discharge; and bleeding and/or sexually transmitted infections. Behavioural signs can encompass changes in relation to how the child used to behave, for instance: becoming withdrawn; refusing to undress for sporting activities; self-harming; eating disorders; and unexplained amounts of money. Other red flags can include sexual knowledge and language which is not appropriate for a specific age group and being picked up from school or other activities by people who are not known to be part of the child's family. Sometimes the abuse involves sexual exploitation where children and young people are sexually exploited for money, status or power. Child sexual exploitation can also happen without physical contact, namely online.

Physical signs that sexual exploitation might be occurring include unexplained physical injuries and sexual health problems. Behavioural changes can include being distressed or withdrawn; going missing for short and long periods of time; secretiveness; and disengaging from previous friendships and existing social networks.

PHYSICAL ABUSE

Physical abuse can involve beating and hitting; shaking; suffocating; drowning; burning; scalding; poisoning; and any other form or means of causing physical harm.

Physical signs that it might be occurring can consist of marks and bruising in areas of the body where they are unlikely to appear in everyday activity; black eyes; broken bones; and bite marks, scald marks, and burns such as cigarette marks. It can also include signs that might indicate a child was restrained or strangled and injuries to the soles of the feet. Injuries which are not consistent with the explanations provided by the child or those responsible for her/his care are a reason for concern.

Behavioural manifestations of physical abuse can include recoiling when touched; a reluctance to go home; avoiding getting changed in front of others for sports or other activities; wearing clothing fully covering arms and legs even on warm days (although this may also be done for cultural and/or religious reasons). The child or young person can also display aggressiveness or be withdrawn; engage in drugs and/or alcohol misuse; attempt to run away; appear sad; and be excessively willing to please and display behaviours that are not consistent with developmental stage.

EMOTIONAL ABUSE

This form of abuse is always present in any form of maltreatment. However, it can also occur on its own, and can include any of the following, or a combination, of:

- Consistently ignoring and rejecting a child;

- Using degrading language and behaviours towards a child;

- Acting in a detached manner in response to a child's attempts to interact;

- The child witnessing the ill treatment and bullying of another;

- Causing a child to frequently feel afraid or endangered;

- Convey to a child that they are valued only as far as they meet the needs of another person;

- Convey to a child that they are worthless, inadequate and not loved;

- Ridiculing and making fun of a child;

- Corruption and exploitation of children.

Physical signs that emotional abuse might be taking place can include inconsistent weight or growth patterns; delayed development (physical, or emotional); and self-harm marks. In terms of behaviour the child or young person may display inconsistent, and at times unpredictable behaviour; be withdrawn; showcase unexplained underachievement at school; engage in self-harming; display excessive attention seeking; and experience difficulty relating to others and forming relationships. Bed-wetting and sleep disturbances can also occur.

NEGLECT

Neglect is defined as a failure in meeting a child's basis needs (physical, psychological, emotional) and can include (among others):

- Failure to provide shelter, food, and adequate clothing;

- Abandonment;

- Inability to respond to a child's emotional needs;

- Failure to protect a child from emotional and physical danger;

- Inability to provide safe supervision (including through caregivers who are inadequate);

- Failure to ensure appropriate medical care and treatment.

Physical signs of neglect can include poor personal hygiene, including unwashed clothing; a lack of energy as a result of inadequate or poor food intake; being consistently hungry, thin or having a swollen stomach, a pronounced lack of muscle tone and with bones appearing to stick out; and having untreated skin or hair conditions (e.g., rashes, fleas, lice). Medical or dental problems which are not taken care of can also occur. Behavioural manifestations that suggest neglect might be occurring can encompass being withdrawn; having difficulty connecting with others and making friends; anti-social behaviour; stealing or begging for food; excessive attention seeking; and alcohol or substance misuse as well as faltering growth.

Children often get bumps and bruises through play times, which **does not mean** that they are being abused. Each injury needs to be considered with due attention to the child's age, background (e.g., if they play a lot of sports that could involve minor injuries, or if they help their family with labour intensive activities such as farming), location of the injury on their body and the explanation given. Many of the injuries occurring in the educational setting will be relatively minor involving cut fingers and grazed knees, but some injuries will be more serious and may require more involved or urgent treatment. Every setting must have a first aid policy and at least one qualified first aider on the staff team. Teachers need to try to identify as best as possible the cause of the injury and if explanations for it make sense. If there is reason to believe that the injury could be due to abuse, then further action as outlined in the following needs to be taken.

Specific safeguarding issues also include bullying, influences of extremism leading to radicalisation; trafficking and/or exploitation; female genital mutilation (FMG); forced marriage; domestic abuse; and children missing from education. Please consult DfE (2019) policy for further information on different types of abuse.

What to Do If You are Concerned About a Child or Young Person's Well-Being

Suspicion or evidence that a child or young person has been or is at risk of harm can come from various sources. For instance, it can be the child or young person confiding in you, or perhaps physical and behavioural signs displayed by the child/young person that raise suspicions in your mind. Or, observations made in your day-to-day work environment have led you to be concerned about the professional conduct of a fellow teacher, staff member, volunteer or other person with access to learners at your school or educational environments where you work. Perhaps you witnessed self-destructive and or self-harming behaviour by a learner at school. Regardless of the nature and source of the evidence (proven or not) you must act.

To do nothing is not an option. Inquiries about child deaths revealed that although people *suspected* that abuse was taking place, they did not act owing to fears of getting it wrong: in short, they were not quite sure it was happening. While you *should not* by any means investigate the situation, you have a **duty** to pass on and discuss your concerns and all information you have on the specific learner and situation with the dedicated safeguarding lead in your school, your manager or call social services for further guidance. This includes allegations made by other people; disclosure(s) made by a child or peers; your observations in terms of signs that abuse might have or be occurring; or that there is a risk of it occurring. In exceptional circumstances, such as an emergency where a child is in immediate danger or at risk of harm, or where there is a genuine concern that appropriate action has not/will not be taken, you should speak directly to children's social care services. You should also inform your designated safeguarding lead that you have done or will be doing so as soon as possible.

Possible options in such scenarios include initiating a conversation with the child or young person (if it is appropriate to do so in relation to child's age and specific circumstances) in order to let the child know you are there in case the child needs someone to talk to. This will also help you to understand whether your concerns are legitimate or not. The Safeguarding and Child Protection policy at your institution will outline what you should do when you talk to a child in a one-to-one meeting: this will ensure that you protect yourself from any future allegations. However, in general terms, keep in mind the following:

- It is likely that privacy is very important to the child or young person concerned. Therefore, choose a quiet time and place to initiate this conversation.

- The following phrases may help as a starting point for the conversation: 'I have noticed lately that you seem'; 'Is everything OK?'; 'Can I have a word with you?'; 'I am concerned about you. Is everything alright?'.

After the conversation you may find that the child or young person is just going through a difficult time temporarily, or that there is a problem (other than abuse) which you or your institution can offer support with, or direct them towards other relevant sources of help.

What to Do If a Child Confides Abuse to You

It may be that a child or young person confides or tries to confide abuse to you. Sometimes the child or young person may start by saying something like: 'I need to tell you something, but can only do so if you promise not to tell anyone else'. It is important that you present a positive and welcoming attitude about the child wanting to speak to you, and patiently listen to what they have to say while reassuring them it is important that they tell you what is that he/she intended to say so that you can help. However, it is **extremely** important that you let the child know that *you cannot promise confidentiality*, as there may be situations where you need to share information with others without the child's consent (The Adolescent Self -harm Forum, 2016).

If the child or young person decides not to proceed with the conversation, you still need to report to your designated safeguarding lead, manager or child services, that the child approached you but decided not to go ahead since you could not promise confidentiality. You should also provide any information which is (or may be) of assistance to the case. If the child/young person goes ahead with the conversation, you need to know how to appropriately respond in such a situation. Here are some guidelines (adapted from Baker et al., 2019; NSPCC, 2020):

- **Be welcoming, even if the time is in inconvenient**. It may have taken a great deal of courage for the child or young person to approach you and they may not want to do it again.

- **Find a quiet place where the conversation won't be interrupted** but bear in mind any guidelines on being alone with a learner.

- **Stay calm**, go at the child's pace and do not make assumptions or speculate.

- **Listen carefully and do not interrupt.** Avoid expressing your own views on the matter. A reaction of shock or disbelief could cause the child to 'shut down', retract or stop talking. Do not ask the child or young person to repeat the disclosure or make a written statement.

- **Communicate in a way that is appropriate for their age AND communication method.**

- **Ask questions for clarification only**.

- **Let them know they've done the right thing.** Reassurance can make a big impact to the child who may have been keeping the abuse secret.

- **Tell them it's not their fault.** Abuse is never the child's fault and they need to know this.

- **Say you will take them seriously.** A child could keep abuse a secret from fear they won't be believed. They've told you because they want help and trust you will be the person who will listen to and support them.

- **Do not make promises you cannot keep** (e.g., 'everything will be OK') and as stated earlier, don't promise to keep the conversation a secret since you will need to share it with either the safeguarding lead at your organisation or with children's social services.

- **If emergency help is required, don't delay in getting it.**

- **Don't talk to the alleged abuser.** Confronting the alleged abuser about what a child has disclosed to you could make the situation **a lot worse** for the child.

- **Explain what you'll do next.** Explain to the child you'll need to report the abuse to someone who will be able to help.

- **Make notes as soon as possible afterwards**, recording exactly what was said using the child's words. Record the time, date, place and context of the disclosure. Record statements and observable things, not your interpretations or assumptions, always keeping it factual.

- **Don't delay reporting the abuse.** The sooner the abuse is reported after the child or young person discloses the better. Furthermore, the details will be fresher in your mind and action can be taken quickly. Report the disclosure and hand over your record to the designated teacher or children's social services as soon as possible.

Promoting Safe Practice in the Use of ICT, the Internet and Social Media

While there are many recognisable benefits, uses and purposes for the use of technology, internet and social media in music education, the use of technology has nevertheless become a significant component with regard to many safeguarding issues. Given the risks and dangers associated with internet use, teachers and educators need to put measures in place which prevent harm to children and young people in the educational contexts where they work.

For effective measures to be put in place, there needs to be an identification of possible online safety issues and risks. Various mechanisms by which to intervene and escalate any incidents as appropriate need to be laid out side-by-side with the identified issues and risks. Also, educating staff and learners about online safety is essential. Risks surrounding online safety can be broadly grouped into three categories: content, contact and conduct. For definitions and examples of each of these categories, see Table 8.1.

Table 8.1 Categorisation of risks to online safety

Risk category	Definition	Examples
Content	Being exposed to illegal, inappropriate or harmful material.	• Access to illegal, harmful or inappropriate images or other content (including radicalisation/extremism materials, hate sites and pornography). • Ignoring age ratings in games (leading to exposure to violence often associated with racist language and substance abuse). • Lifestyle websites, for example pro-anorexia/self-harm/suicide sites. • Content validation: how to check the authenticity and accuracy of online content. • Unauthorised access to, loss of or sharing of personal information.
Contact	Being subjected to harmful online interaction with other users.	• Grooming. • Cyber-bullying in all forms. • Identity theft (including 'frape' i.e., hacking Facebook profiles) and sharing passwords.
Conduct	Personal online behaviour that increases the likelihood of, or causes, harm.	• Privacy issues, including disclosure of personal information. • Digital footprint and online reputation. • Sharing/distribution of personal images with and without an individual's consent or knowledge. • Sexting (sending and receiving of personally intimate images) also referred to as SGII (self-generated indecent images). • Copyright (little care or consideration for intellectual property and ownership – such as music and film). • Potential for excessive use with repercussions on the social, emotional development and learning of the child/young person. • Generating large bills through overuse of mobile phones, gaming, sites and apps.

Source: Adapted from Ofsted (2013)

Learners should only use school computers that have the appropriate filters installed. A filter is a program or section of code designed to assess input or output information in accordance to pre-set criteria and process the information in accordance to pre-set courses of action. This way filters are able to remove or hide unwanted items or information, blocking access to potentially harmful online material from staff and learners in accordance to previously set criteria (i.e., by categorising online content into for example: pornography, gambling, gaming, social media, etc.). The use of filtering systems can prevent access to content promoting:

- Unjust of prejudicial treatment of people with protected characteristics;

- Substance abuse displays, or content which promotes the illegal use of drugs or substances;

- Extremism, terrorism and terrorist ideologies;

- Violence or intolerance;

- Malware;

- Compromising of systems including anonymous browsing and other filter bypass tools;

- Sites hosting malicious content;

- Pornography and displays sexual acts or explicit images;

- Piracy and copyright theft including illegal provision of copyrighted material;

- Self-Harm or showing displays of deliberate self-harm (including suicide and eating disorders);

- Displays of violence or anything which promotes the use of physical force intended to hurt or kill.

(UK Safer Internet Center, 2020, p. 2)

Although helpful, no filtering system can be considered as fully secure and effective and it needs to be complemented with good teaching and effective supervision. The UK Safer Internet Centre recommends that Filtering System Features meet the following principles:

- **Age appropriate, differentiated filtering:** this includes the ability to vary filtering strength appropriate to different ages and roles.

- **Circumvention**: the extent and ability to identify and manage technologies and techniques used to circumvent the system, for example VPNs, proxy services and DNS over HTTPS.

- **Control:** the ability and ease of use that allows schools to control the filter themselves to permit or deny access to specific content.

- **Filtering Policy:** the filtering provider publishes a rationale that details their approach to filtering with classification and categorisation as well as other blocking.

- **Group/Multi-site Management**: the ability for deployment of a central policy and central oversight or dashboard.

- **Identification**: the filtering system should have the ability to identify users.

- **Mobile and App content**: mobile and app content is often delivered via entirely different mechanisms from that delivered through a traditional web browser. To what extent does the filter system block inappropriate content via mobile and app technologies (i.e., beyond typical web browser delivered content)?

- **Multiple language support**: the ability for the system to manage relevant languages.

- **Network level:** filtering should be applied at 'network level', i.e., not reliant on any software located on users' devices.

- **Reporting mechanism**: the ability to report inappropriate content for access or blocking.

- **Reports:** the system offers clear historical information on the websites visited by your users.

(ibid., 2020, pp. 2–3)

Schools, institutions and organisations providing educational activities and private teaching studios should have a policy which outlines and governs acceptable ICT use. This should be shared and explained clearly to other staff members, learners and parents alike so that boundaries are set and so that they are aware of how they can safely use the internet. Such policies should include guidelines on:

- Appropriate use of emails, mobile phones, social networking sites and websites;

- The importance of passwords and guidance on password safety;

- Appropriate use of digital images;

- Safe use of removal data storage devices;

- How school internet access will be monitored, including identification of learners' internet searches;

- Incident reporting, including responding to incidents of misuse and safeguarding children and young people.

It is beyond the scope of this book to provide detailed guidelines on each of the points mentioned previously, as the advice and guidelines will differ depending on the type of educational context being considered, the technology available and their purposes. However, what follows are some general principles to help ensure that you meet essential relevant elements of safeguarding. With these, you will want to follow/develop appropriate safeguarding procedures depending on the specific nature of your work and role.

If you suggest to learners that they access particular content or online materials, ensure you always check the sites beforehand and guide learners to these sites. If you are using a web search for content, make sure to check the search terms and results first so that you use appropriate words for your search. In lessons where internet use is pre-planned, learners should be guided to sites checked and confirmed as suitable for their use. Open-ended searches such as 'find images' or 'find information on' are discouraged. Teachers and staff should continuously check that the material accessed by learners is indeed the intended material and monitor safe use by checking what is actually being accessed and viewed by learners. If internet research is set for homework, specific sites will be suggested that have previously been checked and deemed safe for use by children and young people. Teachers should then advise parents to supervise the learner's internet access at home.

Always use the safety mode for YouTube, and with Google use the Safe Search settings. Employ Digital Leaders in schools who are there to promote online safety among their peers. A strong password or PIN code should be used to safeguard personal data, and these should be used at all times and changed regularly. Learners should not share their passwords, and you should remind them not to. Ensure that both you and your learners log out of all sites when you have finished the work required in order to prevent hacking of personalised data (e.g., Gmail, Facebook, etc. remain logged in to personal accounts until they are deliberately logged out). If you suspect a child has been a victim of cyberbullying, you must retain the evidence and encourage the child to change their password(s). Report the content directly to the website, webmaster or network administrator, and raise your concerns with the designated safeguarding officer and/or senior management in your school or organisation. Allow them to decide what to do with the evidence while you give support to the learner.

Ensure that you strictly follow your school/institution's IT safeguarding and usage policies. Keep and check records of parental permissions that have been granted/not granted, and which must be adhered to when taking images/videos of learners. In many cases schools and institutions restrict teachers and staff from using privately owned equipment for capturing photos or videos of learners and there will also be relevant policy on what images from school events can be used on social networking sites. Some parents may object to images of their children being on social networking sites. Possible ways forward with regard to this is to ask parents/carers to sign an agreement stating that they will not share photographs taken at any school event through any public medium. Or, more simply, prohibit parents from taking any photographs during the event and notify them that the school will take official photographs which parents can then subsequently access. Whatever decisions are made with regard to this, they need to be **clearly communicated to all parents** alongside an explanation of the reasons behind the decision.

Considering the earlier points, as a teacher you must make sure you know the school's policy regarding posting of pictures or videos of learners' performances and/or lessons. Only use password protected devices to download the material, and keep the material password protected and ensure that only appropriate and approved pictures and videos are posted. Make sure that the material is only accessed by those having permission to access it and always confirm prior to posting that signed parental consent for posting pictures/videos has been obtained.

If parental consent was obtained, and the material is appropriate for posting, ensure that children and young people featured in the digital material are not identifiable (i.e., do not provide their full name and personal details). To create another layer of safety, several schools have their own parent portal with rigorous filter settings. In large schools, on the advice of a marketing team, it may be that you as a teacher do not have any permission whatsoever to take pictures/videos or post any material online. Ensure you are aware of what you are allowed/not allowed to do within the limits of your role at a particular institution.

Digital communications with learners and parents/guardians/carers should be on a professional level and only carried out using official school systems. Many schools/institutions and organisations make the point that **under no circumstances** should staff contact learners, parents/carers or conduct any school business using personal e-mail addresses and furthermore that school e-mail is not for personal use.

Teachers and educators in the UK should also be aware that email communications can be subject to Freedom of Information requests, so all correspondence needs to be professional, courteous and respectful. Confidential information and information covered under the Data Protection Act, if being sent by email, should be sent through secure email systems which are usually provided by a school's ICT team. Personal or sensitive data belonging to staff or learners should not be stored on the local drives of desktop or laptop PCs used for educational activities. If it is necessary to do so, the local drive must be encrypted.

Teachers working in their own studios (and those owning tuition businesses) should ensure that personal information such as email addresses and phone numbers will only be exchanged with the parents of the learner. Additionally, and no less important, learners should **not** be added as 'friends' on social media platforms, and privacy settings should be kept up to date on social media sites. It is wise to simply refrain from commenting on these in a public forum or public discussion. Text messages can be particularly problematic. Therefore, do not communicate with learners using text messages, and if a learner texts you, do not reply and inform the parent and (if working in a school/institution) let your designated safeguarding lead or manager know also.

Learners should adhere to the rules and guidelines set out in the Behaviour Policy and Mobile Phone/Interactive Watches Policy regarding mobile technology usage in schools. Particular attention needs to be given to ensure that pictures or videos are not captured in settings where children and young people are, for example, changing clothes prior to PE or musical performances. To avoid any potential problems, learners should be required to put their phone and mobile gadgets in a lockable container prior to getting changed.

RESPONDING TO INCIDENTS OF MISUSE

Misuse of ICT, internet and social media (as a result of infringements of policies and guidelines in place) can occur when people are not well informed nor have full understanding of the policies in place and how to enact them. It can also simply be through irresponsible and careless behaviour, or more rarely, deliberately. Yet, it is important to keep in mind that misuse can only be referred to as such whenever there are clearly outlined guidelines for good practice. The extent and implications of misuse need to be considered through a risk assessment, and this should preferably be undertaken prior to it occurring.

Some misuse can be addressed through sanctions outlined in the Promoting Positive Behaviour policy. Other may need to be referred to your manager; a designated safeguarding officer; agencies such as child social services and the police; and/or to technical support staff for further actions such as filtering and other safety procedures to be put in place, fixed or enhanced. Specific actions to be taken for responding to specific misuse should be outlined in the policy. If the online safety-related incident involves a learner, the nature of the incident, the learner's age and any other factors that might be impacting upon the child and whether or not the misuse is illegal need to be considered. It is also necessary to consider whether or not to involve agencies. Teachers have a responsibility to refer a child to Children's Social Care when it is believed or suspected that a child:

- Has suffered significant harm;

- Is likely to suffer significant harm;

- Has developmental and welfare needs which are likely only to be met through provision of family support services.

Avoiding Risks and Possible Consequences to Self When Working With Children and Young People

Some children may misinterpret actions which are perfectly innocent in their intention, particularly if the child has previously experienced abuse. Physical contact that you may find acceptable may come across as intimidating to a child. Teachers need to abide by the guidelines on the *use* or *non-use* of touch as stated in the specific safeguarding and child protection policies in the context(s) where they work.

There are various and oftentimes contradictory views across different cultures with regard to the use of touch for the purposes of demonstrations in educational contexts. This is particularly true in vocal and instrumental music education. For instance, in the UK many educational settings have a no-touch policy meaning that teachers cannot use touch for educational demonstration purposes, or any other purpose, including greeting or hugging a distressed child. It can be said that at least partially, this exists in order to prevent allegations of child abuse being made against teachers. However, in post-Soviet states, also known as the former Soviet Union, touch is an integral element in instrumental music teaching: it is used widely by teachers to demonstrate/model excellent performance. Regardless of cultural views on whether touch *should* or *should not* be used in music teaching contexts, it is important to consider as a whole the importance of preventing risks for learners and for oneself as a teacher.

In order to avoid risks and possible consequences to self when working with children and young people individually, in groups and as a class, *unnecessary physical contact should be avoided* and only used whenever there are learning benefits which cannot be achieved through other demonstration and modelling strategies. For example, teachers can, instead of using touch, ask learners to observe and listen to how the teacher performs the required task. While observing and listening might work for some learners, from my own teaching experience I am aware that this is not always the case. Therefore, it may be that in some specific circumstances touch *is* the most effective learning strategy.

If your specific teaching context operates a no-touch policy and you consider touch a helpful element for teaching and learning in music, prior to using touch, you must discuss with your designated safeguarding lead or manager the possibility of developing a policy of seeking consent for the use of touch for the purposes of pedagogical demonstrations. In such instances, the policy must include considerations on the following aspects: under what circumstances touch may be used and why? How will consent be obtained from the child, parents, line manager and safeguarding lead? What other precautions may be required? For example, concerning a policy which will cover a teacher intending to show a bow hold, they should first state that they wish to do so and why, explaining why it is needed, and seek consent from learners. This should be communicated to parents prior to it occurring, via a number of ways: verbally; through the safeguarding and child protection mechanisms; and newsletters. It should also be explained clearly to learners before they begin individual lessons.

Learners and parents should be given the option of either consenting or not consenting (in writing). Precautions put in place can be such that parents attend the lessons, especially when the setting is that of one-to-one lessons; that the designated safeguarding lead attends the lesson; that lessons occurs near a window and in an open-door environment, or as otherwise stated in the relevant policy. The need for explicit considerations on the use or non-use of touch in safeguarding and child protection policies, applies whether you work in your own teaching studio or you are a member of staff or a visiting tutor.

In sum, and to conclude this chapter, in order to successfully develop safe learning environments and prevent risks for learners and oneself as a teacher, ensure the following:

- Be fully aware of the safeguarding and child protection in place at your school or institution and abide by it fully. The policy should include guidelines and procedures for addressing concerns about abuse, disclosures and allegations. Be aware whether or not the policy advocates a no-touch approach? If there is provision for touch in the context of teaching demonstrations, be clear under what circumstances and what provisions for consent request and precautions you must follow.

- Ensure you know the members of staff designated to take lead responsibility for safeguarding and child protection in your school/institution. They will be able to clarify elements of the policy, provide further advice and guidance and receive any safeguarding concerns you may have and also act on them.

- Ensure your work context (be it a school, institution, own studio or other) has the following policies in place, aligned with current context specific legislation and make sure you fully understand their content and procedures. They are: a safeguarding and child protection policy; a whistle-blowing policy (usually this is an integral element of the child protection policy); an equality and diversity policy (aimed at preventing and dealing with discrimination, harassment and bullying); an anti-bullying policy including cyberbullying; an acceptable use of technology policy, including the use of mobile phones; a temporary visitor policy; a safer recruitment policy; and a code of conduct. Ensure the policies are revised and updated at least on a yearly basis, and whenever is required.

- Ensure one-to-one lessons take place in a spacious place, preferably with a window, and where your teaching can be seen by others as it takes place. Having a teaching assistant or another colleague in the room while you teach would be highly recommended, but in reality, this is not always possible. Closed-circuit television (CCTV) recordings can be useful to demonstrate your conduct, and should there be any concerns raised, they can be used if recording permission is obtained (from learners, parents and institutions) and where there are robust policies and procedures on safe data storage and data handling. An open-door policy where parents are invited to attend the lessons, particularly if you work in your own studio, is another way around this. If you provide lessons in learners' own homes, ensure there is **always** a responsible adult in the house at the day and time of the lesson, and that the lesson takes place in a common area of the house, with windows and an open door.

- If you teach online, ensure that the platform you use is safe and secure, that you and your learners are in a common area of the house (e.g., living room or kitchen), that you dress in appropriate work clothes (no pyjamas) and that a parent, guardian or a responsible adult is in the room with the learner for the entire duration of the lesson.

- Be open and prepared to listen to children and young people, remaining continuously aware of their needs and behaviours. Likewise, be aware of your own behaviour and that of your colleagues. **Always** act if you have any concerns about a child or young person. **Not acting is not an option.**

Reflective Questions

1. Outline current legislation, guidelines, policies and procedures for safeguarding children and young people in your own country. Compare these with those found in the UK context (outlined in this chapter) and explain how these can be applied to your teaching.				
• Download CW Resource 7 which contains the UK government advice on safeguarding. If you are not based in the UK, search for specific legislation on this topic in your country. After reading these documents consider how they may converge or differ and what the implications are for your teaching.	Aligned with CME, Level 4 Unit (U) or Area of Study (AOS) and Assessment Criteria number of ABRSM (2014) and TCL (2013, 2019)			
	ABRSM		TCL (2013)	
	U6:	6.1.1.	U6:	1.1
			TCL (2019)	
• Apart from the legislation mentioned above, it is advisable to become familiar with other pieces of related legislation such as the Children Act 1989 and the United Nations Convention on the Rights of the Child. References for these can be found in the references section and these can be easily found online.			AOS4:	2
• Read the Child Protection policy of your specific institution and consider how it compares to the pieces of legislation mentioned above				
• If you teach in a self-employed capacity, and do not currently have a child protection policy, you need to create a policy. Your policy needs to agree with the country specific legislation of where you exercise your teaching work and outline considerations for all contexts of your work (e.g., face-to-face teaching, online teaching, one-to-one, group, etc.)				

2. Explain the roles of different individuals and agencies involved in safeguarding children and young people in their musical learning in the UK and note any differences in relation to your own country (if you are not based in the UK).

	ABRSM		TCL (2013)	
• Clearly and succinctly articulate the role of at least the following individuals: legislators; local authorities; Children's Services; school principals; head teachers; designated safeguarding officers; and, your role as a music teacher/educator.	U6:	6.1.2	U6:	1.2
			TCL (2019)	
• If you are not based in the UK, consider the differences and similarities with the roles described in this chapter in relation to the UK context.			AOS4:	2.1.1

3. Explain what to do when children and young people are ill or injured.

	ABRSM		TCL (2013)	
• Consider what you will do when you suspect that abuse might be occurring, but do not have evidence.	U6:	6.2.1 6.3.1	U6:	2.1 3.1 3.2
• Outline the principles and boundaries of confidentiality and when and how to share information.			TCL (2019)	
• Explain what you will do upon evidence that abuse is occurring.			AOS4:	2.1.2 2.1.3 2.1.4 2.1.5 2.1.6

4. Outline the boundaries for appropriate and inappropriate touch when supporting learners' music making and how music teachers can avoid risks and possible consequences for themselves when working with children and young people.

	ABRSM		TCL (2013)	
• Consider the child protection policy in your context and what it states regarding the use of touch for musical demonstration purposes. Is the policy fit for purpose? Are there any policy suggestions or changes you would like to discuss with your Designated Safeguarding Officer?	U6:	6.4.2 6.5.1	U6:	5.1
			TCL (2019)	
• What precautions do you take to ensure that you abide by the Child Protection policy of your institution/context?			AOS4:	3.1.1 3.1.2 3.1.3
• What precautions do you take to prevent risks and allegations being made against you by a child, parent, or work colleague?				

5. Consider how you promote safe practice of ICT, including the use of internet, online activities, mobile phones, social media and music technology in your teaching.				

	ABRSM		TCL (2013)	
• Consider the three types of risks to online safety outlined in Table 8.1 (i.e., content, contact and conduct) and explain what actions you take to ensure online safety. Most of these actions should also be part of your school, institution, or studio policy. • If you teach online, what policies and procedures do you follow to ensure safety for you and your students and to prevent unfounded allegations against you?	U6:	6.4.4	U6:	4.4
			TCL (2019)	
			AOS4:	2.1.5 2.1.6

Notes

1. School governors generally are parents of children at the school, members of the school staff, authority governors nominated by the local education authority, members of the local community (appointed by the rest of the governing body) and/or representatives of any sponsoring bodies. They are tasked with providing the school with a clear vision, ethos and strategic direction, holding the headteacher to account for the educational performance of the school and its pupils, and overseeing the financial performance of the school, ensuring its money is well spent.
2. School Principal/Head teacher is the staff member of a school responsible for the management of the school.
3. The children barred lists consists of a database of people who are not allowed to work with children and vulnerable adults in regulated activities.

Further Reading

Department for Education (DfE) (2019). *Keeping children safe in education Statutory guidance for schools and colleges on safeguarding children and safer recruitment (DfE-00130–2019)*. DfE.

Office for Standards in Education (Ofsted) (2013). *Inspecting e-safety briefing for section 5 inspection*. Ofsted.

References

Associated Board of the Royal Schools of Music (ABRSM) (2014). *Level 4 certificate for music educators: Assessment framework*. ABRSM.

Baker, H., Miller, P., Starr, E., Witcombe-Hayes, S., & Gwilym, C. (2019). *Let children know you're listening: The importance of an adult's interpersonal skills in helping to improve a child's experience of disclosure*. NSPCC Learning.

Department for Education (DfE) (2019). *Keeping children safe in education, statutory guidance for schools and colleges part one: Information for all school and college staff (DfE-00129–2019)*. DfE.

National Society for the Prevention of Cruelty to Children (NSPCC) (2020). *What to do if a child reveals abuse?* www.nspcc.org.uk/keeping-children-safe/reporting-abuse/what-to-do-child-reveals-abuse/

Office for Standards in Education (Ofsted) (2013). *Inspecting e-safety briefing for section 5 inspection.* Ofsted.

The Adolescent Self Harm Forum (2016). *Self-harm guidelines for staff within school and residential settings in Oxfordshire* (4th ed.). NHS Primary Care Trust.

The Children Act 1989 (commencement and transitional provisions) Order 1991 No. 828 (C. 19) (1991). www.legislation.gov.uk/uksi/1991/828/contents/made

The Children Act (2004). www.legislation.gov.uk/ukpga/2004/31/contents

The UK Safer Internet Center (2020). *Appropriate filtering for education settings.* The UK Safer Internet Center. www.saferinternet.org.uk/advice-centre/teachers-and-school-staff/appropriate-filtering-and-monitoring

Trinity College London (TCL) (2013). *TCL level 4 certificate for music educators: Specifications.* TCL.

Trinity College London (TCL) (2019). *TCL level 4 certificate for music educators, areas of study.* TCL.

United Nations General Assembly (1989). *Convention on the rights of the child.* Treaty Series, vol. 1577. www.refworld.org/docid/3ae6b38f0.html

9 Promoting Collaboration and Partnerships to Support Musical Learning

To Guide Your Reading

- What are the characteristics of effective partnership planning and working?
- How do we establish relationships and collaborative partnerships to support children and young people's music learning?
- How should we evaluate the effectiveness of partnership learning, particularly in relation to its impact on children and young people's musical learning and experiences?

Introduction

Music teachers and educators typically work in partnership with their learners, learners' parents, other schools and the wider community. Developing partnerships and collaborations requires the ability to identify key issues and being able to think 'outside the box' in order to find solutions to problems as they arise. In so doing, they provide better quality learning experiences for learners. This requires taking the initiative to create or help shape a shared vision and goals with relevant key stakeholders as well as understanding the processes of planning, delivery and evaluation. Starting with defining different types of partnership work, where collaboration is highlighted as the highest form of working together, the core attributes of partnership work are introduced at the start of this chapter. This is followed by a section on the combined use of Design Thinking and Design Flow methodologies for initiating and establishing partnership work. Next, considerations on developing effective partnerships with parents, schools and the wider community are made. The chapter concludes with insights on how to evaluate the effectiveness and impact of partnership work.

Why are Partnerships Important?

Partnerships are crucial for:

- Building knowledge. By enabling the creation of links between public knowledge and practitioner knowledge, partnerships generate new knowledge and opportunities for learning for all.

- Adding capacity and supporting efficiency by providing added knowledge and also (potentially) funds for undertaking key activities.

- Widening curriculum choice and access, and providing more options for learners via shared initiatives, courses and facilities.

- Promoting the broader welfare of learners by utilising a more holistic approach to meet their needs.

- Supporting school improvement by drawing on the resources of other institutions to help solve problems, share expertise, raise expectations and address the needs of particular groups of learners.

(Hill, 2008, p. 18)

Developing partnerships where the benefits listed earlier materialise is not always easy or straightforward. A survey conducted by Ofsted (2012) on music partnership work, undertaken in primary and secondary schools in England, highlighted that only ten of the 59 schools visited were making 'outstanding' or 'good' use of partnerships to improve musical outcomes for all groups of learners and obtaining good value for money. Moreover, in the one-to-one instrumental music context, Creech's (2009) work revealed a number of difficulties in the teacher-parent-learner relationships which prevented the establishment of the "harmonious trio" types of partnership and interaction (more ahead).

It is true that excellent work has been done at international, national and local levels, as evidenced by partnerships developed between a variety of organisations supporting music, musicians and music education initiatives in schools, community, institutional and informal environments. To learn more about some of these initiatives, please see CW Resource 5. However, given that too many children and young people around the world still do not receive a good enough music education, and given that all too often musical partnerships don't provide long term impact (Ofsted, 2012, partnership report), there remains much to be done.

Types of Partnerships

Teachers can establish various types of partnership work. Broadly speaking, this can range from networking and co-ordination to cooperation and collaboration (Cribb, 2009). The type of partnership and degree of formality involved will determine the processes, structures and forms of leadership required:

- **Networking** is done more at a person-to-person level and includes sharing best practices and information which is mutually beneficial. For example, learning how another school has dealt with a specific challenge which may also be affecting other schools, or how a local studio teacher has increased learner numbers.

- **Co-ordination** occurs mostly at the programme level, for example sharing educational provisions for a class where there are only few learners registered, by co-ordinating delivery within another school or arranging for another local teacher to take up a group of learners for a given period of time (in cases of possible illness, work breaks and maternity and paternity leave, etc.).

- **Cooperation** involves co-ordination implicitly, but with higher levels of shared work, although still limited to specific programmes of study and where cooperation occurs through the sharing of resources such as staff, learning resources and venues. For example, in organising a masterclass with a renowned teacher, it is paid for by learners of a number of local teachers sharing the costs through collective fund raising.

- **Collaboration** involves working together as separate entities to solve common problems, which are not solely programme specific. Specific problems in music which could potentially be tackled through collaboration include the need for increasing elective choices in music by young people at secondary schools (e.g., GCSE and A level options); increasing young people's employability prospects in music; improving girl's participation and attainment in music technology; improving boy's participation and retention levels in choral music; and improving music teaching and learning provision.

Collaboration is the highest form of working together, as it demonstrates a high commitment of all involved in attempting to solve a common problem affecting its learners and young people. It is particularly advantageous whenever the objectives met could not have been achieved by individuals or schools working alone (Cribb, 2009). Benefits of collaborative partnerships include:

- **Access to increased resources**: this may include being able to benefit from expertise of staff working at another school through the collaborative venture, the sharing of expensive equipment (for example, a music production and recording studio) or the availability of a wider variety of musical instruments and specialist teachers.

- **Sharing of risks:** this includes, for example, implementing a new idea for a programme which has not been tested yet or sharing the costs for recruiting staff to work across schools.

- **Enhancing efficiency:** access to increased resources and sharing of risks. Combined, this contributes to an enhanced efficiency overall.

- **Sharing of learning:** working collaboratively will reflect itself in immense opportunities for learning and growth for all involved, within and beyond the collaborative project in itself.

- **Achieving a moral purpose with respect to children and young people:** this refers to developing a moral consciousness vis-à-vis advocating excellent learning opportunities for all children and young people.

The elements that follow were identified by Kerr et al. (2003) as core attributes of partnership working. They can be transposed onto conceptualising partnerships in music education also. The definition of each of these key elements contributes to the definition of the type of partnership being established and shapes much of the processes and dynamics of partnerships. How so? Let us consider the following:

- **Participation:** who are the participants and what type of roles and participation will they have in the partnership?

- **Relationships and trust**: trust is a key element in bringing and keeping people together. It contributes to the level of effectiveness of the partnership. Hence, we must ask: how can relationships be forged, and higher levels of trust established, between all involved and at various levels or participation? Trust is an essential element in building effective partnerships and is the glue that holds and keeps a partnership together. To ensure trust is developed, we must both enact and promote the use of the following behaviours: talk straight; demonstrate respect; create transparency; know right and wrongs; show loyalty; deliver results; get better at what you do; confront reality; clarify expectations; practise accountability; listen first; keep commitments; and extend trust (Covey, 2006).

- **Co-ordination, facilitation and leadership**: what structures, processes and procedures will be in place for co-ordination, facilitation and leadership? Obviously, this will depend on the type of work that needs to be undertaken, as well as the duration and resources available.

- **Communication:** how will communication be carried out between all involved, and when? How can it be ensured that communication is always done in a respectful and welcoming manner (both verbal and written)?

- **Structural balance:** This refers to the structures and processes in place, including hierarchical structures. While a lack of structure can create confusion and no sense of direction, contrariwise *too much* structure can constrain initiative and dynamism. This is especially true of music education. How can a reasonable balance be achieved?

- **Diversity and dynamism:** partnerships bring together disparate people and ideas, and for this very reason they are dynamic. How will an inclusive, respectful and welcoming environment be created and promoted?

- **Decentralisation and democracy:** how can it be ensured that participants at all levels and in various roles take part in decision making? How will they shape the direction of travel of the partnership work? This will require negotiation. Therefore, we must consider: how can negotiation processes be arranged in order to resolve disagreements in proactive ways?

- **Time and resources:** partnership planning needs to consider the time and resources required for the partnership to materialise effectively, including at the planning stage. This includes building plans for succession planning in case a partner needs to stand down or in case other partners or members need time off. It is important to consider the level and responsibilities given to members and those participating and whether these can be shared among people.

- **Monitoring and evaluation:** effective partnership and collaborative work requires careful monitoring and evaluation carried out at various points in time in order to ascertain if a change of methods, direction or other actions are needed to enhance the impact of such work or to improve processes which may have turned out to be more challenging than originally anticipated.

Although we tend to have a preference for working with people we have worked with before (due to levels of trust previously established), by working only with people we already know, we unnecessarily limit ourselves and the desired outcomes. It is a fact that working with new partners may increase the risks involved, but it also may offer new and interesting benefits.

Initiating Partnership Work

At the early planning stages of partnership work, I suggest using Design Thinking Methodology (Quayle, 2017; Simon, 1996). This can ensure that the partnership is contextualised in a clear understanding of the current needs of learners in your working context, side-by-side with a clear understanding of the needs or priorities of potential partners.

Design Thinking has been used by many innovators in science, engineering, businesses, literature, art and even music to solve problems using human-centred techniques in creative and innovative ways. The first stage in Design thinking methodology is called **empathise**, meaning that designing meaningful solutions requires first and foremost an ability to empathise with the people for whom we are designing and to understand/anticipate what their needs are/will be. This means involving your learners in the process by, for example, asking them what they would be interested in developing further and encouraging them to investigate their own priorities, preferences and aims. This has the added advantage of helping learners feel valued, appreciated and included; it also promotes their active participation and engagement in the initiative.

The second stage is to **define.** After obtaining learners' views on what matters to them, there might be a variety of different views, preferences and conflicting opinions regarding pedagogic priorities. Defining these requires finding common themes, combining ideas and thinking more widely to ensure that the initiative can be meaningful to all, without losing its main, core identity. At the same time, this stage is about identifying your learners' needs and reflecting upon your insights in terms of what could be done and would be useful to them. You should also consider what could be of interest to potential partners since you are looking to establish shared purposes.

The next stage is **ideation**. This stage is about having ideas, challenging assumptions and creating innovative solutions to problems. The ideas you come up with need to relate to the information you obtained during the stages of empathising and defining. Now, in the ideation stage, you are required to think 'outside of the box' and as creatively as possible in order to come up with innovative meaningful solutions. It might be that what is relevant to you and your learners is not, for some reason, as appealing to potential partners. If this is the case, make a list of partnership ideas that you think might be appealing for your potential partners. Then try to combine what might be appealing to them with what is relevant to both you and your learners. This type of work has the potential to generate innovative ideas which combine disparate, yet complimentary ideas which can enrich music education for a group or groups of children and young people in the context where you work. It can also offer you opportunities to expand your work into areas you may not have considered previously.

After you have assembled some ideas, in order to ensure they are meaningful to learners, you will move on to the next stage of the design thinking methodology, namely to **prototype** one or two of the most relevant ideas by sketching them out in more detail. At this point, I suggest that when prototyping your ideas, you consider the four elements of the Design Flow proposed by Chapman and Hadfield (2010), which are purpose; agency; processes; and structure.

Having passed through the design thinking methodology stages of empathising, defining and ideation, you are now well placed to define a **purpose** for each idea you aim to prototype. This should be framed as a vision statement, expressing the values and beliefs behind this initiative (preferably well-aligned with those of the participants and institutions involved). The **purpose** refers to the overall direction of the partnership, particularly with regard to questions such as what is there to do? What are the goals? What are the shared goals which are relevant for each partner leading to improved co-ordination of programmes, policies, delivery and consequently better outcomes?

Furthermore, shared values reflecting respect for the contributions of all partners, as well as understanding and acceptance of differences, combined with an absence of status barriers, will result in more active and impactful engagement overall. The vision statement of the partnership, rooted in its purpose, clarifies the purpose and direction while also inspiring people to work together towards shared success. The statement should describe in a **concise** and **brief** way the ideal result being aimed for. Evidently, this will necessarily require careful and thoughtful thinking ahead, and setting future-focused and yet realistic, attractive and credible goals for the partnership.

Apart from goals for the partnership (overarching statements), you must also establish and consider learning outcomes for the learners. These can include questions such as what are learners expected to develop, learn and do at different stages of the project? What are they expected to have achieved when the project is completed? Knowing the answers to these forms an essential component of being able to successfully evaluate the partnership's impact. Considerations should also be made with regard to what stakeholders and partners are expected to achieve (both jointly and separately). Expectations for learners and partners will, of course, be different. However, what matters is that when all expectations are set, though they might seem disparate when separate, when coming together they result in all pieces of the 'puzzle' painting a clear picture of *what* and *how* this will be achieved.

Concerning **agency,** consider what kinds of collective agency need to be developed and implemented. This implies defining who the partners and stakeholders are and defining what you will do together, what you might do separately for the purposes of the partnership and what resources will you share (if any).

In relation to **processes**, you need to consider what processes need to be implemented to ensure that the partnership work is successful. Here, considerations need to be made regarding roles and responsibilities; for example, who is in charge of the project, and who keeps an eye on it? What boundaries, forms of governance and policies are required? When and how will evaluation take place? (more on evaluation ahead). With regard to **structures**, what structures need to be in place to ensure implementation of the project? What resources will be needed (e.g., staff, time, venue, musical instruments, parental involvement and/or engagement)?

You can use the template for planning a partnership available at CW Resource 8 to conceptualise and prototype your ideas for partnership work. Once you have created a prototype for one or two ideas, take the ideas back to your learners and ask them for their views and feedback on what they think about these prototypes. Try to get specific answers in terms of what possible adjustments, changes and improvements are necessary and even, perhaps, attempt to take a democratic decision on what idea to pursue. Of course, this needs to be communicated in suitable ways in accordance with learners' ages and in ways that they can follow. Therefore, ensure that you are mindful of the level of detail you might give. Ideally, and to follow all stages of design thinking methodology, you would test one or two prototypes, perhaps by running a one-off session similar to what the partnership project is about, and gather feedback from all participants and stakeholders. However, there will not always be resources available in music education related partnership work to enable testing of the stage to be materialised. In such cases, the implementation of the project will be *in and of itself* the test, and while potentially nerve-wracking, is also likely to be filled with many learning opportunities.

Developing Effective Partnerships With Parents

Partnerships established between music teachers and parents are crucial in helping parents realise and understand the profound impact music can have on children and young people's lives. Indeed, it is ultimately our responsibility as teachers to make the case for music and raise awareness of its importance. There is no better way to do this than by establishing ways of working together with parents by partnering with them both formally and informally. Creating meaningful partnerships with parents requires an understanding of their needs, being empathetic, welcoming, respectful and developing an inclusive environment where their contributions and their efforts to engage are acknowledged and appreciated.

When developing partnerships with parents, it is important to consider the differences between parental involvement and parental engagement. Whereas involvement is about 'doing to', engagement is about 'doing with'. Initiatives utilising parental involvement are those where teachers and the school or institution have identified an idea, needs or goals and which then tell parents how they can productively contribute to realising these. Examples include teachers asking parents to volunteer to help out with child minding at a music competition, festival or concert; fundraising activities to obtain funds for a music summer programme or holiday scheme; and requesting that a parent attends a parent-teacher meeting where the parent is given information on the child's progress.

Parental engagement, by contrast, is about providing a space for parents to communicate, either individually or in groups. Here, they can say what they think, raise any concerns they might have and discuss what they would like to see done. This can include providing ways in which parents can, for example, have a say on policy making or on how a certain learning programme is developed and structured; asking parents what their needs are in terms of supporting the learning and musical development of their child; and devising ways in which parents can be given the support they need and ways in which they can provide support for a programme.

Design thinking methodology, with its five sequential steps of empathise, define, ideation, prototype and test, exists side-by-side with considering purpose, agency, processes and structures, providing a structured approach for devising parental engagement and with the potential for creative and innovative solutions to be generated. Obviously, there will be instances where parental involvement is the appropriate thing to do, and others where engagement can help with tackling a variety of different problems. Parental involvement and engagement are both important, and research shows that each is in its own way is beneficial; however, engagement has been shown to produce better outcomes for learners, parents, schools and communities (Ferlazzo & Hammond, 2009).

Creating a two-way, safe and open communicative environment where communication between you, parents and other people involved (e.g., staff) can operate effectively is essential. Parents will be keen to engage when they feel that as a teacher you and the institution where you work have a child-centred interest and a vision for the child. They will also be impressed that as a teacher you are totally invested in the child's development. Therefore, you will want to provide parents with personalised communication specifically related to their child. The process should be such that during each encounter with parents you progressively develop positive relationships which will lead to parents' development of a deeper appreciation of their child's potential, strengths and areas of/for improvement. This communication needs to be done at appropriate junctures. More precisely, it must be done in time for actions to be put in place to support the child in a timely fashion. Nowadays, technology can play a useful role in facilitating communication (e.g., email, text messages, Skype, WhatsApp, etc.), and it is possible to establish parental group chats to promote communication between parents but also share information which might be of interest to the group.

It can be said that the purpose of working in partnership with parents in music education is to help parents see beyond the values, beliefs, and aspirations which have shaped and guided *their* parenting styles and practices in order to grasp their *children's* musical potential and the importance music can have in their lives. One example of this is the way that parents often 'construct evidence' that their eldest child is a better musician than his/her siblings, which in turn will influence the siblings' musical identity/identification (Borthwick & Davidson, 2002, p. 71). Parents can promote a child's "musical competence and achievement; a sense of musical identity and accomplishment; and the continuing desire to participate, overcome obstacles and succeed" (McPherson, 2009, p. 95). However, the reality is that they may not always know how to do so, or how to do so appropriately: some parents, for instance, can expect too much from their children, and in such cases it is also beneficial to be able to create realistic expectations within the minds of parents otherwise children can become trapped in a cycle of demotivated resentment towards the entire music education endeavour.

Teachers can provide appropriate support at this level by empowering parents and children to construct positive attitudes towards music and music making. Working in partnership with parents and families demonstrates that the role of the music teacher and educator goes *far beyond* skill development, and implies a need to be aware of "the web of musical meanings with which we all negotiate, and of the intrinsic relationships between learners' social groups, their musical practices, and their overall musical experiences" (Green, 2010, p. 32). This, of course, includes parents also.

The benefits of establishing effective partnerships with parents are wide ranging. They include being able to help parents to foster their children's sense of competence by enabling them to acknowledge children's efforts and traditional hard work. This needs to be complemented with guidance to parents in relation to managing learners' reactions to frustrations by focusing on the learning goals and reminding children that working hard is more important than achieving high grades (McPherson, 2009). Equally relevant is to convince parents not to 'read' their child's musical interest and musical potential from the child's ability to cope with practice (McPherson, 2009). Specifically, it is vital for them to understand that musical accomplishment is not a pathway of linear progression upwards and can, at times, be very frustrating (e.g., the learning of new, more difficult scales at a higher grade). Understanding the use of music for self-expression and creative purposes, realising its importance in the lifecycle process and how they can use music in the family environment for a variety of different purposes should be a major goal for teachers.

Indeed, research has shown that instrumental music teachers recognise the importance of communicating and working with parents (Creech, 2010). However, the type of perceptions which teachers have vis-a-vis their own roles as teachers and the roles of parents strongly influences the types of partnership they develop with their learners and also learner's parents. As a result of observations in the one-to-one violin teaching and learning context, Creech (2009) proposed a model of interpersonal interaction between teachers, learners and parents, containing six different types of interpersonal interactions. I urge you to consider the interpersonal interactions detailed in the following as a way to interpret your teacher-parent and teacher-learner partnerships. Furthermore, you should also consider whether there is potential for altering your interaction patterns as you see fit in order to enhance your teaching and consequently your learners' learning.

Solo Teacher: in this type of interaction, the learner is expected to accept guidance in a relation characterised by power in favour of the adults. The teacher believes in his or her ability to control the extent to which learners become competent and also considers parents as an asset.

However, the teacher demonstrates a narrow zone of tolerance for incompatibility with his or her expectations and preferences, with harmony prevailing (at least between teacher and parent) where parents comply with the teacher's expectations. The teacher is not sensitive to difficulties parents may be experiencing.

Parents who perceive the teacher as efficacious consider their own responsibility to be to reinforce the teacher's directions. Learners who initially complied with parental wishes may change to an interaction where controlling surveillance measures imposed by parents are rejected.

Dominant Duo: the motivation for learning is driven by the parent-teacher dyad, with the learner being a third party to the parent-teacher transactions. The teacher tries to meet the expectations of the parent and at the same time connect with a learner who may not always share the parent's agenda.

The teacher in this kind of partnership attempts to encompass the divergent preferences and expectations of both learner and parent. Although the parent conveys a sense of high self-efficacy related to the fact that the skills being learned are those with which he or she felt confident with, the learner has low self-efficacy, as demonstrated by the amount of effort he or she is prepared to spend on learning.

Since the teacher is aware of the parents' little regard for the child's individual preferences, the teacher may attempt to compensate by being very responsive to the learner within the learner-teacher relationship.

Dynamic Duo: the teacher sees him/herself as a competent specialist and considers that their role is to concentrate the efforts of both teacher and child on the work that can be accomplished between them. As such, they maintain a distance from parents.

Teachers in this type of interaction tend to portray themselves as isolated and distant from parents not only in time and space but also ideologically and tend to preserve this divide. Parents, who may have provided forms of support in the home perhaps not recognised by the teacher do not feel equal to discussing the subject matter with the professional specialist. Teacher and learner form an alliance where the teacher selects appropriate material for each learner and demonstrates enthusiasm for the subject matter by offering consultation and discussion. The learner may not have been receptive to coercion on the part of the parent to practise, and hence parents, who see themselves as resources for their children rather than agents responsible for shaping the child, may have avoided exerting control and instead have permitted the child to regulate his or her own activities and learning.

Double Duo: in this type of interaction, the teacher's relationship with parents is unilateral or hierarchical, not reciprocal or collaborative. Parents were enlisted to help to achieve their goals, which were determined together with the learner. However, teachers were not responsive in their attitudes towards parents, judging their own views to be superior and sometimes considering that they were doing the parenting which they believe the real parents should be doing.

Teachers in these cases establish strong bonds with their learners, and learners in turn respond positively to the teacher's directions and seek the interest and support of their teachers. In this way, the teacher-learner relationship resembles that of a 'musical parent'. This type of interaction differs from the Solo Teacher type on the grounds that here the learner occupies a diplomatic role, in a partnership where there was little rapport between teacher and parent but where a strong teacher-learner agreement exists and which retains high learner receptiveness to parental support.

Discordant Trio: there is lack of trust in the relationship between parents and teacher and distance is maintained. Teachers find it difficult to deal with criticism from powerful parents, and don't welcome parental views relating to pedagogy, even when parents' insights have to do with their knowledge of the child's ability to cope with particular tasks.

Teachers tend to perceive parents' insights as threatening and as an infringement on the teacher's judgement. In this type of partnership, teacher and learner roles, as implicitly accepted by the teacher, parent and learner alike, are such that: 1) the teacher has a duty to the learner and parent, in relation to educating the learner; 2) the learner has a duty to obey the teacher's instructions related to learning; and 3) the parents' duty, as defined by the teacher, is not to hinder the teacher in the fulfilment of his or her role and responsibilities.

Harmonious Trio: is characterised by a healthy parent-teacher-learner partnership whereby the fundamental needs of developing the learner's trust, autonomy (independence) and initiative towards learning are shared between the teacher, parent and learner.

In this scenario, both the parents and teacher recognise their capacity to promote trust in children and promote autonomy and provide guidance while at the same time fostering independence. Initiative is promoted by engaging with children in motivating ways. Also, parents and teachers enrich one another's roles by meeting each other's needs by working together collaboratively, seeking information and support from each other and engaging in collaborative feedback. Parental involvement and engagement occur at various degrees and differently at different stages of the child's development. It can include attending lessons; helping with practice; attending concerts; and personal involvement (knowing about what was going on for the child within the learning environment).

The teacher integrates parental involvement and engagement into their regular teaching, resulting in parents feeling positive about their ability to make a positive contribution to the learning. Learners achieve a balance of agency (the drive towards independence) and are encouraged in their development as autonomous learners where the adults (both teacher and parents) believed in the learner's musical potential and thus offered emotional and practical support in all musical endeavours.

In the context of partnership work, it is important to consider any potential barriers and challenges and ways to overcome such barriers, whenever possible. As seen earlier, some barriers to the partnership reside in teachers' perceptions of their own role and parents' roles. Careful reflection at this level is important: it allows one to overcome challenges and develop efficient ways of working together harmoniously, preferably in the "harmonious trio" as suggested by Creech (2009). However, there are a number of other barriers which must be taken into account. For instance, setting high levels of expectation thought of as impossible to meet by the child can create unnecessary barriers and difficulties: it has been shown to create tensions within the family and results in children losing motivation (Borthwick & Davidson, 2002). Indeed, a famous Hollywood movie, *Shine* (1996), dealt with this very issue in the context of a young piano prodigy.

A report by Russell and Granville (2005) undertaken in Scotland identified some challenges in establishing partnerships with parents in schools, which can also affect partnerships with parents in music education more generally. These included a lack of time both from parents and teachers to meet and discuss ways for working more closely; teachers and parents preconceived notions and attitudes towards each other's roles; and resistance from parents to forming groups as documented in the report mentioned earlier. There were other specific barriers identified for specific groups of parents: asylum seekers and refugees; parents with disabilities; foster carers; travellers; and parents living in remote locations from schools.

This provides food for thought for reflecting on how we interact with parents: how welcoming we may or may not be; how we communicate that their involvement and engagement is needed, useful and wanted; and how we combat the stereotypical notion that parents need to be necessarily knowledgeable in music to support their children musically. This report also highlights ways to overcome some of the challenges above discussed. Given the usefulness and comprehensiveness of this report, a link to it is provided on the CW Resource 9.

Developing Effective Partnerships With Schools and the Wider Community

Establishing partnerships with schools, community groups or institutions aimed at mobilising, encouraging and supporting people to take action and collectively make a difference to children, young people and families requires the ability to take the initiative and have a strong willingness to actively contribute to society. If any of these qualities are missing, it is unlikely partnerships will materialise or be successful. Planning and developing this type of work requires strong project management and leadership skills. Once you have decided to facilitate this type of work, it is essential that you develop and refine your ability to persuade and empower people to actively engage and communicate in clear ways: why this is of interest to them; where they fit in; and how they can be part of the initiative?

Partnership work developed between schools has been shown to contribute positively to improved learner attainment and at a faster rate in comparison with contexts where partnerships between schools are not occurring (Chapman & Muijs, 2014; Hutchings et al., 2012). These benefits span across schools working together and offer important development and learning opportunities for staff. This can result in enhanced efficiency and quality of work within and beyond the partnership. While being aware of the relevance of the previously mentioned ideas, the question is how to get started? In his model "Framework for Partnership Practice", Hill (2008) emphasises a number of elements which are here adapted to fit the diverse contexts of music education. You may wish to consider these when planning to develop effective working partnerships between schools, or the wider community. They are:

- Building upon current joint working and existing relationships;

- Having a clear understanding of the current performance and needs of your own teaching context/institution/school;

- Having a clear understanding of the performance and needs of potential partners, be it individuals, schools, institutions and/or the wider community;

- Having an agreed focus and purpose for partnership working;

- Having an agreed plan and methodology for partnership working;

- Involving staff in the development of the partnership;

- The availability of dedicated funding to support the establishment of a partnership;

- Learning from other partnerships;

- Involving learners in the development of the partnership;

- Involving parents in the development of the partnership;

- Having a supportive local authority (depending on the scale of the partnership);

- Involving the governing body in the development of the partnership (this depends on the scale of the partnership).

In terms of agreed planning and methodology, it is relevant to ascertain the shared purpose between partners and clearly define what type of partnership is to be developed. Establishing what needs to be done and by whom, as well as the roles and responsibilities and forms of leadership and governance, is also essential. An Ofsted (2012) report on music partnership work in primary and secondary schools in England highlighted that schools where music education partnerships were successful were those where:

- Sustained and significant levels of funding were monitored rigorously and evaluated at different points in time. This allowed for action to be taken when funding was not being utilised well. This ensured good value for money;

- Schools made efforts to ensure that all groups of learners benefited from the partnerships, including the most disadvantaged groups, through monitoring and tailoring of provisions to make it relevant;

- Partnership work was linked to learners' interests, needs and levels of proficiency, through analysis of learner's prior experiences. This contributed to high levels of engagement and effective progress. It also allowed the partnership to complement and support other school related music work;

- Strategies were put in place to ensure that musicians (school teachers and visiting musicians) could learn from each other, leading to sustained work and enhanced learning for learners during and beyond the partnership;

- Headteachers, senior managers and leaders used the partnership to gain more knowledge and insights into music education. This resulted in careful monitoring and evaluation, as well as enhanced professional dialogue with music teachers, better value for money and improved outcomes for learners.

Anticipating potential barriers and detailing solutions for overcoming them is another important aspect in partnership planning and management. Broadly speaking, barriers can be of various types, and Hill (2008) has categorised these as cultural; strategic; operational; and leadership related. *Cultural* barriers are firmly established within the ethos and policies of institutions and can include difficulties in understanding or conveying 'what's in it for us?' and difficulties in engaging people, particularly when the work may involve unpaid work and/ or additional responsibilities. These are also applicable where resistance may occur from a group or groups of people which may be rooted in differences with regard to values, beliefs, perceptions and conceptions concerning the benefits versus efforts and resources required. *Strategic* barriers arise whenever there are conflicting objectives or priorities in the schools involved, leading to pressures on individual roles in relation to accountability and insufficient allocation of funding for the project to be sustainable in the long term. *Operational* barriers can transpire whenever there is an incompatibility of schedules, timetables, and/or a lack of resources (e.g., funding, transportation and so on). Last, *leadership related* barriers relate to differences in perception and understanding of aims, objectives and expected outcomes by different stakeholders in the partnership. Key staff can become engaged in conflict and a lack of trust between people can arise thereby jeopardising the partnership.

It might not be possible to anticipate all barriers that may materialise. However, attempting to anticipate difficulties and consider strategies or policies that may need to be in place to prevent or minimise problems should they occur is certainly a wise and prepared course of action to take.

Evaluating the Effectiveness and Impact of Partnership Work

Evaluation and quality assurance are essential and need to be planned to be conducted at several stages in the partnership work (both during and afterwards). Monitoring and evaluation at different stages will provide understandings on key issues such as:

- Are the planned objectives being met for all stakeholders?

- What is going well and how can it be capitalised?

- What needs to be improved and how can this be achieved in a timely fashion?

- Are the processes and procedures put in place fit for purpose? If not, what needs to be changed or adapted?

- Are the communication channels being used efficiently? If not, how can communication be improved?

- Are the expected impacts (short, medium and long term) materialising? If not, what needs to be done for improvement to be demonstrated?

Having 'SMART' objectives established from the outset of the partnership (both shared and individual) for all stakeholders will greatly assist in answering the previous questions efficiently. Namely, having objectives which are **S**pecific, **M**easurable, **A**chievable, **R**ealistic and **T**ime-bound (Drucker, 1955). Once objectives have been established and agreed, it is relevant to establish when, where, how and by whom monitoring and evaluation of the work in progress is to be undertaken. It is only through close monitoring and evaluation that success can be guaranteed as this allows for changes and improvements required to be implemented in a timely fashion. Another aspect that needs to be considered is what sort of data (qualitative and quantitative) needs to be collected in order to understand how the partnership is going, whether or not it's being impactful and how this information will be collected and analysed.

Carefully considering the type of data needed is intimately related to the nature of the work being undertaken. Qualitative data can include informal feedback from children, young people, parents, teachers and staff; pre- and post-intervention interviews, focus groups, surveys or questionnaires; teacher and staff notes and observations; children and young people self-evaluations; surveys undertaken with those involved as stakeholders; and planning records and reviews to planning made at meetings etc. Quantitative date can include attendance records; pre- and post-intervention questionnaires; and attainment levels. Establishing partnership performance indicators with regard to processes, resources, partnership management and impact will guide you in terms of the type and nature of information you need to collect.

Impact can only be seen in the context of specific interventions, and it's hard to define exactly. Broadly speaking, it can be said that when we talk about impact in music education partnership work, we are referring to positive outcomes, in terms of *intended* impact but also *materialised* impact (as a result of the intervention). This is meaningful and important because it brings about a change in a recognised social problem. Preferentially, positive impact should be sustained, meaning that it has a lasting effect, lasting after the intervention has ended, and is achieved by the individuals participating in the intervention and their associated communities.

Impact is usually considered in terms of its short, medium and long-term (sustained) effects and can be difficult to measure or quantify. This is especially true in our context given that in music interventions, assessing *how* the intervention may affect, for example, health or attainment, may be difficult to demonstrate practically. Therefore, impact tends to be more frequently measured in qualitative ways based on the experiences of participants, and for this reason it may be difficult to be measure realistically in the long term. Nevertheless, funders and stakeholders need to be convinced that partnership interventions work and are being impactful. Success in terms of obtaining funds rests on the ability to detail the partnership from a point of view of objectives; expected impact; project management; and ways to evaluate both the project processes and impact. Therefore, the importance of efficiently communicating the impact of your work both to stakeholders, partners, participants, community and funders is integrally embedded in the idea of evaluating impact. By doing this effectively, you will create greater awareness of your work and its importance to the wider community but also generate public curiosity on the innovative work you are doing and hopefully develop supporters of your cause. At the same time, you will develop a strong profile as a committed music teacher and educator in your community who is highly professional and credible and thereby increase chances of obtaining funding for projects you are involved in.

Reflective Questions

1. List at least three organisations that work to support children and young people's musical learning in the context of the work you do. Describe the approaches they take. Why is the work they do important?				
• Do an internet search to find music education related partnership work being developed in your local context and in other countries. Consider who are the partners engaged in this, the type of work being done by each, the wider vision and mission of the initiative, the intended outcomes, and objectives. • Outline the expected impacts stakeholders involved aim to achieve. • Consider evidence of impact presented by these organisations. Were there any evaluations of the work described? If so, how were these obtained?	Aligned with CME, Level 4 Unit (U) or Area of Study (AOS) and Assessment Criteria number of ABRSM (2014) and TCL (2013, 2019)			
	ABRSM		TCL (2013)	
	U2:	2.5.2	U2:	5
			TCL (2019)	
			AOS4:	4.1.1

2. Consider your current teaching context, your learners, and their needs. What partnership work could you plan to initiate?				
• Consider applying the principles of Design Thinking methodology to come up with identification of meaningful ideas for your learners and to co-create the idea with them. • Consider developing a template to plan the partnership idea considering aspects such as: description and background of the partnership; common ground for all partners; benefits; objectives; resources required; terms and conditions; and, plan for evaluation of the partnership. • Also plan for different stages of the partnership work, such as initial, implementation and evaluation stages.				
	ABRSM		TCL (2013)	
	U2:	2.5.3	U2:	5
			TCL (2019)	
			AOS4:	1.1.3 1.1.4

3. Define the characteristics of effective partnerships planning and management.				
• Consider the core attributes of working partnerships identified by Kerr et al. (2003) outlined in this chapter, and any other elements you may find useful.				
	ABRSM		TCL (2013)	
	U2:	2.5.1	U2:	5.1
			TCL (2019)	
			AOS4:	1.1.2

4. Explain how effective relationships and collaboration can be established between partners and learners. Consider aspects such as: negotiating working arrangements, agreeing a budget, roles and responsibilities, learning objectives and musical learning activities.				
• You can use the work you have completed in your answer to Question 2 to demonstrate that you have considered the elements outlined here. The template you use for planning your partnership work can be submitted as an appendix to coursework tasks and as an integral element of your CME portfolio.	ABRSM		TCL (2013)	
	U2:	2.5.3	U2:	5.3
			TCL (2019)	
			AOS4:	1.1.3 1.1.4

5. How can you evaluate the effectiveness and impact of partnership work in children and young people's musical learning and experiences?				
• Consider the section on evaluating the effectiveness and impact of partnership work in this chapter and plan for specific and appropriately contextualised ways to evaluate your partnership work. Your plan for evaluation should also be embedded in your partnership template.	ABRSM		TCL (2013)	
	U2:	2.5	U2:	5
			TCL (2019)	
			AOS4:	1.1.5

Further Reading

Hill, R. (2008). *Achieving more together: Adding value through partnership*. Association of School and College Leaders.

Office for Standards in Education (Ofsted) (2012). *Music in schools: Sound partnerships*. Ofsted. www.ofsted.gov.uk/sites/default/files/documents/surveys-and-good-practice/m/Music in schools sound partnerships.pdf

Quayle, M. (2017). *Designed Leadership*. Columbia University Press.

References

Associated Board of the Royal Schools of Music (ABRSM) (2014). *Level 4 certificate for music educators: Assessment framework*. ABRSM.

Borthwick, S. J., & Davidson, J. (2002). Developing a child's identity as a musician: A "family" script perspective. In R. MacDonald, D. Miell, & D. J. Hargreaves (Eds.), *Musical identities* (pp. 60–78). Oxford University Press.

Chapman, C., & Hadfield, M. (2010). Realising the potential of school-based networks. *Educational Research, 52*(3), 309–323. https://doi.org/10.1080/00131881.2010.504066

Chapman, C., & Muijs, D. (2014). Does school-to-school collaboration promote school improvement? A study of the impact of school federations on student outcomes. *School Effectiveness and School Improvement, 25*(3), 351–393. https://doi.org/10.1080/09243453.2013.840319

Covey, S. (2006). *Speed of trust*. Clements.

Creech, A. (2009). Teacher-parent-pupil trios: A typology of interpersonal interaction in the context of learning a musical instrument. *Musicae Scientiae, XIII*(2), 163–182.

Creech, A. (2010). The role of music leaders and community musicians. In S. Hallam & A. Creech (Eds.), *Music education in the 21st century in the United Kingdom: Achievements, analysis and aspirations* (pp. 314–328). Institute of Education, University of London.

Cribb, A. (2009). *Understanding education: A sociological perspective*. Polity Press.

Drucker, P. (1955). *The practice of management*. Heinemann.

Ferlazzo, L., & Hammond, L. (2009). *Building parent engagement in schools*. Linworth Publishing.

Green, L. (2010). Research in the sociology of music education: Some introductory concepts. In R. Wright (Ed.), *Sociology and music education* (pp. 21–34). Ashgate.

Hill, R. (2008). *Achieving more together: Adding value through partnership*. Association of School and College Leaders.

Hutchings, M., Greenwood, C., Hollingworth, S., Mansaray, A., Rose, A., & Glass, K. (2012). *Evaluation of the city challenge programme* (Research Report DFE-RR215) [Department for Education (DfE)]. https://dera.ioe.ac.uk/14820/1/DFE-RR215.pdf

Kerr, D., Aiston, S., White, K., Holland, M., & Grayson, H. (2003). *Literature review of networked learning communities*. NFER and NCSL commissioned research.

McPherson, G. (2009). (2009). The role of parents in children's musical development. *Psychology of Music, 37*(1), 91–110.

Office for Standards in Education (Ofsted) (2012). *Music in schools: Sound partnerships*. www.ofsted.gov.uk/sites/default/files/documents/surveys-and-good-practice/m/Music in schools sound partnerships.pdf

Quayle, M. (2017). *Designed leadership*. Columbia University Press.

Russell, K., & Granville, S. (2005). *Parent's views on improving parental involvement in their children's education* [The Scottish Executive]. www.webarchive.org.uk/wayback/%0Aarchive/20180518065507/www.gov.scot/%0APublications/2005/03/20759/53608

Simon, H. (1996). *The sciences of the artificial* (3rd ed.). MIT.

Trinity College London (TCL) (2013). *TCL level 4 certificate for music educators: Specifications*. TCL.

Trinity College London (TCL) (2019). *TCL level 4 certificate for music educators, areas of study*. TCL.

10 Becoming a *Reflective* and *Reflexive* Practitioner

To Guide Your Reading

- How can you move from being a *reflective* towards a *reflexive* practitioner?
- What different types of reflection are there?
- How do different theories and models of reflective practice converge and diverge?
- How can you best engage in continuous professional development?

Introduction

Good teachers are not born; rather, they are made over time. This occurs via a process that begins with wanting to learn more in order to become a better teacher, and then being perseverant; regularly trying and evaluating new ways of doing things; and being open to feedback from others for improvement. The process requires understanding of what, why and how we do things so that we can connect better with learners and provide them with high quality learning experiences that will facilitate their learning. It also requires being able to challenge and question one's own attitudes, values, assumptions and prejudices and understanding how they might be influencing one's own actions. This chapter begins by briefly defining *reflective* and *reflexive* practice. Insights are provided on how to ensure that reflection as a process can be optimised, followed by an outline of a selection of theories and models of reflective practice, which gradually evolve towards reflexivity. The concluding section offers suggestions for continuing professional development through understandings of what the expectations for teacher development are and offers suggestions of ways in which teachers can keep themselves up-to-date with the latest developments in theory and practice and their community of practice.

Reflective Versus *Reflexive* Practice

If **you** are a teacher, you are certainly engaged in *reflective practice* and possibly also *reflexive practice* in one way or another, more or less consciously, and in more or less structured ways. *Reflective practice* involves reflecting on what we may think has happened on a given occasion, why it has happened in such way, who was involved and what those involved might have felt, thought or experienced (Bolton, 2010). On the other hand, *reflexive practice* is more than reviewing a specific situation. It involves devising ways in which to question our own attitudes, values, assumptions, thought processes, prejudices and habitual actions so that we can better understand our own roles in relation to others (Bolton, 2010). It requires the ability to establish internal dialogues and make use of the support of others in order to achieve an awareness of how we may be perceived by others while also considering ways to change our own behaviour with the aim of improving our teaching and learners' learning experiences.

As a process, *reflective practice* involves a cycle of reflection-action-reflection grounded on self-reflection and evaluation. In turn, this can promote self-awareness and critical evaluation skills and is something that all teachers (should) do at different points in time (Schön, 1991). This can be at various junctures in the overall learning process, for instance:

- Before an action is taken to evaluate possible consequences, for example, through lesson planning – ***prospective reflection***;

- During teaching as you are actually doing it – ***in action***; and

- Thinking after teaching has taken place – ***on action***.

Combined, the insights obtained through various reflections undertaken at different points in time will help you to:

- Better understand your learners and their needs;

- Review a specific event or situation, how you reacted and how this might help you address similar situations in the future;

- Consider outcome(s) that have occurred as a consequence of a sequence of certain events or actions;

- Consider how to practically apply new theories you have learned in your teaching context, and how to develop the skills needed to implement such concepts;

- Consider your personal and professional learning and development needs and devise a plan of action;

- Further develop your emotional intelligence[1] (Goleman, 1998), particularly when reflections include: considerations concerning emotions experienced in sequence of events; or in reference to some other situation, and which thereby lead to development of self-awareness, recognition and management of emotions.

Given that the main aim of reflection embedded in reflective practice is to *improve teaching*, how can insights gained through reflection result in actions being taken to improve the work we do and moreover bring about positive outcomes in our teaching and contribute to our continuous professional development? At this level it is important to:

- **Engage in reflective practice as a conscious, deliberate and preferably structured process, particularly for issues or situations you have identified that would benefit from reflection**. Several theorists and pedagogues have put forward models of reflective practice to ensure a level of structure in the process. The next section provides a brief overview on some of these models, moving both chronologically and conceptually towards reflexive practice. It will be useful for you to develop a clear understanding of the main concepts behind these models and practically trial implementing a few of them to find out which resonate better with you at a personal and professional level. You can also select a combination of models for your use.

- **Keep in mind that reflection is something you do primarily for yourself, and keep a record of your reflections in the form of a diary**. A record of your reflections will be beneficial for revising, acknowledging and evaluating your own progress in development. However, it can also be used as evidence of continuous professional development. As such, others involved in your development may read it (e.g., mentors, direct line managers and so on). Formats for recording your reflections vary widely, and so does the terminology people use to refer to it at different institutions and places. You might have come across terms such as Personal Development Plan (PDP); Personal Action Plan (PAP); Personal Development Journal (PDJ); or Individual Development Journal (IDJ). There are others which also somehow refer to the same concept, and may be structured in different ways in different institutions. The format **you** adopt for **your** reflection will depend on whether there is an institutionalised process that you are required to follow, or if you are given the freedom to create and use a format that suits you best. Reflections can be made using notebooks, loose pages, computer files, online journals and so on. Generally speaking, whether you are following an institutionalised template or creating your own, it is advisable that your reflections implicitly or explicitly contain descriptions of the situations and/or events you have chosen to focus upon, as well as your analysis and evaluation of these situations or events, your conclusions and how this reflection can inform your future teaching practice.

- **Keep your diary spontaneous and informal. Consider your preferred ways of doing things and schedule regular times to record your reflections. Your** diary provides **you** with a highly personalised opportunity to establish a dialogue with yourself and more closely connect theory and practice. At times, this may be challenging; as with music itself, you may find yourself uncovering elements and processes which are new, unusual or maybe even boring an old hat. This is a *personal* and *subjective* document that you are writing **for yourself**. For instance, if you have a visual learning preference, you can include diagrams, charts and other elements, as long as these help your process of reflection. If talking out loud helps you reflect more efficiently, you can make audio recordings of yourself and these audio files can be compiled together into an audio diary. Or, if required, typed into a written journal/diary and then be used as a basis for further reflections. In either case, reflective practice is to be undertaken over time, and it's important to have regular periods of time which are set aside for you to sit down reflect upon and record your practice (written, audio, other). If the process is to be overseen by a mentor, manager or colleague, remember to agree **from the outset** the type of formats which are acceptable.

How can we optimise self-reflection in order to ensure that we move from being solely *reflective* to also become *reflexive* practitioners? How can one maximise the process? These questions have been addressed by various theorists who have proposed a variety of different models and considered different, yet interrelated, reflection types. All these various reflection types (when used effectively) work symbiotically and can lead to increased levels of self-awareness and understandings on how to move forward. These models provide a structured process that one can follow for undertaking reflective practice. Additionally, the use of a combination of different models provides opportunities for seeing and considering things from different angles and thereby allows you to gain multiple insights as a result.

A Selection of Theories and Models

Different theories and models of reflection have placed emphasis upon different aspects involved in the process of reflective practice. While some have focused upon the conditions that prompt (or are conducive to) engagement in the reflective process, others have considered different types of reflection. Specifically, what needs to be analysed and how results obtained through engagement in reflective practice and reflective thinking can be further used.

John Dewey's early work, entitled *How We Think: A Restatement of the Relation of Reflective Thinking to the Educative Process* (1933), is based upon the ideas of several earlier educators and philosophers. It is considered a seminal work within the field. Dewey considered teaching to be the implementation of a scientific theory and emphasised reflections on teaching as a deliberate, conscious, active and rational process wherein considerations and problems vis-à-vis teaching are analysed logically and where ideas are organised and linked together in meaningful ways. Dewey's conceptual ideas underpin most models and theories of reflection within the educational process. In Dewey's words, reflective thinking is an "active, persistent and careful consideration of any belief or supposed form of knowledge in light of the grounds that support it, and further conclusions to which it leads" (Dewey, 1933, p. 118).

Dewey (1933) made a distinction between reflective thinking and routine thinking. He considered actions *resulting from* reflective thinking as 'intelligent actions' since they have originated from rational considerations of a specific aspect of something rather than solely from impulsive thinking. He believed that reflection was very useful for making sense of events or situations which were difficult to explain, challenging or that created feelings of confusion or even a sense of wonder and awe. In his view, these situations or events were to be resolved through reflection and conceptualised as persistent and reasoned thinking with an end goal in mind, in a cyclical recursive process encapsulating the following sequential steps: experience, reflection, conceptualisation and experimentation (leading itself to new experiences). Recalling the event/situation, and using questions aimed at exploring why things happened the way they did, thereby enabled insights into what actions could have possibly been taken instead in order to achieve a different outcome. Since the publication of Dewey's pioneering work, several theories and models have encapsulated his core ideas concerning reflection and thinking. However, Dewey's notions on reflection have been challenged over the decades by a number of other theorists in this area. The most prominent critique of this model is that it relies heavily upon reflection *as the process of* thinking about action, not linking it well enough with the process of actions taken *as a result of* reflective thinking.

In this regard, Schön's work (1991, 1983, 1987), partly based on the work of Dewey (1933), identified two types of reflection: 'reflection on action', which is undertaken retrospectively after the action has taken place; and 'reflection in action', done while the actions are happening, namely, 'thinking on your feet'. He suggested that by engaging in reflection *on action*, teachers build a repertoire of previous experiences and scenarios which help to inform their future actions in relation to new or unexpected events. In turn, this enables a faster and more appropriate response. Furthermore, reflection-in-action is considered by Schön as a pivotal part in the process of reflection, allowing for a continuous investigation, interpretation and reflective conversation with oneself, through active experimentation concerning aspects which may be challenging. This provides opportunities for the use of information gained through reflections on past experiences to inform and guide new actions. Therefore, 'reflection-in-action' offers a way of using past experiences, reflection and action to experimentally solve problems as they occur.

This process involving experimentation, reflection and action combined, is cyclical, as the problem is continuously interpreted, framed and reframed and solutions are systematically sought. From this, new ideas that are generated are trialled in the classroom environment with a view to solving the problem or offering various possible solutions. Schön considers previous experiences as a source of knowledge to be highly useful in the reflective practice process. However, to be successful it requires that teachers have appropriate experiences to draw upon. Building on Dewey's work, Schön has more efficiently linked reflection to professional development and professional practice. He argues that by engaging in reflective practice, teachers can make links between explicit knowledge[2] and hidden or tacit[3] knowledge. However, neither Schön nor Dewey specify what content and circumstances of reflections would be useful to consider.

To some extent, the Experiential Learning Cycle, devised by Kolb (1984) and later simplified by Pedlar et al. (2001) (who made it clearer and more operational), provides a framework within which to organise the basic components of a Personal Reflection Model. It preconises that reflection should begin with identification of an experience which will be used for reflection ('Concrete Experience' or 'the What?'). This is then followed by considerations on the content of the experience from one's own perception of the situation while devising what needs to be considered, discussed or evaluated (that is, 'Reflective Observation' aimed at reviewing and reflecting on the experience or on 'What happened?'). Subsequently, insights and learnings are grasped from the experience ('Abstract Conceptualisation' or the 'so What'?). The last phase in the cycle involves reflecting upon what needs to be done to generate improvement, to cause solutions and/or learning to materialise, including considering own assumptions, values and behaviour ('Active Experimentation' or in other words, 'now What?'). This reinforces the notion that reflective practice should result in action of some sort and also become *reflexive*. Kolb notes that individuals tend to have a preference for focusing more intensely on one part of the cycle to the detriment of other segments: for instance, by focusing more on the 'Abstract Conceptualisation', that is the 'so What?' phase in Pedlar's model. This is not a problem *as long as* other areas of the cycle are not neglected, and individuals aim to obtain a balanced level of competence in **all** parts of the reflective cycle.

In this model reflection is considered as a metacognitive activity wherein teachers are asked to consider their own thinking processes, values, beliefs and understandings. Sellars (2017, p. 12) highlights a list of questions related to oneself drawn from the work of Gardner (1983). People are able to use this reflection model as they approach each stage of Kolb's model (1984). This is outlined in more detail in the following:

* **What?**

  Why have I decided to focus upon this experience as a focus for reflection? Why is it important that I purposively and consciously reflect upon this experience at **this** point in time?

* **So what?**

  What do I consider the focus here to be?
  How am I prioritising the aspects I focus upon in relation to my reflection?
  Why am I prioritising the aspects in a particular way?

Do my priorities reflect my beliefs and values with regard to teaching as a professional and ethical activity in relation to the ways which I am developing as a teacher?

• **Now what?**

Is it necessary that I take action, or just think about what actions could be taken if the circumstances permit materialisation of action?
Do I have what is required to make well-informed decisions on what actions to take?
Is it possible for me to realistically take a particular action?
What personal, social and ideological influences can/will impact the action I plan to take?
Are the actions I plan to take well aligned with my ethical and moral perspectives on effective teaching and the role of the teacher?
While Schön's work is more concerned with development of expert practitioners in the context of professional practice, Kolb's model is highly theoretical and does not take into consideration the effect of emotions and feelings in the process. Conversely, Boud et al. (1985) argue that since emotions have a strong role on how people recall events, reflection can only be valid from a learning point of view when it considers emotions associated with the event or situation in consideration. It is important to understand why certain, specific emotions occurred and the implications of this in the process. In this way, reflection can become a more integral and complete process.

Gibbs' Reflective Cycle (1988) offers a framework for examining experiences, which lends itself particularly well to reflection on repeated experiences as well as considerations on feelings and thoughts. It contains six recursive and sequential stages:

• Description (what happened?)

• Feelings (what were you thinking and feeling?)

• Evaluation (what was good and bad about the experience?)

• Analysis (what sense can you make of the situation?)

• Conclusion (What else could you have done or done instead?)

• Action plan (If faced again with the same situation what will you do?)

Table 10.1 contains possible questions which can be used at each stage to support reflection using this model.
  In addition to the previous models, which are heavily centred on individual reflection and subjective, individual perceptions, Brookfield (1995) suggests

Table 10.1 Possible questions to guide reflection when using Gibbs Reflective Cycle (1988)

Gibbs Reflective Cycle stages	Possible questions that can help guide reflection
Description of the experience.	• What happened, when and where? • Who else was present? • What did you and the other people do? • What was the outcome of the situation?
Feelings and thoughts about the experience.	• What did I feel during the situation? • What were my feelings before, during and after? • What do I think other people were feeling about the situation? • What do I think other people feel or think about the situation now? • What was I thinking during the situation? • What do I think about the situation now?
Evaluation of the experience, including considering what was good and what needs improvement.	• What went well? • What didn't go so well and requires improvement? • How did I and other people contribute to the experience (positively and/or negatively)?
Analysis to make sense of the situation.	• Why did things go well? • Why did some things perhaps not go so well? • What sense can I make of the situation? • What personal knowledge or input from others can help me understand the situation?
Conclusion: what you learned and what could have been done differently?	• What did I learn from this experience? • How could this have been a more positive experience for everyone involved? • What skills does this situation highlight that I need to develop?
Action Plan for preparing to deal with similar situations in the future, or how to act upon learning needs identified and undertake changes you might find appropriate.	• If I had to do the same thing again, what would I do differently? • How will I develop the required skills or obtain knowledge I need? • How can I make sure that I can act more efficiently next time?

that the process of reflective practice is enhanced by looking through four different lenses:

• **Autobiographical, both as teacher and learner**: to allow deeper understandings of the beliefs, values and assumptions that underpin what you say and do as a teacher and learner, and how these may influence what you do both consciously and instinctively.

- **Through our learners' eyes**: by considering feedback from your learners on your teaching and even by imaginatively placing yourself in the learner's position to obtain insight on whether or not your learners take the meanings you intend from your teaching.

- **Through our colleagues' eyes**: this requires engaging in reflective conversations with colleagues and peers and asking them to observe your teaching and provide you with honest, constructive feedback. Often colleagues and peers can see aspects that we might not be aware of. They can provide constructive feedback enabling reflection on previously unconsidered aspects or considerations on previous assumptions, and hence help to inform decisions on future actions.

- **Through theoretical literature:** this requires being well informed and up-to-date with regard to latest developments in your field and being able to apply both teaching and learning related theories to your practice. It also encompasses being able to use various models of reflective practice, to enable seeing aspects from different viewpoints and thus become a better practitioner.

Continuing Your Professional Development

When considering continuous professional development (CPD), it is important that you have a solid understanding of what the expectations for teacher development are in the contexts where you work. This is especially true in music teaching contexts where many different sets of skills and subject specific knowledge are required and can vary widely from one context to another. While searching for a model of professional development that could be applicable to music teachers as a whole, I came across the CPD framework for teachers and educators used by the British Council (2017). This framework is built on a set of professional practices, enabling analysis of skills and self-awareness features which are in constant interaction. It is a comprehensive model and can easily be transposed and used as a basis for music teachers and educators in the context of their own CPD. With this understanding, I have therefore only slightly adapted the framework to make it more suitable for music teachers (see Table 10.2)

Being a reflexive teacher engaged in continuous personal and professional development requires consideration of where you are at with regard to each of the aspects mentioned in the previous framework, as well as other elements you consider relevant. You must also consider what you need to be doing in order to improve and grow as teacher. At this level, it is crucial that **you** take ownership and responsibility for your own professional development by identifying strengths, weaknesses, learning needs and matching opportunities for development through constant self-evaluation and reflection of your own teaching. Engaging in feedback discussions with your learners, colleagues and other professionals is important for critically challenging your own perspectives with

Table 10.2 A proposed Continuous Professional Development (CPD) model for music teachers

Professional practices	• Knowing and being proficient in the subject you teach in the music context where you operate • Understanding the teaching context • Understanding how teachers and students learn • Planning, managing and moderating teacher and student learning • Demonstrating effective teaching behaviour (including scaffolding, modelling, demonstration and others (see Simones, 2019's framework) • Researching and contributing to the profession • Taking responsibility for your own professional development
Enabling skills	• Music skills required to operate in the specific teaching context • Communicating effectively (verbally, gesturally, musically) • Team working skills • Thinking critically • Building relationships • Effective organisational skills • Increasing motivation • Leadership/supervisory skills
Self-awareness features	• Openness • Conscientiousness • Interactivity (verbal, gestural, musical – both isolated and combined) • Empathy • Resilience

Source: Adapted from Continuing Professional Development Framework for teachers and educators by the British Council (2017)

the perspectives of others in relation to your current teaching practices. It is also useful to obtain suggestions from more experienced colleagues on which strategies you might want to implement and when. This needs to be considered side by side with insights on what is currently considered as best practice in the field, and therefore you need to continuously ensure that you keep up-to-date with this. There are numerous ways to keep yourself up-to-date, for example:

• Being a member of music professional associations or committees (a non-exhaustive list can be found in CW Resource 10);

• Attending training programmes, courses and events such as conferences (for some training programmes and conferences see CW Resource 11);

• Networking with other professionals, either through events or using social media professional networks, and positively contributing to online forums and discussions (for some social media groups, see CW Resource 12);

- Keeping track of and being up-to-date with publications in the field (articles, books, policy reports etc.) through various subscriptions and readings. If you are employed within higher education, it is likely you will have free access to some of these via your institutional credentials. Most allow you to register for electronic updates (for a list see CW Resource 13);

- Visiting other institutions and organisations and understanding more about the work of other colleagues;

- Evaluation of feedback from your learners, colleagues and others;

- Reflecting on experiences and keeping a record of your own improvements/achievements;

- Skills development, particularly through identifying needs in development;

- Observing the teaching of colleagues and other teachers;

- Continuous self-reflection;

- Studying for relevant qualifications;

- Voluntary work;

- Researching in your context of work and contributing further to the music teaching and learning community.

It is through experience, both in *reflective* and *reflexive* practices, that we can come to understand what, why and how we do things as teachers. Thereby, we become ready to adapt and change who we are in a lifelong process of continuous personal *and* professional development. The extent to which you engage in the process will define how integral it will become in your own being helping you strengthen your day-to-day teaching in whatever music context or contexts you operate. As a highly proactive teacher who wants to improve the quality of the teaching you can offer, you will become confident in your ability to draw the best out of each learner and be empowered to take each day in your teaching as a new beginning.

Reflective Questions

1. Describe and compare some of the models of reflective practice you have come across, either through your reading of this book or elsewhere. Choose the approach you will undertake to reflect on your own professional practice for the purposes of your personal action plan.				
• Consider the main ideas proposed by each model and select one or two models you identify yourself more with to use for reflecting on your professional practice.	Aligned with CME, Level 4 Unit (U) or Area of Study (AOS) and Assessment Criteria number of ABRSM (2014) and TCL (2013, 2019)			
	ABRSM		TCL (2013)	
• Explain how your selection of a model or models is based on your own preferred ways of learning.	U3:	3.1.1	U3:	1.1 1.2
			TCL (2019)	
• Consider when and how you will implement the model? For instance, will you keep a written or audio recorded diary? Will you aim for reflection immediately after each lesson, at the end of the day, or at the weekend?			AOS1:	1.1.2 1.1.3
• What resources will you need to collect all the information you might require in support of your reflections (e.g., collecting feedback from learners? Colleagues, mentors?)				

2. Explain how your role fits in the broader context of music education and identify opportunities for further development, learning and progression.				
• Outline your role as a music teacher/educator in your teaching context.				
	ABRSM		TCL (2013)	
• Consider your community of practice and ways in which you can be an active participant in the dialogue, exchange of knowledge, research etc.	U3:	3.2	U3:	2.1 2.2 3.1 3.2 3.3 3.4
• Consider your own priorities and aims for yourself as a teacher. What learning and development needs do you have in relation to attaining the aims you set for yourself and for your learners within your role and beyond?			TCL (2019)	
			AOS1:	1.1.4 1.1.5 2.1.1 2.1.2 2.1.3 2.1.4

3. Evaluate how professional practise has developed through becoming a *reflective* and *reflexive teacher.*				
• Consider what learnings you have possibly taken from your successes, challenges, failures, and mistakes, and how these contributed to your learning and development. Provide concrete examples. • Outline the role of feedback from others in helping you become *reflective* and *reflexive* and improve your teaching.	**ABRSM**		**TCL (2013)**	
	U3:	3.1.3 3.1.4	U3:	1.3 3.1 3.2 3.3 3.4
			TCL (2019)	
			AOS1:	1.1.4 2.1.1 2.1.2 2.1.3 2.1.4

4. Evaluate own knowledge and performance against professional standards and identify and prioritise appropriate formal and informal development opportunities.				
• What are the standards and benchmarks required in your teaching context/s? How does your knowledge and performance compare to these? • What are the priorities for development you have identified (rank them into short, medium and long term)? • What opportunities (formal and informal) are there for you to develop further towards or beyond the stated standards and benchmarks? • What is required for you to make use of the above opportunities (e.g., time, money, other)?	**ABRSM**		**TCL (2013)**	
	U3:	3.3.3 3.3.4 3.4.1 3.4.2 3.5.1	U3:	4.1 4.2 5.1 5.2 5.2
			TCL (2019)	
			AOS1:	2.1.1 2.1.2 2.1.3 2.1.4 3.1.1

5. Considering your answers to the previous questions, produce a detailed, realistic, and specific plan for your own professional development. Use appropriate sources of support in order to establish, process and evaluate the effectiveness of the plan.				
• Use *reflective* and *reflexive* practice, alongside other sources of feedback (learners, colleagues, mentors) to help you identify needs and opportunities for development. • Create aims and objectives for development, ranked by priority and consider including a timeline for when you want to have achieved the aims and objectives you propose to achieve. • Outline the activities you will have to do to achieve the proposed aims and objectives. • Put a plan in place to evaluate the effectiveness of your plan at different points in time. • Keep revising your plan as needed – this is an ongoing document for the duration of your life as a teacher.	ABRSM		TCL (2013)	
	U3:	3.4.1 3.4.2 3.5.1 3.5.2 3.5.3 3.6.1	U3:	All the learning outcomes for this unit
			TCL (2019)	
			AOS1:	1.1

Notes

1. Emotional Intelligence, as a psychological theory, was developed by Peter Salovey and John Mayer. It refers to the ability to perceive and understand emotions and emotional knowledge. This requires the ability to regulate one's own emotions with a view to promoting intellectual and emotional growth. Daniel Goleman (a science journalist) has authored a number of books on emotional intelligence wherein he describes five essential components in the process: self-awareness, self-regulation, internal motivation, empathy and social skills.
2. Explicit knowledge refers to knowledge that is easy to communicate, store and share as it can be expressed through words, numbers, codes, musical notation and mathematical or scientific formulae.
3. The term **hidden** or **tacit knowledge** was introduced into philosophy by Michael Polanyi in 1958 in reference to the fact that 'we can know more than we can tell'; and such knowledge in many instances cannot be conveyed adequately through verbal means. This type of knowledge only emerges through practise within appropriate contexts and transmitted in co-shared social contexts, commonly called the 'community of practice'. Examples of this type of knowledge include playing a musical instrument, driving a car, riding a bike.

Further Reading

Bennett, D. (Ed.). (2012). *Life in the real world: How to make music graduates employable*. Common Ground.

Brookfield, S. (1995). *Becoming a critically reflective teacher*. Jossey-Bass.

Sellars, M. (2017). *Reflective practice for teachers* (2nd ed.). Sage.

Smilde, R. (2012). Change and the challenges of lifelong learning. In D. Bennett (Ed.), *Life in the real world: How to make music graduates employable* (pp. 99–123). Common Ground.

References

Associated Board of the Royal Schools of Music (ABRSM) (2014). *Level 4 certificate for music educators: Assessment framework*. ABRSM.

Bolton, G. (2010). *Reflective practice: Writing and professional development*. Sage.

Boud, D., Keogh, R., & Walker, D. (1985). Promoting reflection in learning: A model. In D. Boud, R. Keogh, & D. Walker (Eds.), *Reflection: Turning experience into learning* (pp. 18–40). Routledge Falmer.

British Council (2017). *Continuing professional development (CPD) framework for teacher educators*. British Council. www.teachingenglish.org.uk/sites/teacheng/files/Teacher Educator Framework FINAL WEBv1.pdf

Brookfield, S. (1995). *Becoming a critically reflective teacher*. Jossey-Bass.

Dewey, J. (1933). *How we think: A restatement of the relation of reflective thinking to the educative process*. D.C. Heath & Co Publishers.

Gardner, H. (1983). *Frames of mind: The theory of multiple intelligences*. Basic Books.

Gibbs, G. (1988). *Learning by doing: A guide to teaching and learning methods*. Further Education Unit.

Goleman, D. (. (1998). *Working with emotional intelligence*. Bloomsbury Publishing.

Kolb, D. A. (1984). *Experiential learning: Experience as the source of learning and development* (Vol. 1). Prentice-Hall.

Pedlar, M., Burgoyne, J., & Boydell, T. (2001). *A manager's guide to self-development* (4th ed.). McGraw-Hill.

Schön, D. A. (1983). *The reflective practitioner: How professionals think in action*. Temple Smith.

Schön, D. A. (1987). *Educating the reflective practitioner: Toward a new design for teaching and learning in the professions*. Jossey-Bass higher education series.

Schön, D. A. (1991). *The reflective practitioner: How professionals think in action*. Ashgate.

Sellars, M. (2017). *Reflective practice for teachers* (2nd ed.). Sage.

Simones, L. L. (2019). Understanding the meaningfulness of vocal and instrumental music teachers' hand gestures through the teacher behavior and gesture framework. *Frontiers in Education, 4.* https://doi.org/10.3389/feduc.2019.00141

Trinity College London (TCL) (2013). *TCL level 4 certificate for music educators: Specifications*. TCL.

Trinity College London (TCL) (2019). *TCL level 4 certificate for music educators, areas of study*. TCL.

Index

Note: Page numbers in *italic* indicate a figure and page numbers in **bold** indicate a table on the corresponding page

ABRSM *see* Associated Board of the Royal Schools of Music (ABRSM)
abstract/symbolic notation 57
abuse: child confiding about 218–219; emotional 215; neglect 216; physical 214; sexual 214; understanding and recognising 213–216
academic attainment aided by music 78–79
adaptive mastery-oriented learners 54
adolescent: categorisation of 3; listening to music 44; *see also* young people
adopted symbols 57
affective domain of learning 130, *130*
agency: collective 239; musical 21, 239; personal 30, 35
applicants to Certificate for Music Educators (CME) 4
application form for Certificate for Music Educators (CME), Level 4 12
areas of study in Certificate for Music Educators (CME) 8
assessment in music education 193–205; criterion 198–199; formative 194, 196–198; methods and tools 200–203; projects 201–202; records of learners' achievements 202; reflective questions 204–205; self- and peer assessment 202–203; summative 194, 198–200; teacher-designed tasks and tests 201; work samples and portfolios 201
Associated Board of the Royal Schools of Music (ABRSM) 2, 3, 6, 8
attainment value 107
auditory perception impairment 97

aural learning style **95**
authentic learning 32
autonomy: being fulfilled by music 109, **111**; of learners 56

Bandura, Albert 26
Barrett, Margaret 58
behaviour: inappropriate 112–117; promoting positive 110–113, 119
behaviourism 26
Bloom's taxonomy of learning 130, *130*
boys: choral singing 161; musicality of 42; singing 48
Bruner, J. S. 27

candidates for Certificate for Music Educators (CME) 4, 8–9
Center for Applied Special Technology (CAST) 125, 144n1
Certificate for Music Educators (CME) *see* CME
chanting 46
children: categorisation of 3; cognitive constructivism 26–28; confiding abuse 218–219; improvisation by 62–64, 154; innate musicality of 20–21; learning experiences of 41–42; listening to music 43–45; motivations for instrumental music learning 52–56; musical identities of. 40–43; musicality of 19–36; musical learning by 2; musical self-expression of 40–68; nature *versus* nurture 25–26; participating in community music 179, 182–184; Piaget's stages

of development 26–28; safeguarding in music education 209–231; very gifted 99–102; Vygotsky's zone of proximal development 27; *see also* young people
Children Act (1989) 211, 229
Children Act 2004 211
Children Act (Scotland) 211
Children and Social Work Act 2017 211
Children Order (Northern Ireland) 211
choral singing 161
classical music, listening to 45
CME 2, 7; assessor 4; candidates of 4, 8–9; units 4
CME, Level 4 7–16; application stage of 12; areas of study 8; choosing course provider 11; eligibility for 10; entry requisites of 10; interviewing for 13–15
cognitive benefits of music 75–79
cognitive constructivism 26–28
cognitive domain of learning 93, 130, *130*
collaboration and partnerships in musical learning 233–251; cooperation 235; co-ordination 235; design thinking methodology 237–239, 240; evaluating effectiveness and impact of 247–249, 251; importance of 233–234; initiating 237–239; key attributes 235–237; networking 234; with parents 240–245; reflective questions 250–251; with schools and communities 245–247; types of partnerships 234–237
collaborative learning 134
collective agency 239
comic-strip type noises 46
communicational development benefits of music 74–75, 81
communication in collaboration and partnerships in musical learning 236
communicative musicality 20
communities of practice 4, 32–33
community: collaboration and partnerships in musical learning 245–247; musical opportunities and 162
community music 176–185; assessment 196; ethics of care in 181; facilitation and workshops 181–185; facilitation of 5; hospitality in 180; principles and approaches to teaching 178–180

community musicians 6, 176–180
competence: being fulfilled by music 109, **111**; of learners 56
composing assessment 195
concrete-operational stage of child development 27
contact zone of cultures 104, 105
contexts in musical learning 22–25
continuous professional development (CPD) 261–263, **262**, 266
conventional notation 57
cooperation in musical learning 235
co-ordination in musical learning 235, 236
counter-culture 102
course providers, choosing 11
creativity 56–57, 79, 81, 148, 154, 160, 174
cross-cultural groups 103
culture: as barriers in partnerships in musical learning with schools and communities 247; teaching and 102–106
cyberbullying 223

Dalcroze 187n1
dancing 64–65
Data Protection Act 224
decentralization in collaboration and partnerships in musical learning 236
definition in design thinking 237
deliberative learning 28
designated safeguarding officer (DSO) 212
Design Thinking Methodology 237–240
development section in teaching 173
Dewey, John 256–258
diary of reflections by teachers 255–256
didactic approach to teaching 63, 165, 179, 183–185, 188n7
differentiation in teaching 134
Digital Audio Workstations (DAW) 60–61
Disc Jockeys (DJs) 5
discordant trio in parent-teacher interaction 243
diversity 89, 118; in collaboration and partnerships in musical learning 236
domains of learning 130, *130*
dominant duo in parent-teacher interaction 242
double duo in parent-teacher interaction 243

DSO *see* designated safeguarding officer (DSO)
duty of care 210, 211
dynamic duo in parent-teacher interaction 242–243

early years *see* young children
educators *see* teachers
email communications. 224
emotional abuse 215
emotional intelligence 266n1
emotional well-being aided by music 79–80
empathy 112, 237
enculturative learning 22
environment in instrumental music teaching **172**, 173
equality 89, 118
Eraut, M. 28
ethics of care in community music 181
ethnicity and musical identities 42
ethnic majority group 103
ethnic minority group 103
ethos of reception 105
ethos of teaching 125
Experiential Learning Cycle 258
experiential learning style 93
explicit knowledge 266n2
exploration notation 57

facilitation 33; in community music 177
facilitators in community music 181–185
feedback 139, 173, 176, 184–185, 196–197
filter system for internet use 219, 221
financial constraints as barrier to school learning 90
formal learning in music 23–25, 34
formal operations stage of child development 27
formative assessment 194, 196–198
framework in instrumental music teaching **172**, 173
freedom of expression *versus* structured learning 160
free-flow vocalising 46

Galton, Francis 25
Gardner's theory of multiple intelligences 93–94
gender and musical identities 42
generalist teachers 151–152
General Teaching Council (Wales) 6

Gibbs, G. 259
Gibbs' Reflective Cycle 259–261, **260**
gifted children 99–102
girls: musicality of 42, 161; singing 48
group improvisation 62
group teaching 164
guardians *see* parents
guided discovery in teaching 135
guided learning in music 23–25

harmonius trio in parent-teacher interaction 167, 244
hidden knowledge 266n3
hospitality in community music 180

ICT and safeguarding children in music education 219–225, 230
ideation in design thinking 238
idiomatic stage of musical composition 59
IDJ *see* Individual Development Journal (IDJ)
implicit learning 28
improvisation 62–64, 154
inclusion 88–89, 118
inclusive learning environments 124–141, 143; preparing for development of 87–117; reflective questions 118–119
independent learning 186
Individual Development Journal (IDJ) 255
inductive approach to teaching 134
infants: categorisation of 3; communicative musicality of 20
informal learning in music 22–23, 34, 168, 196
informational barriers to music learning 91, 92
information and communications technology *see* ICT
innate musicality 20–21
instrumental music 4, 5, 163–176; approaches to teaching 165–168, 173–174, **172**; assessment 196–197
instruments *see* musical instruments
integration of information impairment 97
intellectual benefits of music 75–79, 81
intelligence: aided by music 77–78; multiple types of 93–94
interactive music learning 146, 147
intercultural groups 104
internet and safe practices in using 219–225, 231

interview for Certificate for Music Educators (CME), Level 4 13–15
intrapersonal barriers to music learning 91

'knowings' for Certificate for Music Educators (CME) 13–15
knowledge: explicit 266n2; hidden 266n3; know-how and 30–31; tacit 266n3
Kolb, D. A. 258–259

language, unacceptable 115
language skill benefits of music 75–76
LCM *see* London College of Music (LCM)
leadership 161; as barriers in partnerships in musical learning with schools and communities 247
leading music learning *see* music teaching
learners: adaptive mastery-oriented 54; beliefs about intelligence and ability 106–107; definition 4; feedback from 139; knowing their educational context 128; in Learning Power Theory (LPT) 29–30; maladaptive helpless-oriented 54; motivating 54–55; musical background of 155; records of achievements 202; in relationship with teachers 166–167; self-regulated 55–56
learning *see* music learning
learning activities 133–136; structured *versus* less structured 154–155
learning dispositions 30, **31**
learning identity 30
learning outcomes and objectives 4, 128–133, **129**; achievable 131–132; measurable 131; realistic 132; SMART acronym 129–133; specific 129–131; timely 132–133
Learning Power Theory (LPT) 2, 19, 28–33, 124, 125
learning relationships 32–33, **32**
learning styles 92–94, **95**
lesson plans 174, 186; checking for understanding 136; considering potential risks and hazards 137–139; considering resources 137; creating a timeline 137; creating inclusive 126–141; developing lesson conclusion 136–137; developing the lesson introduction 133; knowing

your learner 128; outlining learning outcomes and objectives 128–133, **129**; planning learning activities and teaching methodologies 133–136, 142; reflecting and delivering 139–141; reflective questions 142; summary **140–141**
listening to music 43–45
literacy skills aided by music 76
Locke, John 25
logical learning style **95**
London College of Music (LCM) 6
LPT *see* Learning Power Theory (LPT)

maladaptive helpless-oriented learners 54
manipulative stage of musical composition 59
master-apprentice model of lessons 165
memory difficulties 98
mentoring 15–16, 165–168, 174
mentors 9, 12
metacognitive skills 54–55
method in instrumental music teaching **172**, 173
MIROR 61, 68n2
monitoring in collaboration and partnerships in musical learning 237
motherese 20
motivation 106–109; promoting and developing 54–55, 109–110, 119
movement identity 65
movement play 64–65
movement vocalising 46
"Mozart effect" 77
multicultural groups 103
multiple intelligences theory 93–94
music: facilitating instead of teaching 153; fulfilling psychological human needs 109, **111**; multidimensional benefits of 74–81; participatory 155; prevalence of 21–22; value of 34, 107–108
musical agency 21
Musical Bridges initiative 158
musical development 25–33, 60, 67; nature *versus* nurture 25–26
musical engagement by children 41–42
Musical Futures 23, 162, 168
musical identity 40–43; developing 107–109
musical instruments, motivations for learning 51–56; motivations for learning 52–56

musicality: of children 19–36; innate 20–21
musical notation 56–62; inventing 58–60
musical play 64–65
musical self-expression 40–68, 148, 174;
    improvising 62–64; movement play
    64–65; playing musical instruments
    51–62; reflective questions 66–68;
    singing 45–51; technology and 60–61, 67
musical worlds 22–25
music composition 56–57, 58–59
music curriculum 152–153
music education: gender-based
    stereotypes 42; safeguarding children
    in 209–231
musicianship of listening 44
music learning 22–25; assessing 193–205;
    assessing music 193–205; authentic 32;
    barriers to 90–92, 118; collaboration
    and partnerships in 233–251;
    collaborative 134; defining 29–30;
    deliberative 28; difficulties with 96–99;
    domains of 130, *130*; enculturative 22;
    implicit 28; independent 186; informal
    22–23, 34, 168, 196; Learning Power
    Theory (LPT) 2, 28–33, 124, 125;
    motivation for 106–109; planning
    for inclusive 124–141; scaffolding
    168–176; use of play 134
music learning environments 2, 154;
    inclusive 118–119, 124–141, 143
music listening 43–45
music making experiences 161
music notation *170*
music teachers *see* teachers
music teaching: approaches to 165–168;
    community music 176–185; context
    13; early years 147–150; group 164;
    instrumental music 4; interactive
    146, 147; methodologies 133–136,
    142, 162; obtaining feedback from
    139; online 163; parent-teacher-child
    relationship 167, 242–245; philosophy
    13, 33; in primary school 150–157;
    providing feedback 173, 176; reflective
    questions 186–187; routes of 4–6; in
    secondary school 158–163; through
    music and not about music 159; video
    recorded 164–165; of vocal and
    instrumental music 5–6, 163–176

narrative songs 50
National Guidance for Child Protection
    2017 211

nature *versus* nurture 25–26
neglect 216
networking in musical learning 234
notation of gesture/enactive 57
notation of instrument 57
no-touch policy with students
    225–226, 230

observation as assessment in music
    education 200
Office for Standards in Education *see*
    Ofsted
Ofsted 150, 151, 158, 161
online safety practices 219–225,
    220, 231
online teaching 163
Orff, Carl 187n2

PAP *see* Personal Action Plan (PAP)
parents 4; feedback from 139;
    musical interactions with children
    20; role in young children playing
    instruments 52; supporting
    gifted children 100–101; teachers
    developing partnerships with
    240–245
participation in collaboration and
    partnerships in musical learning 236
participatory music 155
partnerships in musical learning
    233–251; collaboration 235;
    cooperation 235; co-ordination
    235, 236; developing with parents
    240–245; evaluating effectiveness
    and impact of 247–249, 251;
    importance of 233–234; initiating
    237–239; key attributes 235–237;
    networking 234; with schools and
    communities 245–247; types of
    234–237
Paul Hamlyn Foundation 23, 158
PDJ *see* Personal Development Journal
    (PDJ)
PDP *see* Personal Development Plan
    (PDP)
Pedlar, M. 258
peers: assessment in assessment in
    music education 202–203; feedback
    from 139; self-directed learning of
    songs with 49–50; tutoring 135
perceptual benefits of music 75–79
perceptual learning modalities 93
performance assessment 195–196

Personal Action Plan (PAP) 255
personal agency 30, 35
personal development benefits of music 74–75, 81
Personal Development Journal (PDJ) 255
Personal Development Plan (PDP) 3, 9, 15, 255, 266
personal expressiveness of musical composition 59
personality influencing learning style 93
Personal Reflection Model 258
PGCE *see* Postgraduate Certificate of Education (PGCE)
PGDE *see* Professional Graduate Diploma in Education (PGDE)
physical abuse 214
physical aggression 114–115
physical barriers to music learning 91–92
physical learning style **95**
physical well-being aided by music 79–81
Piaget, J. 26–27
"Pillsbury Study, The" 20
pitch 47, 48
play, types of 134
pop music, listening to 45
positive behavior 110–113, 119
Postgraduate Certificate of Education (PGCE) 6
practicing 175
practitioner *see* teachers
praxis of teaching 124–125
pre-operational stage of child development 27
pre-school: categorisation of 3; singing in 45
primary school and teaching music 150–157
production of standard songs 47, **47**
professional development of teachers 261–263, **262**, 266
Professional Graduate Diploma in Education (PGDE) 6
projects as assessment in music education 201–202
protecting children *see* safeguarding children in music education
prototyping in design thinking 238

psychomotor domain of learning 130, *130*
purpose in collaboration and partnerships in musical learning 238

QTS *see* Qualified Teacher Status (QTS)
Qualification and Credit Framework (QCF) 8
Qualified Teacher Status (QTS) 5

reactive learning 28
recapitulation in teaching 173
recognition of prior learning (RPL) 9, 10
records of learners' achievements as assessment in music education 202
reflection, theories and models of 256–261
reflection in action 257
reflection on action 257
Reflective Cycle (Gibbs) 259–261, **260**
reflective questions: assessment in music education 204–205; collaboration and partnerships in musical learning 250–251; inclusive learning environments 118–119; leading music learning 186–187; learning and developing musicality 34–35; multidimensional benefits of 81; planning for inclusive teaching and learning 142–143; on reflective and reflexive practitioner 264–266; self-expression through musical identities 66–68
reflective teachers: professional development of 261–263, **262**, 266; reflective questions 264–266; *versus* reflexive 253–256, 265; theories and models of reflection 256–261
reflexive music technology 61, 68n1
reflexive teachers 2; *versus* reflective 253–256, 265; reflective questions 264–266
relatedness: being fulfilled by music 109, **111**; of learners 56
relationships, learning 32–33, **32**, 35
respect 112, 113
rewards 116
reworking of known songs 46
risks and hazards in teaching 137–139, 143
Rogoff, B. 28
Rousseau, Jean-Jacques 25
RPL *see* recognition of prior learning (RPL)

safeguarding children in music education
    209–231; abuse recognition 213–216;
    avoiding risks 225–228; child
    confiding abuse to teacher 218–219;
    handling suspicion of abuse 217–218;
    roles of individuals and agencies
    211–213; safe practices in using
    technology, internet and social media
    219–225, 231
Safeguarding Vulnerable Groups Order
    2017 211
sanctions 116–117
scaffolding 27, 168–176
Schön, D. A. 257–258
school principals/head teaches and
    safeguarding children in music
    education 212
schools: as barrier to music learning
    90–91; collaboration and partnerships
    in musical learning 245–247; offering
    music learning 150–157
secondary school and teaching music in
    158–163
self-assessment in assessment in music
    education 202–203
self-determination theory 109
self-directed learning of songs alone 49
self-expression through music *see*
    musical self-expression
self-harm 115
self-regulated learners 55–56
sensorimotor stage of child development 27
sensory stage of musical composition 59
sexual abuse 214
singing 45–51; for animation 46;
    choral 161; inventing songs 50–51;
    participatory 161; production of
    standard songs 47, **47**; self-directed
    learning of songs alone 49; self-
    directed learning of songs with peers
    49–50; spontaneous 46
Skinner, B. F. 26
SMART objectives 129–133; for
    collaboration and partnerships in
    musical learning 248
social development benefits of music
    74–75, 81
social learning style 26, **95**
social media and safe practices in using
    219–225, 231
society as barrier to music learning
    90–91
solitary learning style **96**

solo teacher in parent-teacher
    interaction 242
songs: with conventional features 51;
    inventing 50–51; learning songs
    taught by others 48–49; narrative
    50; production of standard 47, **47**;
    reworking of known 46; self-directed
    learning of 49–50; writing 63
spatial-reasoning aided by music 77
specialist teachers 150–151
speculative stage of musical composition 59
spontaneous singing 46
Statutory Guidance Keeping Children
    Safe in Education 211
structural balance in collaboration and
    partnerships in musical learning 236
structured *versus* less structured learning
    activities 154–155
sub-culture 102
subjective-task values 107
summative assessment 194, 198–200
Suzuki method 187n3
symbolic knowledge 28
symbolic stage of child development 27
symbolic stage of musical composition 60
systematic stage of musical composition 60

tabula rasa 25
tacit knowledge 266n3
tactile receptors impairment 97
TCL *see* Trinity College London (TCL)
Teacher Behaviour and Gesture (TBG)
    framework 168, **169**–**170**
teacher-designed tasks and tests 201
teacher modelling 167
teachers: becoming qualified music
    teachers 5–6; behaviours **169**;
    Certificate for Music Educators
    (CME), Level 4 7–16; creating
    inclusive lesson plans 126–141;
    cultural diversity and 102–106;
    demonstrating and modelling
    169, 171–173, 176; developing
    partnerships with parents 240–245;
    gestures **169**–**170**; handling
    inappropriate behaviour 112–117; as
    a learner 155; no-touch policy with
    students 225–226, 230; observation
    as assessment in music education
    200; planning for inclusive teaching
    environments 124–141; professional
    development of 155, 261–263, **262**,
    266; promoting and developing

motivation 109–110; promoting positive behaviour 110–113, 119; reflective *versus* reflexive 253–256, 265; roles of 2; and safeguarding children in music education 212–213; seeking support 155, 162; solo 242; specialist 150–151; supporting gifted children 100–101; tasks and tests in assessment in music education 201; teaching behaviors of 168–176

teacher talk 166, 171

teaching *see* music teaching

teaching qualification for music teachers: CME, Level 4 7–16

Teaching Regulation Agency (England) 6

technology 60–61; musical identities and 43; musical self-expression and 60–61, 67; responding to misuse of 225; safe practices in using 219–225, 231; in teaching 163–165, 175

thinking and problem solving skills 135

third cultural space 104, 105

time in collaboration and partnerships in musical learning 237

touching students and safeguarding children in music education 225–226, 230

transcultural groups 103

Trinity College London (TCL) 2, 3, 6, 8

trust in collaboration and partnerships in musical learning 236

UK Safer Internet Centre 221

unacceptable language 115

United Kingdom and safeguarding children 210–211, 229

United Nations Convention on the Rights of the Child 210, 229

Universal Design Learning 2, 125–141

verbal learning style **95**

vernacular stage of musical composition 59

very gifted children 99–102

video recorded teaching 164–165

visual learning style **95**

visual perception impairment 97

visual-spatial intelligence aided by music 77–78

vocal music 163–176; approaches to teaching 5–6, 165–168; assessment 196

vocal pitch-matching development (VPMD) model 47, **47**

Vygotsky, L S. 27

warm-ups in teaching 173

Wider Opportunities Scheme 150, 151

work samples and portfolios as assessment in music education 201

workshops in community music 181–185

young children: composing and inventing musical notation 56–62; interacting and playing musical instruments 52; learning music learning for 6, 147–150; musical play 64–65; singing 45–51; teaching music to 147–150

young people: listening to music 42, 44; motivations for instrumental music learning 52–56; musicality of 19–36; singing 48–51; *see also* adolescent; children

zone of proximal development 27